NATURE AND ANTIQUITIES

Nature and Antiquities
The Making of Archaeology in the Americas

Edited by
PHILIP L. KOHL, IRINA PODGORNY,
AND STEFANIE GÄNGER

THE UNIVERSITY OF
ARIZONA PRESS

TUCSON

The University of Arizona Press
www.uapress.arizona.edu

We respectfully acknowledge the University of Arizona is on the land and territories of Indigenous peoples. Today, Arizona is home to twenty-two federally recognized tribes, with Tucson being home to the O'odham and the Yaqui. Committed to diversity and inclusion, the University strives to build sustainable relationships with sovereign Native Nations and Indigenous communities through education offerings, partnerships, and community service.

© 2014 The Arizona Board of Regents
Chapter 9. "Manifest Destiny as the Order of Nature" © 2014 Alice Beck Kehoe
All rights reserved. Published 2014
First paperback edition published 2025

ISBN-13: 978-0-8165-3112-7 (cloth)
ISBN-13: 978-0-8165-5499-7 (paper)
ISBN-13: 978-0-8165-3925-3 (OA ebook)

Cover designed by Leigh McDonald
Cover illustrations from the Revista de Exposição Anthropologica Brazileira, 1882.

Publication of this book was made possible in part by funding from the Wofford College History Department. The support of Wellesley College for the preparation of the index is also gratefully acknowledged.

Library of Congress Cataloging-in-Publication Data
Nature and antiquities : the making of archaeology in the Americas / edited by Philip L. Kohl, Irina Podgorny, and Stefanie Gänger.
    pages cm
    Summary: "Nature and Antiquities analyzes how the study of indigenous peoples was linked to the study of nature and natural sciences. Leading scholars break new ground and entreat archaeologists to acknowledge the importance of ways of knowing in the study of nature in the history of archaeology"—Provided by publisher.
    Includes bibliographical references and index.
    ISBN 978-0-8165-3112-7 (cloth : alkaline paper)
    1. Archaeology—America—History—19th century. 2. Archaeology—America—History—20th century. 3. Archaeologists—America—History. 4. Natural history—America—History. 5. Interdisciplinary approach to knowledge—History. 6. Anthropology—America—History. 7. Indians—Antiquities. 8. America—Antiquities. I. Kohl, Philip L., 1946– II. Podgorny, Irina, 1963– III. Gänger, Stefanie.
    CC101.U6N38 2014
    930.1—dc23
                                2014007786

Printed in the United States of America
♾ This paper meets the requirements of ANSI/NISO Z39.48-1992 (Permanence of Paper).

To Maribel Martínez Navarrete, friend and colleague

There is a sense in which Europe was the prisoner of its shepherds and barbaric origin. The savage state cannot be discovered in its history, and has had to be invented, under the name of the state of nature, by poets, lawgivers and philosophers. In America the thing really exists, and the two continents form a vast laboratory in which European speculative experiments can test their hypotheses regarding the human mind by observing it in a state as close as is possible for humans to the condition of frugivorous or carnivorous animals. . . . This is the point at which "America" becomes the prisoner of "Europe's" limited understanding of itself. The concept of "nature" preceding "history" in the organization of social life, evolved in Europe, is about to be imposed upon America, as a means whereby "Europe" understands both "America" and itself, and given the radical inequalities of power between the two, the understanding and government of the self is very different from the understanding and government of the others.
—J. G. A. POCOCK, *BARBARISM AND RELIGION*, VOL. 4: *BARBARIANS, SAVAGES AND EMPIRES*

Contents

Acknowledgments ix

Introduction: Nature in the Making of Archaeology
in the Americas 3
Stefanie Gänger, Philip Kohl, and Irina Podgorny

Part I. Interplays

1. Skulls and Idols: Anthropometrics, Antiquity Collections,
   and the Origin of American Man, 1810–1850 23
   Miruna Achim

2. Finding the Ancient in the Andes: Archaeology and Geology,
   1850–1890 47
   Joanne Pillsbury

3. Place-Names and Indigenous Languages: Samuel Alexander
   Lafone Quevedo and British Antiquarian Methods in
   Nineteenth-Century Argentina 69
   Máximo Farro

Part II. Settings

4. Fraternal Curiosity: The Camacho Museum, Campeche,
   Mexico 91
   Adam T. Sellen

5. The Many Natures of Antiquities: Ana María Centeno
   and Her Cabinet of Curiosities, Peru, ca. 1832–1874 110
   Stefanie Gänger

6. From Lake Titicaca to Guatemala: The Travels of
   Joseph Charles Manó and His Wife of Unknown Name   125
   Irina Podgorny

7. Visualizing Culture and Nature: William Taylor's Murals
   in the Hall of Northwest Coast Indians, American Museum
   of Natural History   145
   Susan Roy

Part III. Narratives

8. Arrows and Sciences: Odd Displays for Another Brazil,
   1840–1882   169
   Maria Margaret Lopes, Mariza Corrêa,
   and Irina Podgorny

9. Manifest Destiny as the Order of Nature   186
   Alice Beck Kehoe

10. Saving the Natives: The Long Emergence and Transformation
    of Indigeneity   202
    John S. Gilkeson

    Selected Bibliography   221

    Editors and Contributors   234

    Index   239

Acknowledgments

The editors would like to thank the Amerind Foundation and its gracious and supportive director, John Ware, for hosting the Wenner-Gren sponsored seminar "The Naturalization of the Past: Nation-Building and the Development of Anthropology and Natural History in the Americas" in Dragoon, Arizona, in 2002. That meeting ultimately gave rise to this book, and we would like to acknowledge all those who participated in the 2002 conference, initiating a dialogue among scholars from different national backgrounds who were interested in the early development of archaeology in the Americas. These include J. Marks, G. Penny, O. Restrepo, H. Benavides, M. Rutsch, N. Dias, C. Loza, M. M. Lopes, and J. Briceño. In particular we extend our thanks to Curtis "Kit" Hinsley, who first suggested that the Amerind Foundation could provide the perfect venue for our seminar. Kit joined I. Podgorny and P. Kohl as co-organizers of the initial conference, and his collaboration proved essential to its success.

We would also like to thank Allyson Carter and her indefatigable staff at the University of Arizona Press. They have supported our efforts from the project's inception and have helped us immeasurably with their edits and suggestions. We also acknowledge the supportive comments of the three anonymous reviewers chosen by the University of Arizona Press; their criticisms and suggestions were most helpful, greatly improving and sharpening our final text.

We are extremely grateful to the Max Planck Institute for the History of Science in Berlin, where Irina Podgorny first met Stefanie Gänger during a visiting fellowship and brought her on board this project. We thank A. Alonso, S. Faiad, A. Martínez, and A. Miranda for their contributions to this endeavor. PIP 0116 (CONICET, Argentina), Wellesley College, and the Department of History, Wofford College, helped cover some of the essential publication expenses, and we thank IKKM-Bauhaus Universität Weimar, and in particular Julia Tarsten, for her help with editing the bibliography. We, of course, also thank our colleagues and the contributors to this volume for their good will, forbearance, and patience to bring closure to this long-planned project. Needless to say, the project never would have reached press without the unstinting support of our families: spouses, children, and significant partners alike. We know their help was essential.

Finally, we would like to dedicate this volume to Dr. M. Isabel Martínez Navarrete, Grupo de Investigación Prehistoria social y económica, Instituto de Historia—Centro de Ciencias Humanas y Sociales (Consejo Superior Investigaciones Científicas). Maribel first introduced I. Podgorny and P. Kohl to each other, believing correctly that their archaeological and anthropological interests sufficiently overlapped and could lead to fruitful collaborative work, an evaluation that we believe has been clearly confirmed by this current work. Maribel has played an essential role in the formation of numerous international collaborative projects, perhaps most notably her successful development of Spanish-Russian investigations with Dr. E. N. Chernykh and his colleagues in their metallurgical studies in the southern Ural Mountains at the important Late Bronze mining center of Kargaly. We believe everyone involved in this project, and other such projects that Maribel has helped establish, would acknowledge her central, indeed indispensable role in these international collaborative works. Everyone tacitly recognizes her help, but not many have publicly acknowledged it. Our short dedication here is meant to correct this unfortunate oversight. *Muchas gracias, Maribel.* Your help was essential to our project, and we strongly believe it should be recognized and recorded.

NATURE AND ANTIQUITIES

Introduction

Nature in the Making of Archaeology in the Americas

Stefanie Gänger, Philip Kohl, and Irina Podgorny

The assimilation of the inhabitants of the Americas to what men and women in the Old World knew and believed in the sixteenth century threatened to subvert not only theology or philosophy but also history.[1] Long into the eighteenth century, the narratives designed to account for Eurasian phenomena failed to provide a history of ancient America, "with the result that it became marginalized or alienated," as John G. A. Pocock phrased it.[2] The "savage condition"—the "state of nature"—imposed on America along with "the concept of 'nature' preceding 'history' in the organization of social life," could be described through natural philosophy, as Enlightenment scholars contended, but the term *history* was not applicable to the peoples inhabiting the new worlds opened to Europeans by their discoveries:[3] even the Inca and Aztec empires—which several northern European authors of the eighteenth century refused to accept as ancient civilizations—lacked "letters and money" and thus could not possibly "act publicly" or remember their doings, as was necessary to have a "civil history."[4] At a time when historical evidence encompassed registers and genealogies, annals and coins, and other classical or biblical sources, and when even those traditional literary sources that had long spoken of ancient America—primarily the accounts of the early-colonial chroniclers—were losing their credibility, the study of the past of America's peoples was without fundament; it had neither an epistemological nor a material basis.[5]

It was precisely because the inhabitants of the New World were "very nearly excluded from 'history' as it came to be imagined" in the eighteenth century[6] that European and Spanish American authors writing about the past, the land, and the peoples of America at that time began to look to novel and unusual forms of evidence, to substantiation from fields such as linguistics, natural history, and geology,[7] but also—notably in Creole clerical accounts from Spanish America—to myths, stripped of their fabulous accretions, and to the testimonies, artifacts, and images wrought by Amerindians.[8] The notorious eighteenth-century "dispute over the New World" between European and American intellectuals revolved not only around European diatribes against tropical America but also, as Jorge Cañizares-Esguerra has argued, around historical methodology and epistemology:[9] it addressed the key question—one British American historiography was to take up only much later, in the nineteenth century[10]—of how, and, above all, on the basis of what material evidence, should the history of the New World be written "from scratch."[11]

This volume is concerned with the early history of how men, and some women, defined and corroborated a language, a method, and a body of material evidence for the study of ancient America in and beyond the nineteenth century. While it does not presume to cover the entirety of this query, the volume presents ten essays tracing a series of episodes and meaningful conjunctures in the process of how contemporaries wrote and rewrote the history of the New World. The particular emphasis of all contributions rests on how they did so by appealing to both "nature" and "antiquities," the material remains of America's pre-Columbian inhabitants.

Historians of archaeology have long and eloquently entreated archaeologists to acknowledge the importance of fields such as antiquarianism in the history of their discipline;[12] they have paid less attention, however, to the constitutive role of "ways of knowing" that ensued from the study of nature—to the part engineering or anatomy, "curiosity," botany, natural history, or geology played in the history and in the making of archaeology. In this vein, some of the contributions to this volume trace how conventions, practices, and concepts from natural history and the natural sciences underlaid and affected the basic tenets of the emerging discipline of archaeology in the nineteenth century. Other articles set out to uncover, reassemble, or adjust our vision of collections and research that historians of archaeology have long disregarded or misrepresented because their nineteenth-century makers would refuse to comply with today's disciplinary borders and study natural specimens and antiquities in conjunction, under the rubric of the chorographic, the curious, or the universal. Again, other contributions trace the sociopolitical implications of studying nature in conjunction with "indigenous peoples" in the Americas—the many men and women who claimed or were attributed "descent from, and historical continuity with, the original inhabitants of nation-states prior to the arrival of settlers who have since become the dominant population" (Gilkeson, chap. 10). These authors inquire into what it meant and entailed to comprehend the inhabitants of the American continent in and through a state of nature.

The overall argument of the book rests on the assumption that there was, well into and beyond the mid-nineteenth century, no self-evident set of practices for the retrieval, collecting, and display of the material evidence of America's pre-Columbian societies, that there was not even an established set of discourses for their study, description, or depiction. Collecting is usually thought to have become more specialized from around 1800. It was some time, however, before the location of ethnographical displays would be settled and before "ethnographic objects" began to be treated as a distinct category.[13] In fact, with very few exceptions—the opening of the Salle des antiquités américaines in the Paris Louvre in 1851 or the foundation of the Peabody Museum of Archaeology and Ethnology at Harvard in 1866—the majority of museums and private collections of the nineteenth century brought American antiquities together with industry and nature.[14] Several museums—both state and private—in Europe and the Americas throughout the nineteenth century were established as general or "universal" collections, including antiquities and exotica along with local and foreign plants, animals, and rocks; historical relics, numismatics, and mineralogy; mummified bodies, paintings, or a narwhal's horn (see, e.g., Lopes on Brazil's National Museum, chap. 8).[15] Others—such as the collections the fraud Manó assembled in the service of the Colombian Republic (Podgorny, chap. 6)—brought crafts together with animals and plants, minerals and archaeological remains, within the logic of chorography, the natural history of places—a town, a region, or a nation-state—over time: man-made things were thought to spring like characteristic plants or vernacular architecture "from the soil."[16] Again, other collections—across the Americas and Europe alike—united antiquities and nature long into the nineteenth century under the rubric of the curious: of the items' novelty, their absurdity, their "pleasing" aspect, or their diverse and fascinating forms (Gänger, chap. 4; Sellen, chap. 5).

When looking back, historians of archaeology and of collecting have often been tempted to impose "the dividing lines habitually used to segregate the various disciplines" on their objects of study, "thoroughly mutilating (them) in the process" by "artificially" isolating specimens "according to the requirements of the history of those particular domains."[17] For the purpose of this volume, however, we chose to see these collections as evidence of how nineteenth-century collectors, travelers, and scholars still moved in a relatively "fluid space, ripe with conceptual possibilities" (Achim, chap. 1), one where antiquities could enter into a wider range of material and epistemological associations. The study of the antiquities from the Americas was emergent and evolving in Europe and both North and Latin America throughout the "long nineteenth century"—from the Atlantic Revolutions around 1800 up to the Great War (for the period between 1890 and 1914, see Kehoe, chap. 9)—and the collections and studies these decades produced are testimonies to a range of endeavors and possibilities that, though they were to fade and weather in the long run, still left their mark on the discipline.

The contributors to this volume argue that it was precisely for the lack of any disciplinary obligation or certainty that men and women with an interest in America's antiquities drew on practices and discourses with which they were familiar from their professional training as engineers, linguists, or physicians; from collections they had heard of or visited; and from their readings of manuals of natural history, philosophical texts or newspaper reports to find the words for describing, the conventions for ordering, and the practices for retrieving their objects of study. Some of the earliest archaeological excavations in the eighteenth century were organized by military engineers—men who knew "how to dig, how to record, draw up plans, how to take measures"—and their drawings and images were to mark the empirical foundations of archaeology in the Americas and Europe.[18] In eighteenth-century Spanish America, collections and studies of Americas' antiquities originated in the framework of expeditions with geographical or botanical purposes, and this association would be formative as well. The plan of the Inca structure at Ingapirca drawn by Charles-Marie de La Condamine, a French mathematician and cartographer and one of the leaders of the French Geodesic Mission to the Viceroyalty of Peru (1735–1746), for instance, is the first measured archaeological illustration in the Andean region.[19] Indeed, many of the antiquaries and "archaeologists" of the nineteenth century shared an openness to all the scientific currents of their time, and several of them had studied or read about medicine, botany, and geology or philology before they developed an interest in archaeology.[20] The artisans employed in mounting archaeological displays in museums, too, had usually first gathered experience in the installation of natural specimens or in the mounting of scaffoldings, and their experiences informed their interests as well as the conventions and aesthetics they applied to man-made things. More broadly, the hallmarks of natural history—immensely popular in nineteenth-century bourgeois circles in Europe and the Americas—underlay the very premises of early archaeology.[21] Indeed, although archaeologists have long been at pains to deny the relationship of their discipline with collecting,[22] archaeology and anthropology across the Americas and the Atlantic, up to the ascendancy of functionalism in the 1920s, allocated a central role to artifacts as data, and the practices of locating, collecting, and exhibiting antiquities were at the heart of practitioners' endeavors.[23]

Gradual acceptance of a chronologically lengthened evolutionary past in the second half of the nineteenth century also ensued from discoveries in geology, biology, and paleontology: in particular, later in the nineteenth century, the excavation of stratified sequences revealed regional differences that could be compared and interrelated (see Pillsbury, chap. 2). The discovery of a European Paleolithic prehistory that stretched back not just a couple of millennia but many thousands of years was closely associated with acceptance of the sometimes unsettling and contentious concepts of organic evolution and natural selection. 1859 was the seminal year that witnessed both the publication of Charles R. Darwin's *On the Origin of Species* and Jacques Boucher de Crèvecoeur de Perthes's discoveries of stone tools found in stratified terraces along the Somme river valley in northern France. Boucher de Perthes's work unequivocally proved the reality of the antiquity of man—the contemporaneity of extinct fauna with a "local savage humanity."[24] In that sense, "savagery" became a reality in Europe's deep past, a time that could be studied by appealing to the natural sciences outside the realm of historiography and its sources.

Ever since antipositivist philosophers of science such as Thomas Kuhn argued in the 1950s and 1960s that theoretical and linguistic changes of science shifted with abruptness and totality, historians of science assumed the impossibility of communication across the breaks of periodization that simultaneously involved theory change and empirical fracture.[25] The field has only recently abandoned this view, forwarding a new vision of science as "an intercalated set of subcultures bound together through a complex set of hard-won locally shared meanings."[26] Historians of archaeology have followed suit, arguing that the history and development of the discipline were not linear but involved multiple coexisting strands—possibilities and practices coalescing and "growing back on themselves."[27] As in other fields of knowledge, the patterns formed by the disciplinary trajectories of archaeology within the encyclopedia of available knowledge were "kaleidoscopic and cacophonous":[28] new ways of knowing were created, but the old ones rarely disappeared—early archaeology in the Americas was a "matter of *complex cumulation* and . . . simultaneous variety."[29] In this vein, this book is not so much a history of archaeology as a history of the sometimes divergent practices and discourses that emerged in relation to the collection, sale, consumption, and study of American antiquities over the nineteenth century, of the ways in which they coexisted and combined with others and, in doing so, created and re-created forms of observation and study.

On the Origins of the Project

The origins of this project are linked to a seminar that was held in Arizona in 2002 titled "The Naturalization of the Past: Nation-Building and the Development of Anthropology and Natural History in the Americas," hosted by the Amerind Foundation and organized by Philip Kohl, Irina Podgorny, and Curtis Hinsley. The seminar was concerned with the historical development of anthropological archaeology in the Americas and its links to the natural sciences and to the process of nation building with an emphasis on the decades between 1860 and 1920. Although this volume continues to operate along some of the original ideas and continues the discussion that brought the participants together back then, it has also undergone significant transformations: the majority of the authors involved in this volume, and one of the three editors—Stefanie Gänger—joined the project over the last three years, while those who did participate in the Arizona meeting have mostly written entirely new contributions, taking up insights and discussions that have shaped the field more recently.

What this volume shares with the first conference, however, is, first, the belief in the importance of adopting a transcontinental perspective, one that brings scholars from North and Latin American academia—Spanish-, Portuguese-, and English-speaking countries—together across linguistic and national divides; second, an awareness of the necessity of linking scholarly endeavors across a range of disciplinary backgrounds—from archaeology to history, and from linguistics to museum studies—in order to get a better understanding of the making of archaeology; and third, and perhaps most importantly, adherence to the first conference's concern with the necessity of writing the history of American archaeology in its historical context—a historical context that encompassed sociopolitical but also intellectual and material dimensions and one in which nature, as a field of intellectual enquiry as much as a cultural trope, was both meaningful and formative.

Writing the History of Archaeology in the Americas

In the past three decades, many studies in the history of archaeology have focused on nationalism as a formative context in the development of the discipline and have studied the role of archaeology in inventing presumed ancestors for groups aspiring to nationhood.[30] Other historians have stressed colonialism and imperialism as formative contexts in the development of the discipline.[31] Studies have also focused on how postcolonial nationalist movements appropriated archaeological discourses and practices in processes of emancipation.[32] While nationalism, political ideology, or reason of state play a significant role in the studies of nineteenth-century Brazil and twentieth-century North America (Lopes, chap. 8; Kehoe, chap. 9; Gilkeson, chap. 10), these themes are virtually absent from most other studies, especially those centering on nineteenth-century Spanish and North America (Pillsbury, chap. 2; Gänger, chap. 5; Farro, chap. 3; Achim, chap. 1; Podgorny, chap. 6; Sellen, chap. 4). This is not accidental: the chapters assembled in this volume show that central governments were sometimes unable, and sometimes simply not invoked, to provide a setting and funds for archaeological practice. Instead, it lay mostly in the hands of gentleman-scholars, *salonnières*, or adventurers, men and women who set up collections in their living rooms, discussed their intellectual concerns in exclusive circles, and financed their studies, excavations, and publications with private fortunes (Gänger, chap. 5; Podgorny, chap. 6; Pillsbury, chap. 2; Sellen, chap. 4).[33] It is perfectly plausible that politics and ideology would have greatly influenced scholarly practices and discourses in times and places where the nation-state constituted the primary financial and institutional setting, but, as the studies assembled in this volume reveal, neither nationalism nor imperialism was the only and in many cases even a significant underpinning of archaeological endeavors undertaken by individuals. This is not to imply the existence of a "normal" archaeological tradition untainted by its historical context. Rather, it is to say that the political was always only one and at times not a terribly significant aspect of a wider historical setting—one that also encompassed protagonists' personal experiences or professional expertise as well as their times' intellectual fashions or social conventions.

Compilations in the history of archaeology have mostly centered on specific—linguistically, historically, or politically defined—regions such as Hispanic South America, the United States, or Europe, bringing about discrete and sometimes impervious historiographies and suggesting incorrectly that linguistic or political boundaries were the single or foremost determinants in the making of knowledge.³⁴ Edited volumes on the history of archaeology that bring together authors working in both North and Latin America remain rare.³⁵ Similarly, in the historiography of museums of natural history across the Americas, studies situating natural history museums in the Americas in a continental perspective—looking for connections between north and south—are scarce:³⁶ the avenue of discussion opened up by Susan Sheets-Pyenson, for example, who examined comparatively the founding and growth of five natural history museums in Canada, Australia, New Zealand, and Argentina, has barely been followed.³⁷ In some cases, the focus on nationalism may have further exacerbated and "naturalized" the perceived divides between countries and regions. A historiography encapsulated within national borders not only obscures America's shared intellectual history, it may even occasion fallacies and misreadings (see Podgorny, chap.6).

This volume breaks new ground by taking the reader all across the American continents from the Southern Cone up to Canada, across the Andes, the Brazilian Amazon, Mesoamerica, and the United States. A Pan-American perspective on the making of archaeology in the nineteenth century is long overdue, especially as a corrective to the prevailing view that Spanish American intellectuals and developments were—in contrast to North American scholars or European travelers—marginal in this process. The idea that the Spanish colonial government and its successor states lacked interest in ancient ruins, for instance—an idea that relates back to narratives about the destruction of buildings, documents, and artifacts in the aftermath of the Spanish conquest—has long been a popular trope in the writings of local elites and foreign travelers of postindependent times but also in more recent historiography.³⁸ This bias in the history of archaeology correlates with a much wider set of discourses in the history of science that has long considered Iberian knowledge production to have been "episodic and marginal"—in isolation from and at odds with North Atlantic scientific modernity.³⁹ Anglo-American historians of science and archaeology have only recently begun to decenter the traditionally Euro- and Anglocentric orientation of the field.⁴⁰ In this vein, a new "global history of science" has emerged, a history of the webs of linkages and intermediaries that made knowledge and its objects travel and change along the way. This volume follows in the wake of these trends: it gives visibility to agents and collections and to knowledge and ideas hitherto unmentioned or relegated to the margins, and it centers on how European and North and Latin American researches fed into and set the context for each other and how both were interrelated through the movement of objects, knowledge, and people.[41] Knowledge about ancient America, at least up to World War I, took form chiefly at the interstices between states and continents.[42] This premise translates both in the structure of the volume—thematic rather than geographical—and in the focus of its contributions on men and women who crossed and defied political and linguistic borders throughout their lives, drawing disperse localities together: physically, as travelers and itinerants (Pillsbury, chap. 2; Podgorny, chap. 6; Achim, chap. 1; Farro, chap. 3), but also intellectually, as readers of, correspondents with, or hosts for scholars from afar (Sellen, chap. 4; Gänger, chap. 5). Practices and discourses about ancient America solidified across, this volume argues, rather than within state territorial boundaries.

The focus on intellectual and material exchange ought by no means to obscure the fact that archaeology traveled a very different course in the Americas and Europe owing to the divergent sociopolitical and biographical biases of early practitioners, to profound differences in the available material and textual record—the Old World textual record was extended back to about 3200 BCE with the decipherment of Egyptian hieroglyphics and Mesopotamian cuneiform in the nineteenth century—and the differing conditions for its physical preservation and survival.[43] We wish to emphasize, however, that despite historical and environmental contingencies, early archaeological practitioners across the Americas and Europe had more in common than is commonly assumed: from furniture to safety practices and from techniques of preservation to logics of exhibition or architectural references, museum practices repeated themselves in every major American and European city.[44] So did archaeological debates: practitioners in Philadelphia, Paris, or Lima alike inquired into the analogies between Mesoamerican and Andean societies and lost civilizations recorded in the Bible or in classical literature; they found a method and a role out of the amalgam of moral and scientific concern with the "Indian" vanishing before the spread of progress in schemes of unilinear evolution (see Achim, chap. 1; Kehoe, chap. 9; Gilkeson, chap. 10),[45] and they gradually came to understand the ancient remains' value for contributing to the understanding of a past that distinguished periods and places (Pillsbury, chap. 2). In short: their practices and discourses, their interests and actions, urge us to see, despite all differences, their intellectual endeavors in conjunction with one another.

With few exceptions, the historiography on the history of archaeological collections, expeditions, and research in the nineteenth- and twentieth-century Americas has focused selectively, not only on specific types of collectibles—usually either pre-Columbian antiquities or natural specimens—but also, and most importantly, on public national museums and exhibitions and on official discourses. This volume, while it includes survey essays on state-based museums and official discourses (such as the politically potent overviews of Alice Kehoe, chap. 9, or John Gilkeson, chap. 10), comprises in its majority studies that point to settings, themes, and constellations hitherto much less visible in the historiography: to miscellaneous, private collections and intellectual endeavors in the "provinces" of Peru, Argentina, and Mexico; to the writings of a Catamarca linguist, the cabinet of a Cuzco lady, or the collection formed by two brothers in Yucatán (Gänger, chap. 5; Farro, chap. 3; Sellen, chap. 4); to the significance of drawings or atlases, of murals or note-taking for our protagonists' understanding and vision of ancient America (Farro, chap. 3; Roy, chap. 7; Pillsbury, chap. 2);[46] and to the role of commerce and fraud and of sociability or entertainment (Podgorny, chap. 6; Gänger, chap. 5) in the early history of archaeology. Most of the studies contained in this volume opt for an approach of *penser par cas*, relying on and making available little known archival material, unpublished images, and rarely recognized publications, including the periodical press of various Spanish American countries. The historiography of American archaeology, both North and South, has privileged for decades the study of grand sociopolitical narratives; institutionalized public settings; and the politics of archaeology, and these by now familiar considerations remain indispensable. It is essential to complement these studies, however, with another history of archaeology—one that is attentive to contingence and nonlinearity, to the smaller scale and the finer grain, to that which is secluded rather than public, truncated rather than formative, and subtle rather than dominant. This book is, therefore, also a plea for zooming in on details, with one eye, while the other watches out for the wider world.

The Chapters

We have divided the volume into three parts in order to draw our readers' attention to the wider historical themes around which the essays gather.

The articles assembled in part 1, "Interplays," share a concern with the interplay and transfers between different fields of knowledge—between archaeological practices or discourses and the methods, terminologies, and modes of substantiation employed in linguistic ethnography, comparative anatomy, and geology. Miruna Achim discusses the coming together of antiquities and human physical remains—bones and skulls—in the same epistemological and physical spaces of early-nineteenth-century travel reports and collections from the site of Palenque, an association, commonplace as it might seem today, that was neither natural nor obvious at the time. Achim traces not only how both traditions formed "an unexpected synthesis of a common search" for the origin of American man but also how this synthesis was emblematic of a time when knowledge about the ancient past of America still "occupied a fluid space, ripe with conceptual possibilities." Achim's article introduces the reader to John Lloyd Stephens, a traveler whose writings make their appearance in a number of contributions in this volume—on Mexico (Sellen, chap. 4), but also on other, more distant areas (Pillsbury, chap. 2; Gilkeson, chap. 10; Podgorny, chap. 6); the effect of Stephens's Pan-American "best seller" on the development of archaeology in the Americas is one of many questions touched on in the volume that opens up new fields of research.

The subsequent chapter by Joanne Pillsbury (chap. 2) studies the effect of the natural sciences on the discovery of a deep pre-Hispanic past—one that extended well before the Inca—through nineteenth-century large-scale archaeological atlases. Pillsbury traces how pictorial conventions from botany, engineering, and geology provided templates for the depiction and eventually the study of antiquities that contributed to a growing understanding of evidence of the passage of time. Máximo Farro's chapter (3), in turn, traces the history of linguistic ethnography in Argentina—and more particularly, the analogies and interdependencies between linguistics and the practices of natural history and antiquarianism in the work of the Argentine Samuel Alexander Lafone Quevedo (1835–1920). Farro's emphasis rests on Lafone Quevedo's method of working with words as pieces of historical research, in the manner of naturalists and antiquarians, collecting, sorting, arranging, and classifying vocabularies and making etymologies as if they were sets of natural history specimens or antiquities.

Achim, Pillsbury, and Farro alike observe how their practitioners dismantled, slighted, or remade disciplinary divides and how they created novel understandings and techniques for and changed the outline of the emergent discipline of archaeology in that process. Particularly in the Americas, part 1 holds, the making of archaeology as a field cannot be adequately understood without taking seriously its relationship with the study of nature—in the shape of natural history, geological fieldwork, or botanizing.

Part 2, "Settings," brings together essays on particular collections and their owners—miscellaneous assortments linking natural specimens and antiquities that materialized at the crossing or in defiance of emerging disciplinary divides. Adam Sellen (chap. 4) studies the collection formed by the brothers Leandro and José María Camacho in early-nineteenth-century Yucatán. As Sellen is able to show, various historical strands gave meaning to the brothers' assembly of pre-Columbian vases, instruments and adornments, colonial weaponry, paintings on canvas, shells, precious metal, colored sands, and types of wood: to some observers the objects' value lay in their meaningfulness as historical documents; to others it lay in their picturesqueness; and to yet others, it lay in the collection's overall function as "microcosms of Yucatecan virtues."

Stefanie Gänger's chapter (5) studies the history of the cabinet of curiosities created by Ana María Centeno de Romainville (1817–1874) in mid-nineteenth-century Cuzco—an assemblage linking Andean antiquities with bright corals, three-legged chickens, and dissected fetuses. Centeno's collection, the article argues, consciously brought antiquities together with natural specimens under the shared rubric of the "curious." Centeno's collection, like the Camacho brothers', is testimony to the variety of reasons and the diversity of settings where antiquities could still be collected, considered, and marveled at long into the nineteenth century.

Irina Podgorny's chapter (6), in turn, traces the itinerary of Joseph Charles Manó across Spanish America, an impostor naturalist who, in the course of his peripatetic life collected, exhibited, and studied anything from botanical, mineralogical, and zoological specimens to archaeological artifacts and from "curiosities" to maps and books. He did so mainly because he was well aware of what Spanish America's governing elites were willing to pay for during the 1870s and early 1880s: collections and reports that conveyed comprehensive visions of their national territories—the diversity and richness of both their natural kingdoms and their arts. Instead of judging the collections of Centeno, the Camachos, or Manó as "unscientific," as many have done, the essays gathered in this section consider the extent to which they are a reflection of a nineteenth-century scientific culture that had not yet established criteria for what exactly American archaeology was to be.

Part 2 closes with a chapter by Susan Roy (chap. 7) on the history of a set of murals by artist William Taylor for the American Museum of Natural History that served as a naturalized backdrop to the material culture exhibits of the Northwest Coast Hall of Indians. Roy's work stresses how a connection between nature and indigeneity was made, not only through representation on the side of the elites in the museum but also by indigenous peoples themselves, to forward legal claims and to reestablish possession: she is able to show how aboriginal leaders appropriated artistic and other cultural narratives about their deep connection to their territory in conflicts over land rights and resources with the settler population.

Part 3, "Narratives," returns to the broader issue of how to write the prehistory and early history of the New World and to the answers men and women across the Americas gave to this question over the long nineteenth and twentieth centuries. The section opens with a look back at the decades following the founding of the Empire of Brazil, when its intellectuals faced the question of how to write a history of Brazil that would encompass the pasts of the native populations. Based on an analysis of the work of the botanist Carl Friedrich von Martius, the expedition of the Comissão Científica de Exploração to Ceará in the late 1850s, and the anthropological exhibition at the National Museum in Rio de Janeiro early in the 1880s, Maria Margaret Lopes's chapter (8) traces how practitioners in Brazil, through a reading of the work of Johann Gottfried von Herder and Giambattista Vico, sought to determine discourses, practices, and settings for the study of their country's indigenous past. Although von Martius and others had first proposed a place for the study of the native population in the realm of history, Lopes observes how the practice was transferred irrevocably to anthropology and the natural sciences toward the end of the nineteenth century. The article unfolds a discussion of several understudied fields—most importantly, perhaps, the effect of an emphasis on the recording of myths and language as material evidence to write the history of the native population of the New World.

Alice Kehoe's chapter (9) traces how archaeological theories and discoveries in the United States cemented a place for indigeneity outside history during the long nineteenth century. She traces, above all, the discourses that equated Native Americans with nature, providing a justification for the conquest and forced removal of Native Americans from their traditional lands and for a denial of Native American history, humanity, and modernity. After denouncing the earlier subjection of indigenous peoples, Kehoe discusses the transformative Native American Graves Protection and Repatriation Act (NAGPRA) legislation of 1990 that has forced the return of skeletal remains and collections of culturally significant archaeological and ethnographic artifacts to the peoples from whom they were taken; this enactment is seen as a milestone ushering in a new era of interactions between First Nations and the U.S. government.

The book closes with a chapter (10) by John Gilkeson, who provides an overview of the emergence and growth of the field of ethnohistory, its insertion in history and acceptance by North American historians, and with it the development of "historicity" for native peoples; his article tells the story of how Native Americans, once viewed as peoples without history, have come to be seen as historical peoples with their own ever-changing and developing pasts. Both Kehoe and Gilkeson conclude optimistically by extending their broad surveys to the present and showing how Native Americans today are actively redefining and making their pasts.

* * *

The articles assembled in this volume study the development of an interest in nature and antiquities in the nineteenth century through small-scale, fine-grained, and contingent studies focusing in their majority on the private realm. In the decades around 1900, several of the most outstanding and prominent of these private collections formed in Peru or Mexico were sold, either to central governments in their countries of origin or, in the absence of an appropriate state policy to hinder exportation, to the period's large collecting museums in Europe and the United States. Intriguingly, and tellingly, the collections disintegrated in the process, with governments and increasingly specialized museums acquiring only one or two specific types of objects, usually those that were intelligible within the framework of the disciplines and models of collecting that consolidated toward the end of the nineteenth century: either pre-Columbian antiquities or fossils or plants. The sale of these collections, but above all their fragmentation en route, bears witness to the end of a time when the study of America's antiquities, its discourses and practices, and its place in a wider epistemological landscape was still "in the making"—a time when the interest in nature and antiquities in the Americas still had many faces and resided in as many, or more, material forms.

To conclude, an anecdote. The historian Marie-Noëlle Bourguet noted an eloquent detail in her analysis of the notebook Alexander von Humboldt kept during his journey in Italy, which he undertook several months after his return from the New World, where he had traveled from 1799 to 1804. Faced with some celebrated sculptures of classical antiquity in Rome, Humboldt, surprisingly, paid but little attention to their aesthetics; instead, after years of observing rocks, examining natural specimens, and measuring heights in Spanish America, his first impulse was, as the scribbles in his notebook reveal, to take out his glasses and instruments, recording the mineralogical composition and taking measurements of the statue.[47] Historians have long, and prominently, claimed Humboldt's gaze was "Imperial" on his arrival in the New World,[48] but, as this episode shows, it had, in a way, at least, become "American" by the time of his departure: his American experience reconfigured his approach to materiality and the past; it altered his perception of the antiquities of the Old World. The nature of antiquities in the Americas had struck back, seemingly, at the heart of the Old World's classical antiquity.

Notes

1. John G. A. Pocock, *Barbarism and Religion*, vol. 4., *Barbarians, Savages and Empires* (Cambridge: Cambridge University Press, 2008), 161.
2. Ibid., 168.
3. Ibid., 157, 76.
4. Ibid., 176–77.
5. See Jorge Cañizares-Esguerra, *How to Write the History of the New World: Histories, Epistemologies, and Identities in the Eighteenth-Century Atlantic World* (Stanford, CA: Stanford University Press, 2001).
6. Pocock, *Barbarism and Religion*, 158.
7. Cañizares-Esguerra, *How to Write the History of the New World*, 6.
8. Ibid., chap. 1, 4.
9. Ibid., 235.
10. Ibid., 5.
11. Ibid., 45.
12. See Alain Schnapp, "Between Antiquarians and Archaeologists: Continuities and Ruptures," in *Histories of Archaeology: A Reader in the History of Archaeology*, ed. Tim Murray and Christopher Evans (Oxford: Oxford University Press, 2008).
13. George W. Stocking Jr., "Essays on Museums and Material Culture," in *Objects and Others: Essays on Museums and Material Culture*, ed. George W. Stocking Jr. (Madison: University of Wisconsin Press, 1985); Elizabeth A. Williams, "Art and Artifact at the Trocadero: Ars Americana and the Primitivist Revolution," ibid., 147.
14. See Christopher Whitehead, *Museums and the Construction of Disciplines: Art and Archaeology in Nineteenth-Century Britain* (London: Duckworth, 2009); Irina Podgorny, *El sendero del tiempo y de las causas accidentales: Los espacios de la prehistoria en la Argentina, 1850–1910* (Rosario: Prohistoria Ediciones, 2009), chap. 2.
15. See also John V. Pickstone, *Ways of Knowing: A New History of Science, Technology and Medicine* (Manchester: Manchester University Press, 2000); Samuel J. M. M. Alberti, *Nature and Culture: Objects, Disciplines and the Manchester Museum* (Manchester: Manchester University Press, 2009), 15–16.
16. Pickstone, *Ways of Knowing*, 72. See also Vladimir Jankovic, "The Place of Nature and the Nature of Place: The Chorographic Challenge to the History of British Provincial Science," *History of Science* 38, no. 1 (2000): 79–113.
17. Krzysztof Pomian, *Collectors and Curiosities: Paris and Venice, 1500–1800* (Cambridge: Polity Press, 1990), 4–5.
18. See Irina Podgorny, "The Reliability of the Ruins," *Journal of the Spanish Cultural Studies* 8, no. 2 (2007):213–33; Joanne Pillsbury and Lisa Trever, "The King, the Bishop, and the Creation of an American Antiquity," *Ñawpa Pacha* 29 (2008): 191–219.

19. Monica Barnes and David Fleming, "Charles-Marie de La Condamine's Report on Ingapirca and the Development of Scientific Field Work in the Andes," *Andean Past* 2 (1989): 175–236; Joanne Pillsbury, "Perspectives: Representing the Pre-Columbian Past," in *Past Presented: Archaeological Illustration and the Ancient Americas*, ed. Joanne Pillsbury (Washington, DC: Dumbarton Oaks Research Library and Collection, 2012), 10–13.

20. Alain Schnapp, *The Discovery of the Past: The Origins of Archaeology* (Paris: British Museum Press, 1993), 280.

21. See Lynn L. Merrill, *The Romance of Victorian Natural History* (New York: Oxford University Press, 1989), 5.

22. As Alain Schnapp has pointed out, the archaeologist is still a collector, albeit "of a peculiar kind" and with a distinctive method (Schnapp, *Discovery of the Past*, 12–13).

23. George W. Stocking Jr., "Philanthropoids and Vanishing Cultures: Rockefeller Funding and the End of the Museum Era in Anglo-American Anthropology," in *Objects and Others: Essays on Museums and Material Culture*, ed. George W. Stocking Jr. (Madison: University of Wisconsin Press, 1985), 114.

24. Peter Conwy Rowley, *From Genesis to Prehistory: The Archaeological Three Age System and Its Contested Reception in Denmark, Britain and Ireland*, Oxford Studies in the History of Archaeology (New York: Oxford University Press, 2007); Glyn Daniel, *The Idea of Prehistory* (Cleveland: World, 1962); A. Bowdoin Van Riper, *Men Among the Mammoths: Victorian Science and the Discovery of Human Prehistory* (Chicago: University of Chicago Press, 1993).

25. Peter Galison, *Image and Logic: A Material Culture of Microphysics* (Chicago: University of Chicago Press, 1997), 794.

26. Ibid., 840.

27. Tim Murray and Christopher Evans, eds., *Histories of Archaeology: A Reader in the History of Archaeology* (Oxford: Oxford University Press, 2008), 3.

28. Donald R. Kelley, "Introduction," in *History and the Disciplines: The Reclassification of Knowledge in Early Modern Europe*, ed. Donald R. Kelley (Rochester, NY: University of Rochester Press, 1997), 2.

29. Pickstone, *Ways of Knowing*, 9.

30. Philip L. Kohl and Claire Fawcett, eds. *Nationalism, Politics, and the Practice of Archaeology* (Cambridge: Cambridge University Press, 1995); Philip L. Kohl, M. Kozelsky, and N. Ben-Yehuda, eds., *Selective Remembrances: Archaeology in the Construction, Commemoration, and Consecration of National Pasts* (Chicago: University of Chicago Press, 2007); Philip L. Kohl, "Nationalism and Archaeology: On the Constructions of Nations and the Reconstructions of the Remote Past," *Annual Review of Anthropology* 27 (1998): 223–46; Murray and Evans, *Histories of Archaeology*.

31. See Stefan Altekamp, *Rückkehr nach Afrika: Italienische Kolonialarchäologie in Libyen 1911–1943* (Cologne: Böhlau, 2000); Henrika Kuklick, "Contested Monuments: The Politics of Archaeology in Southern Africa," in *Colonial Situations: Essays of the Contextualization of Ethnographic Knowledge*, ed. George W. Stocking Jr. (Madison: University of Wisconsin Press, 1991).

32. See Donald Malcolm Reid, *Whose Pharaohs? Archaeology, Museums, and Egyptian National Identity from Napoleon to World War I* (Berkeley: University of California Press, 2002); Margarita Díaz-Andreu, *A World History of Nineteenth-*

Century Archaeology: Nationalism, Colonialism, and the Past (Oxford: Oxford University Press, 2007).

33. On the importance of the private sphere in scientific practices in Latin America, see, e.g., Stefanie Gänger, *Relics of the Past: The Collecting and Study of Pre-Columbian Antiquities in Peru and Chile, 1837–1911*, Oxford Studies in the History of Archaeology (Oxford: Oxford University Press, 2014); Irina Podgorny, "Bones and Devices in the Constitution of Paleontology in Argentina at the End of the Nineteenth Century," *Science in Context* 18, no. 2 (2005): 249–83.

34. José Alcina Franch, *Arqueólogos o anticuarios: Historia antigua de la arqueología en la América Española* (Barcelona: Ediciones de Serbal, 1995); Kohl and Fawcett, *Nationalism*.

35. See Jonathan E. Reyman, ed., *Rediscovering Our Past: Essays on the History of American Archaeology*, Worldwide Archaeology Series 2 (Aldershot: Avebury, 1990); Ludomir Lozny, ed., *Comparative Archaeologies* (New York: Springer, 2011).

36. See Sally Gregory Kohlstedt, "International Exchange and National Style: A View of Natural History Museums in the United States, 1850–1900," in *Scientific Colonialism: A Cross-Cultural Comparison*, ed. Nathan Reingold and Marc Rothenberg (Washington, DC: Smithsonian Institution Press, 1987); Maria Margaret Lopes and Irina Podgorny, "The Shaping of Latin American Museums of Natural History, 1850–1990," *Osiris* 15 (2000): 108–18. See also Flora E. S. Kaplan, ed., *Museums and the Making of "Ourselves": The Role of Objects in National Identity* (London: Leicester University Press, 1994).

37. Susan Sheets-Pyenson, *Cathedrals of Science: The Development of Colonial Natural History Museums During the Late Nineteenth Century* (Montreal: McGill-Queens University Press, 1988). See the work in this line as developed by M. Margaret Lopes and Miruna Achim and I. Podgorny, eds., *Museos al detalle: Colecciones, antigüedades e historia natural, 1790–1870* (Rosario: Prohistoria, 2013).

38. See Irina Podgorny, "'Silent and Alone': How the Ruins of Palenque Were Taught to Speak the Language of Archaeology," in *Comparative Archaeologies: A Sociological View of the Science of the Past*, ed. Ludomir Lozny (New York: Springer, 2011), 527–53.

39. Juan Pimentel, "The Iberian Vision: Science and Empire in the Framework of a Universal Monarchy, 1500–1800," *Osiris* 15 (2000): 18.

40. Ibid.; Jorge Cañizares-Esguerra, "Iberian Colonial Science," *Isis* 96 (2005): 64–70.

41. Sujit Sivasundaram, "Sciences and the Global: On Methods, Questions, and Theory," *Isis* 101 (2010): 146–58.

42. See Marc-Antoine Kaeser, "On the International Roots of Prehistory," in Murray and Evans, *Histories of Archaeology*.

43. See Elizabeth Hill Boone, "The Defining Sample: How We Pursue the Pre-Columbian Past," in *A Pre-Columbian World*, ed. Jeffrey Quilter and Mary Miller (Washington, DC: Dumbarton Oaks Research Library and Collection, 2006), 21–23.

44. Miruna Achim and Irina Podgorny, "Descripción densa, historia de la ciencia y las prácticas del coleccionismo en los años de la revolución, la guerra y la independencia," in *Museos al detalle: Colecciones, antigüedades e historia natural, 1790–1870*, ed. Miruna Achim and Irina Podgorny (Rosario: Prohistoria Ediciones, 2013), 15–26.

45. See Jacob W. Gruber, "Ethnographic Salvage and the Shaping of Anthropology," *American Anthropologist* 72, no. 6 (1970): 1289–99; Marshall Sahlins, "'Sentimental Pessimism' and Ethnographic Experience; or, Why Culture Is Not a Disappearing 'Object,'" in *Biographies of Scientific Objects*, ed. Lorraine Daston (Chicago: University of Chicago Press, 2000). For "salvage" discourses among archaeologists working in the Andes and the Southern Cone in the nineteenth century, see Gänger, *Relics of the Past*.

46. See also Joanne Pillsbury, ed., *Past Presented: Archaeological Illustration and the Ancient Americas* (Washington, DC: Dumbarton Oaks Research Library and Collection, 2012); Anke Te Heesen, "Accounting for the Natural World," in *Colonial Botany: Science, Commerce and Politics in the Early Modern World*, ed. Londa Schiebinger and Claudia Swan (Philadelphia: University of Pennsylvania Press, 2005).

47. Marie-Noëlle Bourguet, "Escritura de viaje y construcción científica del mundo: La libreta de Italia de Alexander von Humboldt," *Redes* 14, no. 28 (2008): 81–95.

48. Mary Louise Pratt, *Imperial Eyes: Travel Writing and Transculturation* (London: Routledge, 1992).

PART ONE

Interplays

CHAPTER ONE

Skulls and Idols

Anthropometrics, Antiquity Collections, and the Origin of American Man, 1810–1850

Miruna Achim

Findings at an Ancient Tomb

In the mid-1840s, John Lloyd Stephens was a best-selling travel author in the United States and abroad. He achieved his first critical and commercial success with his *Incidents of Travel in Egypt, Arabia Petrae and the Holy Land* (1837), which fed the American and English fascination with the lands associated with the Bible. The second "incidents of travel" were located in Greece, Turkey, Russia, and Poland (1838). But his enduring claims to fame were his two books on Central America, Chiapas, and Yucatán, which inflamed the imagination of all future explorers of the region. Lavishly illustrated by the English artist Frederick Catherwood, the *Incidents of Travel in Central America, Chiapas and Yucatan* (1841) sold twenty thousand copies in the first three months after publication.[1] The same year, Stephens and Catherwood returned to Yucatán, resulting in the fourth and last book in the series, *Incidents of Travel in Yucatan* (1843). Besides the impressions of ancient sites, complemented by observations on the political and social conditions of the region, Stephens avidly collected ruins and even bought parts of the pyramid complexes at Copán, Palenque, and Uxmal, intending to ship them to the United States where they would form a new antiquities museum in New York City. Ultimately, his project proved unsuccessful, though it remains synonymous with the outsized romantic ambitions of early-nineteenth-century antiquarianism itself.

Along with objects of a more antiquarian nature, Stephens also collected human bones. In an "incident" that occurred during his second trip to Yucatán, in the hacienda of San Francisco—where, he suspected, the ancient town of Ticul had once stood—Stephens offered his readers a glimpse into the fledgling nineteenth-century practice of bone collecting. Guided by the local priest, Estanislao Carillo, himself a collector and writer on antiquities, and Stephens's go-between with the Indians, Stephens inspected the town, noting the few antiquities that remained: a beautifully crafted vessel and an ancient sepulcher—a four-feet-high "square stone structure," which Stephens thought "had not been disturbed since the earth and stones had been packed down on top."[2] Suspecting there were bones to be found inside, he ordered the Indians to work: after six hours of removing stones with their crowbars, under the "prodigious force" of the beating sun, they came upon a skull and then the rest of a skeleton, which had been placed in a sitting posture "with its face toward the sun, the knees bent against the stomach, the arms doubled at the elbow, and the hands clasping the neck or supporting the head."[3] Unable to disinter the skeleton without damage, Stephens contented himself with some of the bones and the broken skull; adding to his dismay, all the teeth fell out when he tried lifting the skull from the ground, but the Indians picked them up, one by one. "It was strangely interesting," mused Stephens-turned-Hamlet, "with the ruined structures towering around us, after a lapse of unknown ages, to bring to light these buried bones. Whose were they?"[4]

On the evidence of the "rudeness" of the sepulcher, the well-preserved state of the bones, and their closeness to the surface, Stephens deemed it was "impossible to ascribe [the] ruins to Egyptian builders,"[5] as ruins in the Yucatán frequently were in the antiquarian accounts Stephens may have read before his trip. The Indians' concerns over the fate of the bones corroborated Stephens's impressions: "They are the bones of our kinsman," they claimed. "What will our kinsman say at our dragging forth his bones!"[6] So deep was their empathy with the remains that Stephens knew that had it not been for the priest, they "would have covered them up and left the sepulcher."[7] Despite the misgivings of those present, the bones were not reburied but were "born away forever from the bones of their kindred" on "rough journeys on the backs of mules and Indians," and they became "so crumbled and broken that in a court of law, their ancient proprietor would not be able to identify them."[8] Wrapped in "a pocket handkerchief," they would eventually be delivered to Doctor Samuel George Morton in Philadelphia, "known for his research he has bestowed upon the physical features of the aboriginal American races."[9] Stephens hoped that the bones found in Ticul would help Morton answer Stephens's questions regarding Yucatán's original inhabitants.

Morton obliged. On August 9, 1842, during a meeting of the American Academy of Natural Sciences in Philadelphia, Morton presented the skeleton received from Stephens together with four others from Yucatán sent in by Benjamin Norman. "The skeleton, dilapidated as it is, has afforded [Morton] some valuable facts," Stephens commented later, "and has been a subject of some interesting reflections."[10] After reconstructing the skull, Morton found it to have a "remarkably" flat and vertical occiput and an exceedingly small parietal or lateral diameter, no less than five inches and eight tenths, features that identified it with "the same *type* of the physical conformation which has been bestowed with amazing uniformity upon all the tribes on our continent, from Canada to Patagonia, and from the Atlantic to the Pacific Ocean."[11] Like some rare animal fossil, which could be successfully identified with its ideal type in a zoological atlas, the skeleton from Ticul was American,[12] and this in turn corroborated Stephens's hypotheses about the origin of the builders of Yucatán's ancient civilizations. Stephens explains:

> If his [Morton's] opinion is correct—and I believe it is—if this skeleton does present the same *type* of physical conformation with all the tribes of our continent—then, indeed, do these crumbling bones declare, as with a voice from the grave, that we cannot go back to any nation of the Old World for the builders of cities; they are not the works of people who have passed away, and whose history is lost, but of the same great *race* which, changed, miserable, and degraded, still clings around their ruins.[13]

Stephens's account of the skeleton's trajectory from Yucatán to Philadelphia—whence it would return to the pages of Stephens's book, not as crumbling bones, but "affording . . . some valuable facts" about the origin of American civilization—presents us with a two-sided story: on the one hand, Stephens is confident that he has enlisted "science" to prove his theory, and on the other hand, there is the puzzling idea that this pocket handkerchief full of analyzed bone carries the weight to overthrow the speculations of earlier explorers. The presence of these bones in Stephens's travels leads us, his twenty-first-century readers, to map some aspects of the problems of early-nineteenth-century scholarship about American ruins.

Considering bones and antiquities to be objects of a self-consciously "scientific" form of collecting, commonplace as it might seem today, was neither natural nor obvious when Stephens published his *Incidents of Travel in Yucatán*. Antiquities were the subject of antiquarians who, since the eighteenth century, had turned their attention to things and material vestiges, thus developing a program of inquiry that allotted a disciplinary niche for the study of peoples who had left few or no written documents, as was the case with ancient Americans. Bones, on the other hand, were the object of investigation by comparative anatomists, such as Morton, who attempted to establish and impose stable classifications of human races by, to a certain extent, modeling their practice on successes in the comparative anatomy and classification of animals. This essay explores how these two traditions, antiquarianism and comparative anatomy, came together in the same physical space of collecting and in the same epistemological space to form an unexpected synthesis of a common search for America's ancient past.[14]

While it reflected scholarly approximations and alliances around a common question, the conceptual association between bones and antiquities was conditioned by political imaginaries and geographies that determined the limits within which the antiquarian in the present could envision the past. In the conclusion to this essay I explore the more political implications of this association to suggest that as bones and antiquities came together to produce facts about America's ancient past, their study both provided and reinforced strong rationales for driving a gulf between the civilized ancestors, who had left their artifacts and their remains as a signature of their high degree of civilization, and the "miserable and degraded" contemporary Indians who were no legitimate heirs of the long-gone ancients. Ultimately, the association between bones and idols laid out new grounds for the management of Americana, granting the collector/savant title to collect, export, own, and study those vestiges.

Signs and Stones: Antiquarian Interpretations of America's Unwritten Past

At the first encounters between Europeans and Americans in the fifteenth and sixteenth centuries, there was little doubt that sculptured idols, codices, ceramics, pottery, weapons, and ornaments were all part of the material and religious culture of Americans. After the conquest, these objects became the target of systematic destruction, motivated, on one hand, by the conquerors' desire to extract gold and precious minerals to add to the flow of goods to Europe, and on the other, by the missionaries' attempts to extirpate "idolatry," that is, to put a stop to the objects' continuing religious and cultural meanings to the Amerindians.[15] This concerted effort at destruction would be lamented by eighteenth-century scholars who began to write accounts of America's ancient past integrating American ruins into a larger story of European history. Because of the disappearance of written evidence that could have provided explanations of the past, scholars were forced to make do with the material fragments that had escaped destruction. Study of these fragments called for methods of reconstruction and interpretation that were different from those that historians applied to written texts, methods that had been put into practice by antiquarians to retrieve the pasts of European cultures with few or no written remains, such as Stonehenge or the Etruscan civilization. Archaeological historian Alain Schnapp has suggested that the epistemological transition in the eighteenth century from text to object as a reliable form of evidence entailed the modeling of antiquarian practices after those of the natural sciences: antiquarians performed object "autopsies," opening, dividing, and invading objects to explore their materiality through the senses of touch, taste, smell, and above all, sight.[16]

It was in the late eighteenth century that artifacts from America's past came under this kind of scrutiny. Earlier midcentury discoveries at Herculaneum and Pompey, in the Spanish viceroyalty of Naples, were instrumental in the development of an imperial Spanish policy that aimed at the systematic discovery and study of ruins across the empire, contrary to accusations that the Spanish never took an interest in America's ancient past other than to destroy it. The complex at Palenque in Yucatán, for example, was the focus of antiquarian expeditions, which surveyed the site, using the same methods and producing the kind of data engineers employed when sinking shafts for mines or transporting massive weights, or naturalists used to quantify the extent of the empire's potential natural resources.[17] Interest in antiquities was not driven exclusively from Madrid but also emerged endogenously among the educated criollo elite. For instance, in 1790, street work in the center of Mexico City revealed two particularly impressive sculptures, and the city's most famous natural philosophers, Antonio de León y Gama and José Antonio Alzate y Ramírez, engaged in a fast-paced debate over the meanings of the stones. Failing to arrive at a consensus over the iconographic details, they turned to quantitative studies of the statues' volume, weight, and chemical composition without, however, solving the dispute. Yet here were two things the debaters agreed on: the high degree of civilization reached by the ancient

Mexicans and the relevance of antiquarian studies to those committed to writing and understanding local pasts.[18] In part, the material turn in the writings of these American criollos was a matter of political positioning, and it reflected a growing unhappiness with and an attempt to modify the philosophical histories of writers such as Voltaire, who allotted America a less than favorable place in their universal histories of civilization while placing the story of Europe's development at the forefront.[19]

In the nineteenth century, the metanarrative of American antiquarianism tended toward the question of the origins of American man and the various Amerindian cultures. Two questions in particular preoccupied nineteenth-century students of America's past as the vestiges of that past began circulating increasingly from and to the newly independent American nations: who were the builders of America's past civilizations, and how could the discrepancy between America's civilized ancient inhabitants and the "barbarous" contemporary Indian be reconciled. Alexander von Humboldt's writings, particularly his *Vues des Cordillères, et monumens des peuples indigènes de l'Amérique* (Paris, 1810), were a starting point for both of these reflections. Humboldt suggested that America was settled by "Toltecs," who crossed over from Asia and migrated South, building impressive urban complexes on their way—at Teotihuacan, Tula, and Cholula, in central Mexico, in the seventh century and at Palenque in the eleventh—until they settled in Peru, where they gave rise to the Inca civilization. Humboldt claimed that the monuments the Toltecs built provided a picture of the universal progress of humankind holding an intermediate place between those of Scythian tribes and those of the ancient dwellers of Hindustan. After the Toltecs left, central Mexico was occupied by other peoples from the north, such as the Aztecs and the Tlaxcaltecas, who never reached the stage of civilization reached by the Toltecs. The Spanish presence in America annulled all possibility of future progress for them. American Indians would continue to live at the margins of history until they vanished.

The framework of Humboldt's narrative changed little during the nineteenth century, even when its details did. The discovery of ancient mounds in North America was interpreted as confirmation of the unity of America's past civilizations;[20] at the same time, it strengthened the impression of discontinuity between the civilized peoples of the past and the "barbarian" Indians of the present. Some students of America's ruins held that these were originally built by an altogether different people who had become extinct. Others simply amplified Humboldt's idea that the Amerindians, after the fall of the original builders, had morally and physically degenerated. Believers in discontinuity had a hard time agreeing on who the other, civilized ancestors were, and the first half of the nineteenth century saw a proliferation of theories about the origin of American man. As antiquarians transformed new sources of evidence into "readable texts," they put into motion competing epistemic methods that traced the history of the unwritten past via philology, mythology, or the evidence of concrete objects. Protocols for linking American civilization with an assortment of plausible or fantastic origins, from ancient Egypt to China, from Israel to Hindustan, were so diverse and so promiscuously used as to make it difficult to separate cranks from mainstream figures.

The English historian John Ranking, for instance, linked fossil mastodons discovered in America—which he mistook for elephants—with the arrival in present-day Peru of the Moguls and their animals on huge sea rafts, having started off in Japan sometime in the fourteenth century.[21] One theory of American origins stands out among others: the Central American government official and explorer Juan Galindo tried to persuade the members of scientific societies across the Atlantic that America was the origin of all civilization, the birthplace whence all migrations sprang, but as American-founded civilizations flourished in Europe and Asia, those in America slowly degenerated.[22] This extremely abbreviated description of the state of American antiquarian studies shows what a variegated field it was and what variegated methods of reading the evidence sustained it. As new findings became available to Western scholars—through the objects themselves but frequently through reproductions (drawings, engravings, molds, and photographs)—they were combined, often through extraordinary contortions of logic, with older premises. During the early decades of the nineteenth century, human bones became just one of the newer forms of evidence to inform antiquarian studies.

Bone Collecting

Human bones had been collected as relics for hundreds of years, but it was not until the late eighteenth century that they became scientific proof of the physical, moral, and intellectual differences between human groups. The story of how this happened, like that of antiquarianism, is complex and convoluted, and I will sketch out only its basic premises here.[23] Its milestones include the endeavors of naturalists such as Georges Louis Leclerc (Comte de Buffon) and Carl Linnaeus to write man into the natural history of animals and into animal taxonomies, respectively, and to account, at the same time, for the diversity of humankind. By the mid eighteenth century, Linnaeus had classified the genus *Homo* into more than one species, and had organized species into a gradual progression of physical characteristics, from ape to man, whereby some groups of humans were closest to apes. The methods used by comparative anatomists like Georges Cuvier to study and compare animals, where bones played an important role, became relevant for the study of human groups. A series of parameters—such as the proportion of the cranium to the face, the projection of the jaw, and the breadth of the cheekbones—became empirical proof of differences between groups. Thus, in 1770, the Amsterdam anatomist Petrus Camper, as part of a guide to drawing peoples, proposed an aesthetic classification of human groups on the basis of the projection of the jaw, the "facial angle": Europeans' facial angle was the widest (the aesthetic ideal being the Greek and Roman classical profile), while Africans had the narrowest angle of all humans, followed by monkeys, whose angle was superior to that of dogs, birds, frogs, fishes, and so on, down the chain of being. Increasingly, moral and intellectual faculties were predicated on these same physical gradations. "Race," which had been identified during previous centuries with the origin or bloodline of a people, became an increasingly atemporal and fixed notion signified as a natural category and anchored in the body and not on other factors, such as climate, which had played an important role in defining the differences between human groups over centuries. By the nineteenth century, the biological notion of race gained potency in complex historical circumstances: a new phase in European colonialism increased the flow of information about nonwhite peoples in Europe while it made urgent the development of a scientific basis for studying and governing indigenous human beings.[24]

The German anatomist Johann Friedrich Blumenbach accomplished for human comparative anatomy what Cuvier did for animals. A lifelong collector of human bones, particularly skulls, Blumenbach used "facial projection" as a criterion for dividing humankind into five races, from Caucasians (a term coined by Blumenbach on the basis of the purportedly perfect skull of a woman from the Caucasus) to Mongols, Malays, Americans, and Ethiopians.[25] Blumenbach's *De generis humani varietate naturae* (1776) became obligatory references for all future studies of race even when anatomists disagreed on what the principal divisions of mankind should be. Some, such as Julien-Joseph Virey, listed two races, while others, such as Bory de St. Vincent, listed as many as fifteen.[26] Within this discussion, there was little consensus about where to place American man in part because few scholars had access to American skeletons before the third decade of the nineteenth century. During the 1790s, Blumenbach had received a few from his correspondents in Philadelphia; Humboldt would supply him with four, collected during his voyage to the Western Hemisphere: a skull from the upper Orinoco and a decorated trophy head and the skulls of two women from Brazil.[27] But by the 1820s, after most Spanish American countries became independent, the commerce in skulls, skeletons, and mummies widened. In 1823, for instance, Lucas Alamán, the Mexican Minister of Internal and External Affairs, sent Blumenbach the skull of a Mexican Indian.[28]

It was Samuel George Morton (1799–1851), who would make the most of increasingly available American human remains. Born in Philadelphia, Morton studied medicine at the University of Edinburgh at a time when phrenology had a considerable intellectual influence on the study of the human skull. Though Morton would not adhere to the strict specifics linking brain topography to moral and intellectual faculties, he did share the phrenologist's ambition to reveal the physical underpinnings of human intellectual and moral diversity. After returning to Philadelphia in 1824, he became a lecturer in anatomy at the University of Philadelphia and began collecting human skulls for the purpose of measuring and illustrating the differences in skull forms between the five great races of men as classified by Blumenbach.[29] Over the course of his life, Morton acquired 601 animal skulls and 867 human skulls, of which 338 were American and would form the basis of Morton's involvement with the study of American race.[30] Another important part of the collection was ancient and contemporary Egyptian skulls that formed the basis for his *Crania Aegyptiaca*, published in Philadelphia in 1844.

Morton's Philadelphia was a privileged place to be for a scholar interested in Americana because it was there that many networks and peoples trafficking in Americana met. Not a few of these links led directly to Morton's cabinet. As vice president of the American Academy of Natural Sciences—an institution he virtually chaired after 1828, after the academy's president William Maclure went to Mexico—Morton would be the first to unpack shipments of fossils, plant and animal specimens, minerals, human remains, antiquities, and books sent to the academy by travelers from all over the world, especially from within the United States and from south of the U.S. border. It was at the academy that Morton examined, during weekly board meetings, the human skeletons that began to arrive in the mid-1830s. Army surgeons, on the heels of white men's wars against Indians, sent him the remains of mostly contemporary North

American Indians. William Samuel Ruschenberger, a U.S. Navy surgeon stationed in Peru, was another assiduous correspondent who presented Morton with coveted objects such as the embalmed head of a mummy and skeletons from the cemetery of Arica, in the Atacama Desert, and 23 skulls from Pachacamac, the Temple of the Sun, not far from Lima.[31]

In Peru, desert conditions had preserved ancient remains. In Mexico, ground conditions were less favorable, and Morton had comparatively few Mexican skulls for his studies. In the mid-1820s, Joel Robert Poinsett, representative of the U.S. legation in Mexico and an avid collector of Mexican antiquities himself, sent the academy a human skull.[32] Marmaduke Borrough, the flamboyant U.S. consul in Veracruz—who, before his post in Mexico, held an assignment in India, whence he returned to tour the United States with a rhinoceros—was Morton's tireless broker in the bustling Atlantic port, where bona fide merchants and smugglers mingled and goods of all sorts came and left, with or without the blessings of inefficient or corrupt customs officials.[33] In Veracruz, Borrough gathered skulls, antiquities, and objects of natural history and shipped them to Morton together with descriptive letters detailing the provenance of each object.[34] The skulls had purportedly been found in ancient tombs: one was obtained by the academy's absent president Maclure in Acapacingo, sixty miles south of Mexico City; another came from San Lorenzo, east of Mexico City, courtesy of François Carlo Antommarchi, who served as Napoleon's last physician in Saint Helena before coming to Veracruz;[35] six skulls, from unspecified ancient tombs "within the territories of the Otomies, Tlascalan, and Chechemecan" nations, were obtained via José Gómez de la Cortina, coin collector and member on the board of the National Museum of Mexico; and two supposedly Aztec skulls had been donated by Dr. John P. Macartney of Mexico City.[36] In addition to the skulls he personally received from correspondents such as Ruschenberger and Burrough, Morton had access to specimens in other collections: an ancient Peruvian skull in the Peale Museum, a "Toltecan" skull—exhumed in an unspecified location close to Mexico City, together with "a great variety of antiques, vessels, masks, and ornaments."[37] At the same time, Morton traded casts, drawings, and reports with other collection owners. English geologist Joseph Barclay Pentland sent him casts of the six skulls he had unearthed around Lake Titicaca while surveying Bolivia in 1826–1827. From the "English gentleman," Frederick Edmonds, Morton received representations of heads in the form of "relics" (small clay heads) from the Temples of the Moon and of the Sun in Teotihuacan.[38] These painstakingly amassed material vestiges would form the material evidence as Morton applied himself to study the American race.

"The Skeleton Affords Facts"

Morton published various editions of his studies as his collection increased. His conclusions did not essentially change over time, and each subsequent edition confirmed and fine-tuned previous findings. His earliest study of American skulls, also the most systematic, the *Crania Americana; or, A Comparative View of the Skulls of Various Aboriginal Nations of North and South America*, published in Philadelphia in 1839, is an explicit and ambitious exposition of Morton's practice and purpose.[39] It is also, by far, the most lavishly illustrated of his books. Over 400 pages long, the folio volume includes 71 minutely detailed lithographs of skulls, each depicted dramatically full-scale in the center of the page and followed up by descriptions of its provenance and its type and a list of measurements (which included the "facial angle," the longitudinal, parietal, frontal, and vertical diameters, and the internal capacity of each skull). In addition, the book presents a colored world map of racial distribution, numerous smaller woodcuts of skulls and antiquities, comparative tables of measurements, and discussions of Morton's measuring methods and representations of his instruments. It closes with a 22-page appendix, presenting "phrenological remarks on the relation between the natural talents and dispositions of nations and the developments of their brains," authored by phrenologist George Combe.

Morton's racial classificatory system is based on Blumenbach's division of humankind into five races. In contrast with Charles Darwin, whose experiences in Edinburgh fortified his convictions concerning the common origin of mankind, Morton returned to the United States a stern subscriber to multiple origins.[40] Modifying the biblical framework, he argued that the five races were created after the Deluge, independently of each other, on different continents. Having started off separately in their respective geographical locations, races preserved their identities over time. Americans (not including the Eskimo, thought by Morton to be of Mongolian origin) constituted one recognizable race, which occupied the large expanse of land between Alaska and the South Pole. Clustering around race-specific values, skull shape and internal skull capacity were the most important indicators of the stability of race and testified to physical and organic differences that in turn determined the moral and intellectual capacities of each race and its place in the hierarchy of mankind. Morton found that on the average, the Caucasian skull, at 87 cubic inches, was the most capacious of all, "large and oval, its anterior portion full and elevated, its face, small in proportion to the head, oval, with well-proportioned features"; it followed that the Caucasian race was first among the races, "distinguished for the facility with which it attains the highest intellectual endowments."[41] By comparison, Americans came in fourth: their skulls were smaller, averaging 80 cubic inches, "wide between the parietal protuberances, prominent at the vertex, and flat on the occiput, with deep set eyes, low brows, high cheekbones, large and aquiline noses, large mouths, tumid and compressed lips" (fig. 1.1).[42] This was consistent with this race's disposition to covetousness, restlessness, foolhardiness, tendency to superstition, and averseness to cultivation. Though he accepted that the Indian's mind could expand through culture, Morton thought this was unlikely: "after

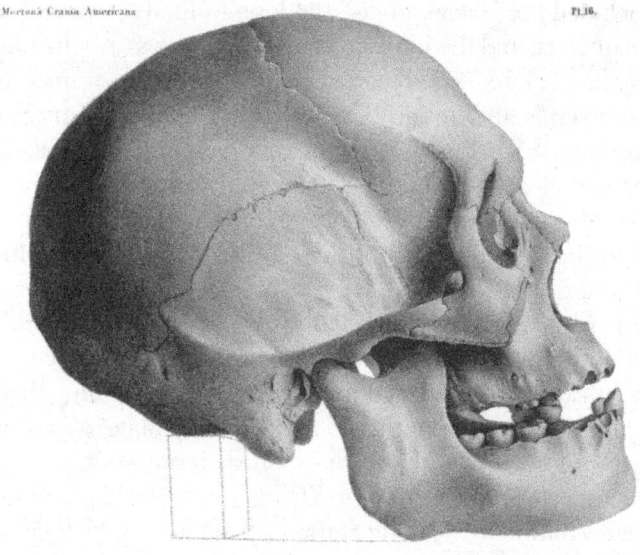

Figure 1.1. Mexican skull, "relic of the genuine Toltecan stock," donated by Joel R. Poinsett to the Academy of Natural Sciences in Philadelphia. Plate 16 in Morton's *Crania Americana*. Whipple Library, Cambridge University.

more than two centuries of contact with civilization, Indians are at the same level as before, have made no improvement."[43] Only the Caucasian skull disposed that race toward change and betterment.

If Americans, limited as they were by anatomy, hardly seemed destined for great cultural achievement, archaeological evidence—increasingly available in the context of the white American advance across the North American continent and the corresponding discoveries of mounds as well as the renewed interest in ancient ruins scattered throughout the regions of the former Spanish empire in the Americas—was proof to the contrary. How to solve the discrepancy between the negative terms in which he described aboriginal Americans with the vestiges of complex civilizations is one of the underlying goals of Morton's *Crania Americana*. A few years later, in his *Crania Aegyptiaca*, he would account for the rise of the ancient Egyptian civilization in a continent peopled by the Negro race by proposing, on the basis of his studies of Egyptian bodies from ancient tombs, that the ruling and cultural elites of ancient Egypt were actually of Caucasian stock and lived surrounded and served by the more numerous "Negro" population.

In *Crania Americana*, Morton created a different distinction, proposing the division of aboriginal Americans into two families: a semicivilized, extinct, Toltecan race, who, after building impressive urban complexes in central Mexico, migrated north and south, leaving behind such vestiges of their passage as the mounds in Ohio and the ancient ruins in Central America and Peru; and the barbarian peoples that roamed North and South America when the first Europeans encountered them and who lived on or near the ruins of Mexico and Peru and on the plains and in the West of the United States. While strongly influenced by late-Enlightenment writers such as Humboldt, who made a distinction between civilized ancient Americans and contemporary Indians, Morton's solution was, at the same time, politically charged, especially in the America of his day, when the issue of who constructed the ancient American civilizations became enormously pertinent to the issue of the rights of the Amerindian groups to territory and resources.

On their face value, Morton's anatomical findings did not support his solution. If American skulls, ancient and contemporary, on the whole had a smaller internal capacity than Caucasian skulls, that difference was particularly dramatic when averages were based exclusively on ancient American skulls. Toltecan skulls from ancient tombs in Mexico, Peru, or the mounds in the United States were even less capacious than those of contemporary "barbarous" tribes by five and a half cubic inches. Especially

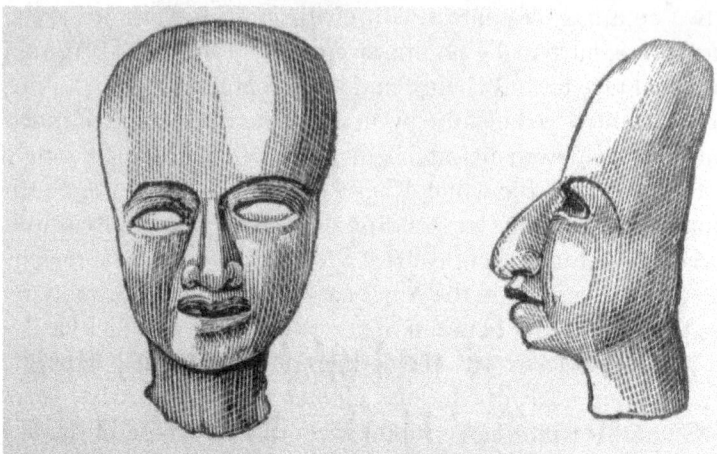

Figure 1.2. Terra-cotta heads collected in Teotihuacan by Frederick Edmunds and reproduced by Morton in his *Crania Americana*, p. 146. Whipple Library, Cambridge University.

incongruous were the results shed by work on ancient Peruvian skulls, which caused George Combe, one of Morton's staunchest allies, to exclaim in a private letter, "There is no living people with heads rationally so deficient as these ancient Peruvians, who are civilized or who construct."[44] Yet Morton would not give up his hypothesis of the intellectual superiority of the Toltecan race: rather, he shifted the grounds for that superiority, explaining that shape was as important a factor as size in the development of intellectual capacities. The Toltec's large anterior chamber was therefore responsible for their greater achievements.

To prove his point, Morton turned to other kinds of evidence that he correlated with the quantitative and qualitative evidence he obtained from skulls: cranial casts, descriptions, and measurements he received from other collectors as well as representations of heads as found in ancient sculptures and reliefs. Objects of an archaeological nature became especially relevant for Morton's studies of ancient Mexican skulls, of which he had relatively few, and he treated antiquarian objects as if they offered unquestionable anatomical proof. Of the small clay figurines from the Temples of the Sun and the Moon in Teotihuacan that he received from Frederick Edmonds, Morton wrote that these "effigies . . . no doubt approach very near to nature, and at least express what those people considered the beau ideal of human physiognomy" (fig. 1.2).[45] They closely followed what Morton would claim to be the typical Toltecan head, "compressed from back to front," with "high and broad foreheads, oval face, prominent cheekbones, and rather tumid lips."[46]

Modern illustrations of Mexican antiquities also served Morton as evidence for his anatomical studies. While he lamented not having seen the two milestones of antiquarian literature, Lord Kingsborough's *Mexican Antiquities* (1830–1848) and Henri Baradère's *Antiquités mexicaines* (1832–1836) before publishing his *Crania Americana*, Morton made the most of the English translation of Antonio del Rio's 1787 expedition to Palenque, the *Description of the Ruins of an Ancient City, Discovered near Palenque*, published in London in 1822. Morton pored over the book's reproductions of reliefs from Palenque with an eye for the typical heads of the Toltecs who, according to antiquarian tradition, settled Palenque during their migration from central Mexico, and his scrupulous attention was rewarded by the discovery of a telltale detail: a "small, inverted skull" in the bottom left corner of one of the plates. The "symmetry and accuracy of the figure" led Morton to believe that the original carver of the relief at Palenque, "accomplished the task with a skull before him," like some seventeenth-century Dutch still-life painter whose goal was to render nature as faithfully as possible. (By the same token, Morton had no doubts respecting the faithfulness of the nineteenth-century reproduction when antiquarians were, in fact, raising questions about the verisimilitude of reproductions.) The head's "great lateral swell, the rather expanded forehead, and the prominent aspect of the vertex of the crown . . ." place the Palenque "skull" halfway between Peruvian heads in the south and those of the Natchez to the north.[47] For Morton, this is as it should be, because Palenque sits on some migration route, between Florida in the north and Peru in the south. Thus, "physical" evidence confirms antiquarian hypotheses.

Two specimens drawn from Del Río's book reflect just how far Morton would go in order to construct proofs of the ideal Toltec head. By "merely omitting such parts of the elaborate head-dresses as are unnecessary to the present purpose," Morton "faithfully transcribe[s]" two heads, stripped bare to their essentials: conical in shape, "very narrow from front to back, and consequently very broad from side to side," with retreating foreheads, low brows, large and aquiline noses, and wide and tumid mouths, they embody the typical Toltec skull.[48] We might object that this proof requires nothing less than a suspension of disbelief, that it is impossible to infer the shape of the head by "merely omitting" the headdress, because it would take for granted that the part above the headdress is the head and not part of the headdress (fig. 1.3). Disquieting as this might sound to a

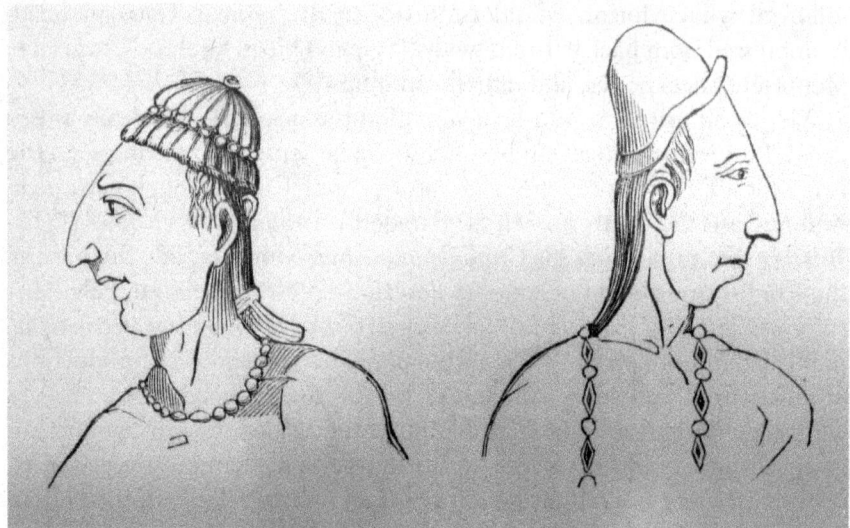

Figure 1.3. Heads in Del Río's *Description of the Ruins of an Ancient City*, stripped of their ornament to prove the shape of the typical Toltec head as represented by Morton in the *Crania Americana*, p. 145. Whipple Library, Cambridge University.

present-day reader, however, Morton's conjectural thinking was an integral part of the antiquarian method, which often imagined and reconstructed the missing or effaced surface of a relief or the collapsed side of a pyramid in the same way naturalists built up specimens on the evidence of bone fragments.

On the other hand, what might appear as indiscriminate use of evidence, whereby Morton relied on man-made artifacts to prove anatomy and vice versa, was a mark of his time, before the strict partitioning of disciplines. In 1839, the same year *Crania Americana* came out, John Delafield published in Cincinnati *An Inquiry on the Antiquities of America*, where he gave speculative answers to the puzzles posed by finds at ancient tumuli discovered in North America. On the basis of "evidence" gleaned from Humboldt's illustrations of monuments in South and Central America, from ancient and modern skulls, and from the cranium of an Egyptian mummy, Delafield concluded that the mounds near Cincinnati had been built by ancient Egyptians. In a similar vein, a decade later, naturalist Richard Owen was called on to examine two children from Central America whose profiles struck many for their similarity to the profiles in the reliefs at Palenque, leading to the belief that the children belonged to an ancient "Aztec" race lost in the jungle, where it inhabited pyramidal complexes.[49] Then, in the mid-1860s, under the aegis of the French Scientific Commission in Mexico, geologist Guillemin Tarayre sought to trace the settling of America from north to south by comparing anatomical evidence (obtained by studying groups of present-day Indians) with archaeological evidence.[50]

Gaping into an open sepulcher in Yucatán, Stephens had hoped the anatomical evidence he gathered on site—scant, fragile, and elusive as it was—would confirm his theory that the ancient builders of Yucatán did not come from Egypt but were aboriginal Americans. Stephens's foray into bone collecting is not simply a chapter torn from the history of physical anthropology but rather a chapter in the antiquarian age of a procedure that was becoming the discipline of archaeology. Two years before Stephens's visit to Ticul, Morton had published *Crania Americana*, where he sustained a hypothesis similar to Stephens's, who might have seen the book or read reviews of it when he returned to New York after his first trip to Central America, before he went back to Yucatán. He might have become convinced that Morton's line of study could corroborate his own. There is a sense in which the two men move in opposite directions to coincide in a space where bones and idols began to be studied together: Stephens, the untiring explorer, turning to bones in his antiquarian speculations; Morton, at the center of his cabinet in Philadelphia, surrounded by skulls, gathering antiquarian proof for his studies of bones.

By the 1840s, American bones and American antiquities came together in different ways. On a basic level, they traveled the same routes and were exchanged among agents in the same networks. They were exhumed or sold by Indians (either working under the command of others or, more rarely, on their own); bought, stolen, and smuggled by self-appointed explorers; transported at some expense, and at some hazard, by land and water; and received by institutions, scientists, amateurs, and private collectors. At the same time, bones and antiquities were brought together in the same fluid epistemological spaces. They were subjected to similar treatments—they would be unpacked, cleaned, reconstructed, measured, analyzed chemically, classified, and displayed—to confirm each other and form a compact piece of evidence of America's unwritten history and to answer questions that were part of a larger puzzle: What was the origin of the people who founded the ancient American civilizations? And what had become of them? What relation did present-day Indians have with these civilized ancients?

El sepulcro del pueblo que fue: The Sepulcher of the People Who Were

The association between antiquarianism and comparative anatomy turned out to be a powerful alliance. The questions posed in the "scientific" domain were not alien to the larger public domain, and treating the epistemological question fails to fully account for the epistemological motive, that is, for the social context in which bones and ground plans of lost cities were cast. Together, bones and antiquities constructed America's civilized past—a past that was claimed nationally or imperialistically with consequences for politics, economics, and national pride—and conditioned the way America's present was imagined. The question of the origin of the people who founded the ancient American civilizations led to the charged question—one of immense relevance to the white and criollo policymakers of Mexico, the United States, and Western Europe—concerning present-day Indians: were they of the same root and branch as the people who left such immense vestiges of culture behind them in the jungles or even under the streets of Mexico City? When combined with the evidence of the ruins and of the bones of enlightened ancestors scattered over the Western Hemisphere, the bodies of contemporary Indians yielded proof of their distance from the past and provided rationales for separating present-day Indians from the lands, natural resources, ruins, and bones that they had been inhabiting, using, or safeguarding for many years.

In 1840, Emmanuel von Friedrichsthal, secretary of the Austrian Legation in Mexico, toured Yucatán and became the first traveler to write on the ruins at Chichén Itzá. On advice from Stephens, whom he had met in New York, Friedrichstahl bought a camera and took the first daguerreotypes of ruins in Yucatán. He amassed an important collection of antiquities, which he took back to Europe in 1841, and kept close notes on his explorations, some of which were published in European journals.[51] Among Friedrichsthal's writings, only one was published in Mexico: a letter on the builders of Yucatán's ruins, written on April 20, 1841, for Justo Sierra O'Reilly, then editor of the periodical *Museo Yucateco*. After marveled descriptions of the ruins at Uxmal and Chichén Itzá, Friedrichsthal hypothesized on the origin of the builders of these monuments and on their relationship with the Indians who resided in the vicinity. He closely followed Morton—to whom Friedrichsthal obligingly sent a skull—in postulating that the whole American continent was inhabited by one single aboriginal race that was created and developed separately of all others. Unlike Morton, Friedrichsthal believed that the ancient monuments scattered over Yucatán had not been built by this race but by another, superior caste of people, probably of Caucasian stock, who employed symbolic writing and mathematical proportion and practiced agriculture and slavery on a scale so large and organized as to enable them to construct massive urban complexes. Aboriginal Indians, whose descendants made up a large part of the population of the Yucatán, were evidently slaves to this enlightened caste, of which nothing remained but beautiful monuments, "dumb epitaphs on the tomb of a people that was."[52]

Friedrichsthal's nostalgia for America's glorious ancient past and his antipathy for its present was hardly an exception among nineteenth-century antiquarians; what makes his letter stand out are the circumstances of its publication. It was published twice, both times by Justo Sierra O'Reilly: the first, as we have seen, in the *Museo Yucateco,* and the second, in the *Registro Yucateco,* in 1845, at the height of Yucatán's separation from the rest of the Mexican republic, on the brink of the caste war of the Yucatán. Friedrichsthal's theories would have surely found favor among Yucatán's elites, who, possibly, would not only have identified themselves with that enlightened ancient caste that governed over the benighted aboriginals but may have well thought of themselves as justified in taking harsh measures against those aboriginals lest they, too, fall like their putative Caucasian ancestors. Two years later, Sierra O'Reilly would travel to the United States to negotiate, unsuccessfully, military help against the Mayan rebels.[53]

The line of intellectual transmission from the civilized first Americans to the civilized nineteenth-century Americans obviously bypassed the barbarous Indians, who did not know how to appreciate or properly use antiquities, land, or natural resources. They failed to cultivate their lands, and their worship and fear of antiquities defied the economy of accepted use in the nineteenth century. The science of the bones added to these claims by making assumptions that actually went against the seeming continuity of the bone record. In place of that succession, two narratives competed: in one of them, the ancestors were of an altogether distinct stalk; in the other, nineteenth-century Indians were the product of centuries of degeneration from the original Americans. In any case, contemporary Indians were no legitimate heirs to the first Americans. Lands and antiquities were being reclaimed, for safekeeping and for producing profit and knowledge. Who was to inherit them? Stephens's excitement at the prospect of buying the pyramids at Copan gives us an idea: "To buy Copan! Remove the monuments of a by-gone people from the desolate region in which they are buried, set them up in the 'great commercial emporium' and found an institution to be the nucleus of a great national museum of American antiquities!"[54]

During the first half of the nineteenth century, before the institutionalization of academic disciplines such as anthropology, linguistics, or archaeology, the search for the origin of American man occupied a fluid space, ripe with conceptual possibilities, of which the alliance between antiquarianism and anatomy was but one. Yet despite the variety of answers to questions about the origin of America's ancient civilizations, to ask who had built the so-called abandoned cities of America's past was to ask who rightfully inherited America's abandoned cities in the present. As American antiquities began to circulate, resulting in their increased value and in questions about rightful ownership, collectors and savants, legitimated variously by institutions, by their role in policymaking, or by their assumption of a place in commerce, needed title to collect, exchange, and display vestiges of America's past. Amateur explorers such as Stephens and Friedrichsthal, among many others, claimed that title from "facts" that derived from the discoveries themselves—the objects literally legitimated the takers by showing that they were built by the intellectual "ancestors" of the takers, be they Caucasians from Egypt or extinct Toltecans with Caucasian-like qualities. In the seemingly objective epistemological space of the science of man was wrought the exclusion of contemporary Indians from their intellectual and physical heritage. Conditioning this epistemological usurpation was the fact that U.S., British, and French savants and collectors had a rather free hand in the domain of the former Spanish empire due to the fact that national legislatures within the weak nation-states that emerged after independence failed to exert control over the collection and extraction of antiquities from Spanish American countries just as they failed to create endogenous industries to exploit their own natural and human resources, allowing foreign enterprise to dominate their economies. Thus, the present-day perception that nineteenth-century archaeologies were dominated by national agendas[55] misreads the reality of the first half of the nineteenth century, which saw the rise of the independent collector and the development of novel rationales for the acquisition of ruins and bodies.

Acknowledgments

While writing this essay, I have benefitted from comments from various publics in Mexico City, Paris, London, and Cambridge. I would like to thank particularly Alejandro Araujo, Laura Cházaro, Jean-Baptiste Fressoz, Carlos López Beltrán, Rodrigo Martínez, Roger Gathman, Silvia Sebastiani, and Nuria Valverde. I am equally thankful to the anonymous reviewers at the University of Arizona Press and especially to the editors of this book, Philip L. Kohl, Irina Podgorny, and Stefanie Gänger, for their useful suggestions.

Notes

1. Helene Littmann, "John Lloyd Stephens," *American National Biography: Supplement 2*, ed. Mark C. Carnes (Oxford: Oxford University Press, 2005), 535. Scholarship on Stephens's travels in Yucatán is considerable; see, among others, R. Tripp Evans, *Romancing the Maya: Mexican Antiquity in the American Imagination, 1820–1915* (Austin: University of Texas Press, 2004).

2. John Lloyd Stephens, *Incidents of Travel in Yucatan* (New York: Harper and Brothers, 1843), 277.

3. Ibid., 278.
4. Ibid.
5. Ibid., 280.
6. Ibid., 278.
7. Ibid.
8. Ibid., 280.
9. Ibid.
10. Ibid., 281.
11. Ibid., 284.

12. The report of the examination was published in the *Proceedings of the Academy of Natural Sciences of Philadelphia* 1 (1841–1843): 203–4.

13. Stephens, *Incidents*, 284.

14. For European collecting of Americana in the first half of the nineteenth century, see, among others, Pascal Riviale, "Europe Rediscovers Latin America: Collecting Artifacts and Views in the First Decades of the Nineteenth Century," in *Collecting Across Cultures: Material Exchanges in the Early Modern Atlantic*, ed. Daniela Bleichmar and Peter C. Mancall (Philadelphia: University of Pennsylvania Press, 2011), 254–68.

15. Scholarship on the extirpation of idolatries is considerable; the seminal work remains Pierre Duviols, *La lutte contre les religions authochtones dans le Pérou colonial: "L'extirpation de l'idolatrie," entre 1532 et 1660* (Paris: Institut Français d'Études Andines, 1971). There were numerous notable exceptions to the program of religiously motivated destruction, such as Fray Bernardino de Sahagún, who, in the sixteenth century collected information about preconquest Mexican religion, theology, ethics, political and social organization, and natural knowledge.

16. Alain Schnapp, *La conquête du passé: Aux origines de l'archéologie* (Paris: Carré, 1993), 11. See also Arnaldo Momigliano, "Ancient History and the Antiquarian," *Journal of the Warburg and Courtauld Institutes* 13, no. 3/4 (1950): 285–315.

17. For eighteenth-century antiquarianism in Spanish America, see José Alcina Franch, *Arqueólogos o anticuarios: Historia antigua de la arqueología en la América*

española (Barcelona: Serbal, 1995). See also Irina Podgorny, "'Silent and Alone': How the Ruins of Palenque Were Taught to Speak the Language of Archaeology," in *Comparative Archaeologies: A Social View of the Science of the Past*, ed. Ludomir R. Lozny (New York: Springer, 2011), 527–54; "The Reliability of the Ruins," *Journal for Spanish Cultural Studies* 8, no. 2 (2007): 213–33.

18. For a detailed study of the debate, see Miruna Achim, "Signos y piedras: La literatura anticuaria en búsqueda de la historia Mexicana," in *Entre textos e imágenes*, ed. Fermín del Pino-Díaz, Pascal Riviale, and Juan J. R. Villarías-Robles (Madrid: CSIC, 2009), 17–26.

19. Jorge Cañizares-Esguerra, *How to Write the History of the New World: Histories, Epistemologies, and Identities in the Eighteenth-Century Atlantic World* (Stanford, CA: Stanford University Press, 2001).

20. See Caleb Atwater's "Description of the Antiquities Discovered in the State of Ohio and Other Western States," *Archaeologia Americana: Transactions and Collections of the American Antiquarian Society* 1 (1820): 105–251.

21. John Ranking, *Historical Researches on the Conquest of Peru, Mexico, Bogota, Natchez, and Talomeco, in the Thirteenth century, by the Mongols, Accompanied by Elephants* (London, 1827).

22. Juan Galindo, "A Description of the Ruins in Copan, in Central America," *Archaeologia Americana: Transactions and Collections of the American Antiquarian Society* 2 (1836): 543–50.

23. My summary reconstruction of the story that follows is based on Claude Blanckaert, "Les conditions d'émergence de la science des races au début du XIXe siècle," in *L'idée de "race" dans les sciences humaines et la littérature (XVIIIe et XIXe siècles)*, ed. Sarga Moussa (Paris: L'Harmattan, 2003), 33–49; see also Bronwen Douglas, "Climate to Crania: Science and the Racialization of Human Difference," in *Foreign Bodies: Oceania and the Science of Race 1750–1740*, ed. Bronwen Douglas and Chris Ballard (Canberra: Australian National University, 2008), 33–98.

24. Douglas and Ballard, *Foreign Bodies*, 43.

25. Della Collins Cook, "The Old Physical Anthropology and the New World: A Look at the Accomplishments of an Antiquated Paradigm," in *Bioarchaeology: The Contextual Analysis of Human Remains*, ed. Jane E. Buikstra and Lane E. Beck (Burlington, MA.: Elsevier, 2006), 33.

26. Ibid.

27. Ibid.

28. Johann Friedrich Blumenbach, *Commercium epistolicum J.B. Blumenbachi aus einem Briefwechsel des klassischen Zeitalters der Naturgeschichte*, ed. F. W. P. Dougherty (Göttingen: Niedersächsische Staats-und Universitätsbibliothek, 1984), 85.

29. The scholarly literature on Morton is considerable; see particularly Ann Fabian, *The Skull Collectors: Race, Science, and America's Unburied Dead* (Chicago: University of Chicago Press, 2010); Robert E. Bieder, *Science Encounters the Indian, 1820–1880: The Early Years of American Ethnology* (Norman: University of Oklahoma Press, 1986); Peter C. Mancall, "'Collecting Americans': The Anglo-American Experience from Cabot to NAGPRA," in Bleichmar and Mancall, *Collecting Across Cultures*, 192–216.

30. Samuel George Morton, *Catalogue of Skulls of Man and the Inferior Animals in the Collection of Samuel George Morton* (Philadelphia: Merrihew and Thompson, 1849), iii.

31. William Samuel Ruschenberger, *Three Years in the Pacific, Containing Notices of Brazil, Chile, Bolivia* (Philadelphia, 1834).

32. Samuel George Morton, *Crania Americana; or, A Comparative View of the Skulls of Various Aboriginal Nations of North and South America* (Philadelphia: J. Dobson, 1839), 152.

33. For contraband in nineteenth-century Mexico, see Walther Bernecker, *Contrabando: Ilegalidad y corrupción en el México del siglo XIX, Mexico City* (Mexico City: Universidad Iberoamericana, 1994). On Burrough, see Fabian, *Skull Collectors*, 38.

34. For these inventories see the Samuel George Morton Papers at the American Philosophical Society (last modified December 26, 2011, http://www.amphilsoc.org/mole/view?docId=ead/Mss.B.M843-ead.xml).

35. Morton, *Crania Americana*, 154.

36. Morton's communication for the July 6, 1841, meeting of the American Academy of Natural Sciences, *Proceedings of the Academy of Natural Sciences* 1 (1841–1843): 51.

37. Morton, *Crania Americana*, 155.

38. Ibid., 146.

39. In addition to shorter articles in journals and magazines, Morton published three different book-length studies of American skulls: *Crania Americana* (Philadelphia, 1839); *Inquiry into the Distinctive Characteristics of the Aboriginal Race of America* (Philadelphia, 1844); and *Catalogue of Skulls of Man and the Inferior Animals in the Collection of Samuel George Morton* (1849). After Morton's death, J. Aitken Meigs, librarian at the Academy, published the *Catalogue of Human Crania, in the Collection of the American Academy of Natural Sciences in Philadelphia* (Philadelphia, 1857) based on Morton's own catalog of his collection.

40. See Adrian Desmond and James Moore, *Darwin's Sacred Cause: How a Hatred of Slavery Shaped Darwin's Views on Human Evolution* (New York: Houghton Mifflin Harcourt, 2009).

41. Morton, *Crania Americana*, 5.

42. Ibid., 6.

43. Ibid., 82.

44. Combe, cited by Bieder, *Science Encounters the Indian*, 77.

45. Morton, *Crania Americana*, 146.

46. Ibid.

47. Ibid., 144.

48. Ibid., 145.

49. In 1853, Owen and Richard Cull, secretary of the Ethnological Society of London, coauthored "A Brief Notice of the Aztec Race, Compiled by Richard Cull; Followed by a Description of the So-Called Aztec Children Exhibited on the Occasion by Professor Owen," *Journal of the Ethnological Society of London* 4 (1856): 120–37. Owen did not think the children were proof of an Aztec race, concluding, "I remark that the figures from ancient Mexican hieroglyphics, copied by Humboldt, Martin, and other ethnologists, bear but a superficial resemblance to the children in

question, whose abnormally-arrested cranial development accords with the artificially flattened or compressed heads of those ancient American people" (137). If anything, for Owen, the children's heads most closely resembled "the head of an idiot preserved in the museum of St. Bartholomew's Hospital," of which Owen provided an engraving.

50. Guillemin Tarayre, *Exploration minéralogique des régions mexicaines suivie de notes archéologiques* (Paris: Imprimerie Impériale, 1869).

51. On Emmanuel von Friedrichsthal's activities in Mexico and Central America, see Arturo Tarracena and Adam Sellen, "Emmanuel von Friedrichsthal: Su viaje a América y el debate sobre el origen de la civilización maya," *Península* 1, no. 2 (2006): 49–80.

52. Emmanuel von Friedrichsthal, "Reflexiones sobre las ruinas de Yucatán," *Registro Yucateco* (1845): 437–43.

53. On the caste war, see Terry Rugeley, *Yucatan's Maya Peasantry and the Origins of the Caste War* (Austin: University of Texas Press, 1996) and *Maya Wars: Ethnographic Accounts from Nineteenth-Century Yucatan* (Norman: University of Oklahoma Press), 2001.

54. John Lloyd Stephens, *Incidents of Travel in Central America, Chiapas, and Yucatan* (New York: Harper and Brothers, 1841), 115.

55. See Margarita Díaz-Andreu, *A World History of Nineteenth-Century Archaeology: Nationalism, Colonialism, and the Past* (Oxford: Oxford University Press, 2007).

CHAPTER TWO

Finding the Ancient in the Andes

Archaeology and Geology, 1850–1890

Joanne Pillsbury

We have a tendency to think of the history of our academic fields in isolation, and yet it is impossible to deny that scholarly innovations within a field have often arisen from interactions between disciplines. This is especially true for archaeology, a discipline that has historically drawn on multiple approaches both theoretically and methodologically. Before the emergence of archaeology as a recognized academic discipline in the middle of the nineteenth century, antiquarian studies before that time were conducted as part of expeditions with very different goals.[1] Untrained in what is now thought of as proper archaeological practice, these scholars were essential to the growth of the bushy evolutionary tree of the discipline, contributing in myriad ways to the development of the field. This chapter explores the intersection of disciplinary approaches in the later nineteenth century in the Andes, particularly in the discovery of a pre-Hispanic past that extended well before the Inca. The present inquiry is part of a larger project on the history of archaeological illustration, with goals of analyzing not only how visual representations of the past influenced an understanding of people and places but also how such representations in turn shaped research design. Inherent to this study are questions about the relationship between scholarly disciplines in the development of a sense of deep time in the nineteenth century as well as the ways in which knowledge is shaped through illustration.[2]

The beginnings of scientific archaeology coincided with a marked growth in exploration and collecting. This boom was born of a convergence of several factors, from a profound shift in thinking about the past in the wake of the work of people such as the geologist Charles Lyell and the biologist Charles Darwin to the insatiable thirst to develop national museum collections. We now know the Inca to have been relative latecomers in the history of the prehispanic Andes, having built on the achievements of earlier states and empires that extended back millennia. But until the late nineteenth century, any understanding of a pre-Inca past was vague and derived largely from historical sources composed in the sixteenth and seventeenth centuries. In those chronicles, a history before the Inca was generally limited to a description of peoples the Inca had conquered in a relatively recent past. When a greater depth of time was mentioned, it was usually in the context of trying to explain how the Inca fit into a global history, such as linking them to figures from the Old Testament.[3] For these early modern writers, evidence was largely derived from the Bible and the classical authors.[4]

The effect of the natural sciences on understanding a pre-Inca past in the nineteenth century can be discerned through the study of large-scale archaeological atlases produced at that time. From the mid eighteenth century, atlases—books of images or diagrams on a particular subject—became a way in which ideas about the past were exchanged through the presentation of physical data in visual form. These luxurious publications, suitable for the libraries of the well-educated and the well-to-do, became the essential proxy evidence of empirically based science.[5] The specific focuses of this chapter are the actual and virtual collections of Andean antiquities assembled in the early years of the Peruvian republic, particularly a striking atlas that was prepared by the German volcanologists Wilhelm Reiss and Alphons Stübel and published between 1880 and 1887.[6]

Reiss and Stübel began their careers in the young science of geology in Europe and were on their way to study volcanoes in Hawaii in 1868 when they stopped in Peru. They never made it to Hawaii and turned instead to excavating at the seaside resort of Ancón, near Lima. Mummy bundles and related finds were spectacularly rendered as chromolithographs in the three volumes of *The Necropolis of Ancon in Peru*, published simultaneously in English and German in New York and Berlin. These luxurious volumes measure 52 cm in height and 39 cm in width and contain some 141 illustrations and limited text. Financed by the Royal Museum of Ethnology in Berlin in exchange for the collections Reiss and Stübel excavated at Ancón, the publication contributed to a growing interest in discovering a global antiquity in the wake of Heinrich Schliemann's triumphant discovery of Troy and presentation of "Priam's Treasure" in the years just before Reiss and Stübel's departure from Europe.[7] As we will see below, collecting in both its forms, as actual gatherings of specimens and as virtual collections in the form of publications, was central in the history of science.

Collecting Plants, Collecting the Past

The interactions between disciplines in the natural sciences and their eventual influence on archaeology cannot be separated from the broader context of imperial collecting in the later eighteenth century and the nineteenth century. Botanical expeditions, in particular, proved to be influential on a number of levels, from providing an initial context in which ancient American antiquities were collected to the development of conventions for their depiction.

Expeditions designed with the express goal of collecting and illustrating antiquities did not become common until the nineteenth century because the value of the past was not yet as immediately amenable to profit-minded imperial powers before that time. But antiquities were occasionally collected as a sideline to military and botanical expeditions in the eighteenth century, providing opportunities for the cross-fertilization of ideas and approaches. The French military engineer Amédée Frézier (1682–1773), along with his near contemporary, the astronomer and botanist Louis Feuillée (1660–1732), recorded Andean antiquities in passing, but a more sustained attention to ruins and the first scientific documentation of them can be attributed to the mathematician and cartographer Charles-Marie de La Condamine (1701–1774). Part of the French Academy of Sciences expedition to the Andes to measure the circumference of the earth, La Condamine is credited with creating the first measured drawings of an ancient American site, Ingapirca, near Cuenca, Ecuador.[8]

Often both botanical specimens and antiquities were gathered on the same expeditions. In 1777, the Spanish botanists Hipólito Ruíz and José Pavón and the French botanist and physician Joseph Dombey set out on a major botanical expedition to Peru. Dombey also collected antiquities, perhaps drawn in part by the botanical imagery on specimens such as the spectacular early-colonial Inca tunic now in the Museo de América in Madrid.[9] These antiquities and others were sent along with botanical specimens to Europe, helping to fuel an interest in a pre-Columbian past.[10]

It is arguably at the intersection of these scientific disciplines and imperial interests that archaeology as a pursuit beyond paper was born. Confronted with the empirical evidence of tangible artifacts, archaeology moved beyond philological concerns to what Daniela Bleichmar has called a "visual epistemology."[11] Here the influence of the natural sciences on archaeology would be striking, for naturalists tended to value pictures more than words: images were superior as a method for presenting data and constructing an argument.[12] For the first time, the visual was becoming central in an understanding of antiquity.

The natural sciences provided templates for the depiction of antiquities. For example, illustration practices first used for botanical studies were later extended to the study of a human past.[13] In the nineteenth century, conventions for depictions and classifications of the natural world were commandeered for archaeology, and the practice of collecting specimens—as systematic collections as opposed to random selections of curiosities—also developed in part out of botany. Collecting is at the core of the history of both the natural sciences and archaeology, both through the comprehensive gatherings of physical specimens and through the virtual collection and presentation of such specimens in publications.[14]

By the eighteenth century, the accurate representation of plant specimens was of paramount importance in the newly globalized context of exchange. Careful observation of plants in their native habitat and meticulous documentation of their physical form was essential in the increasingly competitive world of botanical expeditions.[15] Artists now came along on expeditions, which enabled them to depict their subjects in their fresh, full polychrome glory. Reiss and Stübel continued this tradition, going to great lengths to capture detail and precise color of their subject matter, both in Ancón, but also in their earlier geological studies in Ecuador. There the pair commissioned the painter Rafael Troya to create some sixty oils made in situ of Ecuadorian landscapes, attesting to the importance of images in their scientific enterprise.[16]

Imaging the Past

As with botanical specimens, antiquities were gathered and presented as virtual collections in the form of publications. Although Reiss and Stübel followed many others in the presentation of antiquities, *The Necropolis of Ancon* volumes were a stark contrast to publications of earlier centuries. Works published in the sixteenth and seventeenth centuries contained few if any illustrations. Limitations in printing technologies were certainly a factor in the paucity and character of illustrations, but they were not the only reason for the emphasis on text over image. In the sixteenth and seventeenth centuries, philology was the key to understanding the past.[17] Authority lay in words, not images.

Only rarely derived from drawings made on site, the few illustrations of American antiquities that were included in these early modern works were largely based on textual descriptions and created by artists who had never seen the monuments firsthand. The results were at times fantastical, interpreted as they were through the vernacular of European conventions. The woodcuts from Pedro Cieza de León's 1553 *Parte primera de la chronica del Peru*, for example, inserted Andeans into generic European cityscapes.[18] There was no necessary visual correlation between the place depicted and the visual reality of the place. Illustrations would also be recycled in later publications by the same author or into other, entirely different works.[19]

Originally text-centered, antiquarianism underwent what Peter Burke has called a "visual turn" in the seventeenth century, becoming more interested in the material culture of the past.[20] Images came to take on a larger role in publications, and by the end of the eighteenth century, a greater percentage of them were based on firsthand observation. Instead of just a handful of images, books could include a dozen or more, and they could be larger in size. The influential *Encyclopédie* of Denis Diderot and Jean le Rond d'Alembert, for example, created between 1751 and 1772, contained some three thousand images. Furthermore, aided by developments in copperplate engraving, images and text could be integrated with greater ease.

The earliest important illustrated archaeological publications were the large-scale folios on classical sites that began to be published from the middle of the eighteenth century, such as James Stuart and Nicholas Revett's *The Antiquities of Athens* (1762–1830) and Giovanni Battista Piranesi's varied publications such as the *Antichità romane* (1748) and the *Vedute di Roma* (1778).[21] They were followed by the spectacular volumes of the *Description of Egypt*, published between 1809 and 1828. Unlike Stuart and Revett and Piranesi, whose publications circulated in black and white, some editions of the *Description of Egypt* included a limited number of hand-colored plates.[22] All of these publications were produced in limited numbers, and their inescapably high cost guaranteed they only reached an elite audience.

Lavish folios featuring American antiquities were produced in the first half of the nineteenth century, most notably the delayed publication of the explorations of Guillermo Dupaix.[23] But it was the second half of the century that became the golden age of archaeological illustration. New technologies of representation played a role, including photography, but improvements in lithography and related techniques of reproduction were equally significant. Such developments had a profound effect on sharing ideas and fueling passions in the frenzy of later nineteenth-century collecting.

Popular books on the subject of American antiquities were also published, including John Lloyd Stephens's *Incidents of Travel* volumes. Available in an accessible octavo format with numerous black-and-white engravings by Frederick Catherwood, they were something of best sellers in their day.[24] Photography became a major tool for the depiction of antiquities after Catherwood—Stephens and Catherwood had only limited success with the medium—either as the basis for engravings or reproduced on their own. Sumptuous volumes of photographs of ruins were produced in the second half of the nineteenth century in Mexico, including the striking albums produced by the French traveler Claude-Joseph Désiré Charnay.

Photography came to Peru later, around 1856, but was not used extensively for documenting ruins for another decade.[25] E. George Squier was one of the first to use the medium in Peru to document pre-Columbian remains systematically. His photographs, taken after he served as the U.S. representative to Peru during the guano disputes, were rendered later as engravings in his 1877 *Incidents of Travel and Exploration in the Land of the Incas*. Mistrustful of published historical accounts of the Inca, he set out to record Peru's antiquities, placing an emphasis on the value of the visual evidence: "I carried with me the compass, the measuring-line, the pencil, and the photographic camera; knowing well that only accurate plans, sections, elevations, drawings, and views can adequately meet the rigorous demands of modern science, and render clear what mere verbal description would fail to make intelligible."[26] Squier suggests that some of the ruins may predate the Inca, but he says little beyond his convictions for what he refers to as "an early and comparatively rude past."[27]

As they turned out, however, the engravings in Squier's volume were less about meeting "the rigorous demands of modern science" and more in the vein of a popular account.[28] Charles Wiener's *Pérou et Bolivie*, published in 1880, similarly was a popular account, with over a thousand small engravings of both antiquities and contemporary life.[29] Reiss and Stübel wrote admiringly of Squier in their introduction but were dismissive of their rival Wiener, criticizing his untrustworthy details and images prepared from "familiar photographs."[30]

Complimentary as they may have been about Squier, Reiss and Stübel followed a very different model for their publication, deciding to emulate the costly grand-scale folios produced earlier in the century by Alexander von Humboldt and others. Although antiquities were less of an interest to Humboldt than the natural world, he included illustrations of pre-Columbian remains in his monumental *Vues des Cordillères* of 1810, one of the many lavish volumes he produced. Humboldt was an acknowledged initial model in the private letters of Reiss and Stübel, and even the format of their atlas—in size and orientation—echoed that of the eminent Prussian.[31] But these same letters expressed profound disappointment in Humboldt. Stübel wrote in 1870 that Humboldt's observations on Peru were "absurd, false, and miserable."[32] This opinion is, to a certain degree, reflective of the evolution of scientific discourse over the fifty years that separated Humboldt from Reiss and Stübel.

The universalizing intellectual of Humboldt's day had been replaced by specialists with their minute dedication to detached empirical observation. Lorraine Daston and Peter Galison have written about the rise of "mechanical objectivity" in the nineteenth century, the evolution over time from what was seen as the "meddling" interventions of artists to a preference for the "objectivity" of mechanical reproductions.[33] Photography was part of this evolution, but as Daston and Galison note, the impetus predates the introduction of photography. Illustration—the presentation of scientific data—was surely part of Reiss and Stübel's quibble with Humboldt. His accumulation of images from different sources, the infusions of the classical tradition, and the imposition of rigid conventions of landscape painting at the expense of observed reality would have been an affront to the "objectivity" of Reiss and Stübel. They were, at the end of the day, scientists for whom the protocols of the time depended on standardization.

Humboldt's long shadow fell over Reiss and Stübel in other ways as well, including through the work of one of Humboldt's students, Mariano Rivero, a Peruvian mining engineer with an interest in geology. His volume *Antigüedades peruanas* was later expanded with the help of the Swiss zoologist Johann Jakob von Tschudi and published under the same title.[34] The later edition included a 44 × 57-cm atlas, with 58 color plates, to accompany the text. Originally published in Spanish in 1851, it appeared in English, German, and French shortly thereafter. Influential for many reasons, the Rivero and Tschudi atlas reverberated both nationally and internationally.

Admired by Reiss and Stübel, *Antigüedades peruanas* became one of the first great scientific works of the new Peruvian republic. The Inca—and it was all the Inca at this time, as the earlier, pre-Inca cultures had not yet been identified archaeologically—were presented in the *Antigüedades peruanas* as the founders of the new nation.[35] The first sections of the text volume were devoted to origins, including a discussion of history derived largely from Garcilaso de la Vega (1539–1616) and Fernando de Montesinos (ca. 1600–1651), chroniclers now considered problematic regarding historical data.[36]

The large plates of the *Antigüedades peruanas* illustrate crania, ceramics, and textiles, without scale. Some of the plates, such as those depicting textiles, show a striking fidelity to the original subjects. More often, however, the antiquities and sites are rendered rather loosely, and some illustrations are second- or thirdhand renderings of sites the two men had not visited at the time. The atlas is extensive in its coverage, ranging from Chan Chan on Peru's north coast to Tiwanaku in what is now highland Bolivia.

Interestingly, although Reiss and Stübel created their own atlas a full generation after Rivero and Tschudi, in an era when it would have been possible to produce a volume of photographs, they opted for color lithographs. This was in contrast to their contemporary Alfred Maudslay, a former British diplomat who photographed in the Maya region between 1881 and 1894 and produced his own striking volumes of ruins and antiquities.[37] Reiss and Stübel chose a different path for their atlas, largely eschewing black-and-white photography. They did use photography in the field and photographic devices back in the museum. Furthermore, plates illustrating simple textiles were based on black-and-white photographs. But while their plates benefited from photomechanical techniques, they were ultimately produced by hand, by academically trained painters.[38]

On one level, the choices Maudslay and Reiss and Stübel made were for obvious reasons. Maudslay was photographing buildings and monuments that had lost most of their applied pigments. By contrast, Reiss and Stübel were confronting textiles and other materials that had retained all the vibrancy of their original coloration (fig. 2.1). Stübel wrote of the astonishing quality of the Ancón textiles, comparing them to Gobelins, and marveling at the excellent preservation of the color in particular.[39] Registering the color of the textiles in print was a way to preserve evidence that was considered impermanent.[40] In this sense, Reiss and Stübel echoed their forebears in natural history, particularly those engaged in botanical collection and illustration in the late eighteenth and early nineteenth centuries: illustration was a means to preserve fragile and fleeting characteristics of their physical subject.[41]

Figure 2.1. Wilhelm Reiss and Alphons Stübel, *The Necropolis of Ancon* (1880–1887), plate 16, showing front and back views of a "sumptuous mummy pack." Chromolithograph. Reproduced by permission of the Getty Research Institute, Los Angeles (2992-584).

But Reiss and Stübel's use of color may also have arisen from their backgrounds in geology, a field in which slight gradations in the color of strata were of profound importance. Wilhelm Reiss, born in Mannheim in 1838, went to Italy for his health as a young man and fell in love with fossils and geology. He earned his PhD in geology in 1864 from Heidelberg University and worked in the Canary Islands and elsewhere studying fossils and volcanoes. Alphons Stübel studied chemistry and mineralogy in Heidelberg and Leipzig. He traveled in Egypt and investigated volcanic activity in Italy and Greece. Volcanoes, not antiquities, lured them out of Europe.

Firmly grounded in mineralogy and the geological sciences, Reiss and Stübel adhered to the illustration conventions of their field, largely line drawings and color lithography, for the majority of their published images. Following Lyell's *Principles of Geology* (1830–1833), color became crucial for differentiating sedimentary deposits and other evidence of the passage of time. But even before Lyell, color was understood to be critical to scientific documentation. The German geologist Abraham Gottlob Werner (1749–1817), for example, investigated the stratigraphy of the earth's crust and the chronological succession of rocks. Importantly for this study, his major work was the first modern textbook on the description of mineralogy, *Von den äußerlichen Kennzeichen der Foßilien* (1774), a volume that Reiss and Stübel certainly would have known in their student days.[42] This work contained a comprehensive guide to using color for the description and classification of minerals. Werner's ideas became widespread through various translations and editions, including Patrick Syme's influential revised edition, entitled *Werner's Nomenclature of Colours, with Additions, Arranged So as to Render It Highly Useful to the Arts and Sciences* (1821).[43] Particularly in the wake of Darwin, color became an essential tool of scientific classification not only for strata and the specimens encased within them but also for depicting with accuracy the species that still roamed the earth.[44]

Reiss and Stübel benefited from recent advances in chromolithography, a technique developed in France in 1837. Lithography in general became a preferred method in scientific illustration after 1820 because it allowed an artist's drawing to be reproduced directly, without the intervention of engravers.[45] The technique diminished the translation or interpretative step that inevitably occurred between sketch and copperplate, allowing for a more direct representation of the original drawing or painting. The first large-scale German publication with chromolithographs was Wilhelm Zahn's 1849 volume on classical ornament, and the technique was deployed in landmark publications throughout the nineteenth century, such as Austen Henry Layard's volume on Nineveh.[46] Large-scale volumes using chromolithography were already circulating in South America by the later 1850s, including those produced under the auspices of the Comissão Científica de Exploração, based in Rio de Janeiro.[47]

Reiss and Stübel's extensive use of color is striking in comparison with other archaeological atlases. Nearly all of the plates in *The Necropolis of Ancon* are in color, whereas in other publications color had been usually limited to a few essential images such as maps and frontispieces. Maudslay, for example, used chromolithographs to illustrate his jade finds, but the vast majority of his illustrations were black and white. Arguably, the absence of color helped Maudslay's case, as it gave clarity to complicated images. This is important to register if one acknowledges that most archaeological illustration is ultimately about suppressing data to simplify images in order to make a certain argument. When photography was first developed in 1839—when the daguerreotype technique was announced in Paris—one of its promises, as announced officially, was that it would be an invaluable tool for archaeology, particularly the decipherment of texts.[48] For Maudslay's goal of capturing the complexity of Maya art, the absence of color may not have been a disadvantage but rather a plus, for it allowed for a simplified reading of complicated imagery.

Finding the Ancient in the Andes

Interestingly, color was used to indicate strata in the Andes a century before Reiss and Stübel in the work of Bishop Baltasar Jaime Martínez Compañón. Part of the Spanish Crown's campaigns to collect and know her territories carried out under Charles III (r. 1759–1788), the bishop's nine volumes of watercolors documented both the past and the present of the province of Trujillo, Peru.[49] Inspired in part by the excavations at Herculaneum and Pompeii, themselves sponsored by that same Bourbon monarch when he was Charles VII, king of Two Sicilies, the Andean excavations were arguably more sophisticated than European excavations at the time, particularly with regard to stratigraphy and whole-site documentation. Elsewhere, Lisa Trever and I have discussed his sectional drawing of a tomb—including the gold artifacts illustrated in the bottom stratum.[50] For the first time, there was a sense that the context and the process of the extraction of antiquities rather than simply the objects themselves had become worthy of note.

The bishop's watercolors of the tomb—very close in spirit and composition to his depictions of mines elsewhere in his opus—also reminds us that in the early modern period, archaeology and mining were closely entwined: both archaeological artifacts and ore were considered "treasures from the ground."[51] Irina Podgorny, for example, has illuminated the rhetoric of antiquarians in the 1830s, where Mexican antiquities were referred to as "a golden ore"—one considerably less dangerous to extract.[52] Martínez Compañón's exploration of an incipient stratigraphic method went nowhere, however, as his manuscript languished in obscurity in the wake of Napoleon's invasion of Spain. But these late-eighteenth-century explorations were part of a broader evolution in thinking about the past, a reformulation of approaches to understanding the world and its histories that would gradually coalesce into the nascent fields of geology and archaeology in the first decades of the nineteenth century.

It is important to bear in mind that before the middle of the nineteenth century, the conceptualization of the age of the earth and of human history was most often based on extrapolation from Biblical chronologies. This resulted in what today would seem to be remarkably brief estimations of those histories. In the late seventeenth century, for example, Bishop

James Ussher asserted that the world had been created in the morning of October 23, 4004 BC. Ussher's date was widely accepted and remained a touchstone for decades.

In Peru, knowledge of a pre-Hispanic past was largely derived from the historical accounts recorded after the arrival of Europeans in the sixteenth century. As noted above, the accounts focused on the Inca, the dominant culture in the region at the time of the conquest, with only occasional references to cultures that preceded them. In the sixteenth century, Cieza noted that certain sites such as Chan Chan and Tiwanaku had been built before the rise of the Inca empire. But this brief exploration of history did not extend beyond a few sites, nor did it transfer to individual objects. Until the late nineteenth century, there was little interest in relative chronology, and any sense of history was limited to an immediate pre-Columbian past.[53]

It is clear that developments in the sciences, particularly natural history, had a profound influence on archaeological illustration (inseparable from the related development of collections of archaeological materials), but they also, on a profound level, had an effect on a revelation of a deeper past—a past that preceded the chronologically shallow histories supplied by textual sources. It is important to stress here, however, that this new understanding of the past was born neither in Europe nor in Peru but in the points of intersection between people and ideas from both contexts, as Stefanie Gänger has argued so eloquently elsewhere.[54] Lima became a crucible for a fertile interplay between individuals and scientific disciplines: advances in geological studies in Europe were matched by the studies of dedicated collectors in Lima, who were beginning to identify and classify ceramic styles predating the Inca—in this sense leading rather than following developments in Europe.[55]

Reiss and Stübel spent eight years in South America, traveling in Colombia, Ecuador, and Brazil as well as Peru, the site of their most famous work. They spent a little over a year together in Peru, interacting with members of the local scientific community in Lima, including the Italian naturalist Antonio Raimondi, a resident of Peru for most of his life. Raimondi was among the first to document archaeological remains in that country in a systematic fashion and was himself well versed in geology despite his limited formal education in the natural sciences.[56] Reiss returned to Europe in 1876 for health reasons; Stübel continued researching in Argentina, Bolivia, Chile, and Uruguay, returning to Germany in 1877 via the United States.[57]

Most of Reiss and Stübel's time in South America was devoted to taking scientific measurements and collecting fossils and mineralogical specimens, but they also collected archaeological material on occasion. Stranded in

Lima in late 1874, and disturbed by the unsystematic looting at Ancón, Reiss and Stübel decided to approach the site scientifically. They spent several months at the site in 1875 excavating mummy bundles. These revealed insights into the inhabitants' domestic and ritual lives and "the prevalent views and artistic skill, the bent of taste and colour sense of those times."[58] Reiss and Stübel made sketches and took measurements and photographs at the site; professional artists used these and the collections themselves back in Germany to prepare color lithographs for publication.

In the manner of their geological forebears, the first images in *The Necropolis of Ancon* document the broader context. The introductory landscape images, by Julius Fiebiger of the Dresden Academy, were made after drawings by Stübel. The atlas includes detailed views of the burial contexts, a map of the finds, front and side views of the mummies, scales, and most intriguingly, cross sections, an illustrative technique borrowed from geology (fig. 2.2).

Reiss and Stübel emphasized the importance of the images as presentations of data available for comparison should other burial sites be studied in a similar manner. Avoiding conjecture, "the authors have confined themselves to the faithful reproduction of the objects collected by themselves."[59]

Figure 2.2. Wilhelm Reiss and Alphons Stübel, *The Necropolis of Ancon* (1880–1887), plate 10, showing cross sections of burials. Chromolithograph. Reproduced by permission of the Getty Research Institute, Los Angeles (2992-584).

The text is limited, confined to a brief introduction and short explanations of the objects illustrated. After the initial contextual illustrations, the plates range from the views of mummy bundles to plates illustrating specific finds, from ornaments to utensils, laid out on a plain white background.[60]

The volumes are comprehensive in their coverage, although with some generalizing and/or synthesizing. The cross sections illustrated in figure 2.2, for example, represent a composite view, an "ideal" view derived from observations of the best-preserved burials. The generalizing aspect of this illustration is in keeping with conventions in natural history, particularly botanical illustration, where the specificities and imperfections of any one example are subsumed under an overarching desire to depict an idealized version of a plant, in its most common and complete form.[61]

Reiss and Stübel indicate the sandy strata schematically in figure 2.2, but they stop short of arguing for any sort of superposition or time depth to the mummies found at deeper levels. Yet it seems likely that their understanding of geological strata contributed to the intellectual development of their student Max Uhle, who trained in philology rather than the physical sciences. Uhle's famous delineation of earlier eras was based in part on stratigraphic excavations and the knowledge of superposition, essentially the concept that what was found in lower strata was of greater antiquity than objects found in more shallow layers.[62] Reiss and Stübel state in their text that the cemetery could have been made centuries before the Inca, and in private letters they venture a date of 600–1,000 years before the present, not a bad guess in an age without absolute dating. Many of the objects from the Ancón burial ground are associated with the Wari culture, which is now dated to AD 600–1000, though there were also materials from later cultures in the necropolis.[63]

Reiss's and Stübel's attention on the position of the mummy bundles within a landscape was informed by their experiences in the lava fields of the Bay of Naples, the same fields where Sir William Hamilton and others uncovered the remains of a classical antiquity well below the surface. For it was men such as Hamilton and the geologists who followed him, including Raimondi, who realized that the layering of volcanic strata—the record of repeated eruptions—argued for a greater antiquity of human civilization than was accounted for in the Bible.[64] By the 1780s, mineralogy was being used as a basis for a newly historical interpretation of the earth, a radical repositioning regarding a sense of time and the depth of history.[65] Reiss and Stübel, with their roots in the field of geology and with their intense observation of objects and their contexts, were on the path to revealing the backbone of Andean archaeological chronology, the recognition of antiquities that predated the Inca.

Reiss's and Stübel's atlas was part of a broader scientific current that emphasized images as evidence. Empirical observation—and the presentation of the data derived from such study—meant that images took on new weight. Physical evidence and its images challenged the authority of texts to profound effect. Describing this evolution in thinking in geology from the late eighteenth century and into the nineteenth, Martin Rudwick noted that the distant past had many witnesses beyond verbal reports and records of contemporaries: "objects without words could still be made to tell a story."[66] As fossils were witnesses to nature's past, Andean antiquities could be testaments to a history before the Inca. For Reiss and Stübel, trained in disciplines that depended on empirical observation, the proxy evidence—the illustrations—needed to be meticulous.

Whereas the Rivero and Tschudi atlas was central to the creation of a new Peruvian national identity, the Reiss and Stübel volumes, which were descendants in some ways from *Antigüedades*, were more about the transfer of technologies and understandings of geology to archaeology. *The Necropolis of Ancon in Peru*, unlike *Antigüedades*, is about a dawning realization that the materials they were finding predated the Inca. In their close observation of a single cemetery—their predecessors spent only very short periods at any one site—they argued that the burials belonged to different time periods, some dating back "hundreds" of years.[67] Reiss and Stübel's focused excavations allowed for the development of an idea that a single site may have been used over an extended period of time. To use the felicitous phrase of the French naturalist Georges Cuvier, Reiss and Stübel were "bursting the limits of time" in the manner of their geological forebears.[68]

In the end, however, Reiss's and Stübel's volumes were limited in their influence: only 200 copies of *The Necropolis of Ancon in Peru* were published in English.[69] The costly nature of the volumes may have been one factor that affected the dissemination of their ideas, but their original intentions also remained unfulfilled. Overwhelmed by the quantity of material they collected over the course of their eight years in South America, Reiss and Stübel never published the bulk of their research.[70] The very precision that Reiss and Stübel insisted on for their volumes insured that it would be virtually impossible to ever match Humboldt's thirty volumes. *The Necropolis of Ancon in Peru* was both the peak and the end of the era of the grand-scale archaeological atlases. But Reiss and Stübel's focus on meticulous observation of a single site and the representation of the contexts of the finds infused the thinking of later generations. For Reiss and Stübel, the transference of a sense of deep time gained through the study of volcanic eruptions and their physical legacies opened the door to discovering a distant human past—a history before the Inca.

Acknowledgments

First and foremost, I thank Stefanie Gänger for the invitation to participate in this volume, her generosity in sharing her unpublished research, and her advice on the subject of collecting and the history of science. I also thank Philip Kohl and Irina Podgorny for their helpful editorial suggestions. I owe a profound debt to Julia McHugh, whose help while I was at the Getty Research Institute was fundamental to this paper. Daniela Bleichmar, Juan Pimentel, and Neil Safier have all been stimulating and helpful colleagues through the course of this research. I would also like to thank Luis Felipe Villacorta, director of the Museo Raimondi in Lima, and his assistant, Catherine Turgeon, for their help in illuminating the relationship between Reiss and Stübel and Antonio Raimondi. Monica Barnes contributed to the discussion linking Andean and European histories in the early modern period. Natalia Majluf read an early draft of this paper and provided insightful commentary and suggestions. And finally I reserve my most heartfelt thanks for Edward S. Harwood for his many kindnesses and counsel.

Notes

1. On the history of archaeology, see, among others, Alain Schnapp, *The Discovery of the Past*, trans. Ian Kinnes and Gillian Varndell (New York: Harry N. Abrams, 1993); "Eduard Gerhard: Founder of Classical Archaeology?" *Modernism/Modernity* 11, no. 1 (2004): 169–71; Margarita Díaz-Andreu, *A World History of Nineteenth-Century Archaeology: Nationalism, Colonialism, and the Past* (New York: Oxford University Press, 2007); Gordon R. Willey and Jeremy A. Sabloff, *A History of American Archaeology*, 3rd ed. (New York: W. H. Freeman, 1993).

2. Joanne Pillsbury, ed., *Past Presented: Archaeological Illustration and the Ancient Americas* (Washington, DC: Dumbarton Oaks Research Library and Collection, 2012).

3. For an overview of sources, see Joanne Pillsbury, ed., *Guide to Documentary Sources for Andean Studies, 1530–1900* (Norman: University of Oklahoma Press, 2008). On the linking of Biblical and Andean histories, see especially Monica Barnes, "The Ages of Man and the World According to Hieronymo de Chaues of Seville and Felipe Guaman Poma de Ayala of Peru," in Mary Preuss, ed., *Beyond Indigenous Voices: LAILA/ALILA 11th International Symposium on Latin American Indian Literatures* (Lancaster, CA: Labyrinthos, 1996), 83–88; and "A Lost Inca History," *Latin American Indian Literatures Journal* 12, no. 2 (1996): 117–31.

4. Anthony Grafton with April Shelford and Nancy Siraisi, *New Worlds, Ancient Texts: The Power of Tradition and the Shock of Discovery* (Cambridge, MA: Harvard University Press, 1992); Sabine MacCormack, "Classical Traditions in the Andes: Conversations Across Time and Space," in Pillsbury, *Guide to Documentary Sources*, 23–64.

5. Lorraine Daston and Peter Galison, *Objectivity* (New York: Zone Books, 2007).

6. Wilhelm Reiss and Alphons Stübel, *The Necropolis of Ancon in Peru*: *A Contribution to Our Knowledge of the Culture and Industries of the Empire of the Incas*, trans. Augustus Henry Keane, 3 vols. (Berlin: A. Asher, 1880–1887). Data on the lives and careers of Reiss and Stübel are drawn largely from Andreas Brockmann and Michaela Stüttgen, *Spurensuche: Zwei Erdwissenschaftler im Südamerika des 19. Jahrhunderts* (Unna: Kreis Unna Kulturamt, 1994); and *Tras las huellas: Dos viajeros alemanes en tierras latinoamericanas* (Bogotá: Banco de la República; Biblioteca Luis Arango, 1996); Uwe Carlson, "Reiss y Stübel en Ancón," in *El inicio de la arqueología científica en el Perú, Reiss y Stübel en Ancón: Exposición de litografías de 1875 publicadas en "The Necropolis of Ancon in Peru"* (Lima: Museo de Arte, 2000), 6–9; Stefanie Gänger, "La mirada imperialista? Los alemanes y la arqueología peruana," *Histórica* 30, no. 2 (2006): 69–90; Richard Haas, *Keramikfunde aus Ancón, Peru: Die Tonobjekte der Sammlung Reiss und Stübel im Museum für Völkerkunde Berlin* (Berlin: Mann, 1986), 53–72; "Wilhelm Reiss y Alphons Stübel: La colección del cementerio de Ancon en el Museo Etnológico de Berlín," *Jahrbuch der Staatlichen Ethnographischen Sammlungen Sachsen* 43 (2007): 97–103; Peter Kaulicke, *Gräber von Ancón, Peru: Nach den Arbeiten von W. Reiss/A. Stübel, M. Uhle, R. Ravines, G.R. Willey und C. Huapaya* (Munich: C. H. Beck, 1983); *Contextos funerarios de Ancón: Esbozo de una síntesis analítica* (Lima: Fondo Editorial de la Pontificia Universidad Católica del Perú, 1997); Wilhelm Reiss, *Reisebriefe aus Südamerika, 1868–1876* (Munich: Duncker und Humboldt, 1921); Margaret Young-Sánchez, "Reiss, Wilhelm (1838–1908) and Alphons Stübel (1835–1904)," in Pillsbury, *Guide to Documentary Sources*, 3:568–72. See especially Gänger, "La mirada imperialista?" and Brockmann and Stüttgen, *Tras las huellas*, for a discussion of Reiss and Stübel's social and political views.

7. On the "collection for publication" exchange with the Royal Museum of Ethnology in Berlin (Königliches Museum für Völkerkunde; now the Ethnologisches Museum der Staatlichen Museen zu Berlin), see also Manuela Fischer, "Adolf Bastian's Travels in the Americas (1875–1876)" in *Adolf Bastian and His Universal Archive of Humanity: The Origins of German Anthropology*, ed. Manuela Fischer, Peter Bolz, and Susan Kamel (Hildesheim: G. Olms, 2007), 191–206; and "La misión de Max Uhle para el Museo Real de Etnología en Berlín (1892–1895): Entre las ciencias humboldtianas y la arqueología americana," in *Max Uhle (1856–1944): Evaluciones de sus investigaciones y obras*, ed. Peter Kaulicke et al. (Lima: Fondo Editorial de la Pontificia Universidad Católica del Perú, 2010), 49–62.

8. Monica Barnes, "The Role of Eighteenth-Century French Explorers in the Development of Andean Archaeology," in *Ancient Travellers: Proceedings of the Twenty-Seventh Annual Conference of the Archaeological Association of the University of Calgary*, ed. Claire Allum (Calgary: University of Calgary, 2002), 268–76; Monica Barnes and David Fleming, "Charles-Marie de La Condamine's Report on Ingapirca and the Development of Scientific Field Work in the Andes," *Andean Past* 2 (1989): 175–236; Neil Safier, *Measuring the New World: Enlightenment Science and South America* (Chicago: University of Chicago Press, 2008).

9. Jay A. Levenson, ed., *Circa 1492: Art in the Age of Exploration* (Washington, DC: National Gallery of Art, 1991), 595, no. 452.

10. This interest in an ancient American past in the late eighteenth century and the early nineteenth century was fueled by different impulses in Europe and the Americas, however. In the Americas, a developing sense of separation from Europe on the part of the inhabitants of the viceroyalties of New Spain and Peru awakened a keen interest in

a local and separate past: the young republics, after all, would eventually need their own American antiquity. As early as 1827, Mexico, newly independent of Spain, established the first legislation prohibiting the exportation of monuments and antiquities. See Irina Podgorny, "'Silent and Alone': How the Ruins of Palenque Were Taught to Speak the Language of Archaeology," in *Comparative Archaeologies: A Sociological View of the Science of the Past*, ed. Ludomir R. Lozny (New York: Springer, 2011), 527–53. See also Stefanie Gänger, *Relics of the Past: The Collecting and Study of Pre-Columbian Antiquities in Peru and Chile, 1837–1911* (Oxford: Oxford University Press, 2014).

11. Daniela Bleichmar, *Visible Empire: Botanical Expeditions and Visual Culture in the Hispanic Enlightenment* (Chicago: University of Chicago Press, 2012), chap. 2.

12. Ibid., 61. See also Podgorny ("'Silent and Alone,'" 543) on how the "imitative art" became central to the progress of knowledge.

13. Byron Hamann, "Drawing Glyphs Together," in Pillsbury, *Past Presented*, 231–82.

14. Adam Sellen, "Nineteenth-Century Photographs of Archaeological Collections from Mexico," in Pillsbury, *Past Presented*, 207–30.

15. Bleichmar, *Visible Empire*, 8; see also chap. 3.

16. Alexandra Kennedy, *Rafael Troya (1845–1920): El pintor de los Andes Ecuatorianos* (Quito: Banco Central del Ecuador, 1999). I am grateful to Natalia Majluf for bringing Kennedy's work to my attention.

17. Alain Schnapp, "European Antiquarianism and the Discovery of the New World," in Pillsbury, *Past Presented*, 49–67; Schnapp, *Discovery of the Past*.

18. Pedro Cieza de León, *Parte primera de la chronica del Peru* (Seville: Martín de Montesdoca, 1553).

19. Bleichmar, *Visible Empire*, 80nn3, 4; Barbara Mundy, "Giovanni Battista Ramusio," in Pillsbury, *Guide to Documentary Sources*, 564–67.

20. Peter Burke, "Images as Evidence in Seventeenth-Century Europe," *Journal of the History of Ideas* 64, no. 2 (2003), 273–96.

21. James Stuart and Nicholas Revett, *The Antiquities of Athens* (London: John Haberkorn, 1762); Giovanni Battista Piranesi, *Antichità romane de' tempi della Republica, e de' primi imperatori* (Rome: L'Academia di Franzia, 1748) and *Vedute di Roma* (Rome: Presso l'Autore a strada Felice, 1778). See also Bruce Redford, *Dilettanti: The Antic and the Antique in Eighteenth-Century England* (Los Angeles: J. Paul Getty Museum, 2008); John Pinto, *Speaking Ruins: Piranesi, Architects and Antiquity in Eighteenth-Century Rome* (Ann Arbor: University of Michigan Press, 2012).

22. *Description de l'Égypte; ou, Recueil des observations et des recherches qui ont été faites en Égypte pendant l'expédition de l'armée française* (Paris: Imprimerie Impériale, 1809–1828). See also Edward Said, *Culture and Imperialism* (New York: Knopf, 1993).

23. Guillermo Dupaix, *Antiquités Mexicaines* (Paris: Bureau des Antiquités Mexicaines, 1834–1844); R. Tripp Evans, *Romancing the Maya: Mexican Antiquity in the American Imagination, 1820–1915* (Austin: University of Texas Press, 2004); Leonardo López Luján, "El capitán Guillermo Dupaix y su album arqueológico de 1794," *Arqueología mexicana* 19, no. 109 (2011): 71–81. The Dupaix volumes were produced in both black-and-white versions and editions with some color plates.

24. John Lloyd Stephens, *Incidents of Travel in Central America, Chiapas, and Yucatan* (London: Arthur Hall, Virtue, 1854); Evans, *Romancing the Maya*, 70. Cath-

erwood also produced a limited edition of color lithographs, *Views of Ancient Monuments in Central America, Chiapas and Yucatan*, published in 1844.

25. Carlos Contreras and Natalia Majluf, *Registros del territorio: Las primeras décadas de la fotografía, 1860–1880: Museo de Arte de Lima del 9 de enero al 5 de febrero de 1997* (Lima: Museo de Arte, 1997); Majluf, "Photographers in Andean Visual Culture: Traces of an Absent Landscape," *History of Photography* 24, no. 2 (2000): 91–100; Majluf and Luis Eduardo Wuffarden, eds., *La recuperación de la memoria, Perú, 1842–1942* (Lima: Fundación Telefónica, Museo de Arte de Lima, 2001); Edward Ranney, "Images of a Sacred Geography," in *The New World's Old World: Photographic Views of Ancient America*, ed. May Castleberry (Albuquerque: University of New Mexico Press, 2003), 89–122.

26. Squier, *Incidents of Travel and Exploration in the Land of the Incas* (1877), 3.

27. Squier, *Peru*, 574.

28. There were also mitigating circumstances, and it should be noted that Squier was not in a position to oversee the engravings. See Terry A. Barnhart, *Ephraim George Squier and the Development of American Anthropology* (Lincoln: University of Nebraska Press, 2005); Keith McElroy, "Ephraim George Squier: Photography and the Illustration of Peruvian Antiquities," *History of Photography* 10 (April–June 1986): 99–129; Mariana Mould de Pease, "Ephraim George Squier (1821–1888)" in Pillsbury, *Guide to Documentary Sources*, 651–55.

29. Wiener's ambitious collecting enterprise, however, underway in Peru in the mid-1870s, was undoubtedly something of a spur to Reiss's and Stübel's collecting. Elizabeth Williams, "Art and Artifact at the Trocadero: *Ars Americana* and the Primitivist Revolution," in *Objects and Others: Essays on Museums and Material Culture*, ed. George Stocking Jr. (Madison: University of Wisconsin Press, 1985), 146–66. Wiener's collection of some 4,000 objects in Peru, Bolivia, and Ecuador were initially on display in the Palais de l'Industrie in Paris. This exhibition, in the spring of 1878, attracted high attendance and favorable press (ibid., 151).

30. Reiss and Stübel, *Necropolis of Ancon*, 1:4.

31. Both Humboldt, *Vues des cordillères*, published in 1810, and Reiss and Stübel, *Necropolis of Ancon*, follow a vertical, portrait orientation, whereas the Rivero and Tschudi atlas (Mariano Rivero and Johann Jakob von Tschudi, *Antigüedades peruanas* [Vienna: Imperial de la Corte y del Estado, 1851]) is landscape in orientation. The *Vues des cordillères* measures 58 × 44 cm, with 69 plates; the three volumes of Reiss and Stübel, *Necropolis of Ancon*, as mentioned above, are 52 × 39 cm, with 141 plates.

32. Letter of Alphons Stübel of August 31, 1870, cited in Brockmann and Stüttgen, *Tras las huellas*.

33. Lorraine Daston, "Nature by Design," in Caroline A. Jones, Peter Galison, and Amy E. Slaton, *Picturing Science, Producing Art* (New York: Routledge, 1998), 232–53; Lorraine Daston and Peter Galison, "The Image of Objectivity," *Representations* 40 (Autumn 1992): 81–128; Daston and Galison, *Objectivity*; Peter Galison, "Judgment against Objectivity," in Jones, Galison, and Slaton, *Picturing Science*, 327–59. See also Gänger, "La mirada imperialista?"

34. Mariano Rivero, *Antigüedades peruanas: Primera parte* (Lima: J. Masías, 1841); Mariano Rivero and Johann Jakob von Tschudi, *Antigüedades peruanas* (Vienna: Imperial de la Corte y del Estado, 1851).

35. Luis Felipe Villacorta, "Antonio Raimondi, Archaeology, and National Discourse: Representations and Meanings of the Past in Nineteenth-Century Peru," in Pillsbury, *Past Presented*, 173–206 (see esp. 176–77).

36. See Pillsbury, *Guide to Documentary Sources*, for further discussion of these sources.

37. Alfred Percival Maudslay, *Biologia Centrali-Americana; or, Contributions to the Knowledge of the Fauna and Flora of Mexico and Central America: Archaeology*, 5 vols. (London: R. H. Porter and Dulau, 1889–1902).

38. The original paintings are held in the Leibniz-Institut für Länderkunde in Leipzig, Germany.

39. Letter of Alphons Stübel, February 26, 1875; cited in Carlson, "Reiss y Stübel en Ancón," 9.

40. See Rudolf Virchow's review of *Das Todtenfeld von Ancon in Perú* in *Zeitschrift für Ethnologie* 19 (1887): 151–52. Also a contributing author to the publication, Virchow praises the illustrations, arguing that they will become increasingly valuable as the objects in the collection fade over time.

41. For more on botanical illustration and capturing the transitory, see Bleichmar, *Visible Empire*, esp. 63.

42. Abraham Gottlob Werner, *Von den äußerlichen Kennzeichen der Foßilien* (Leipzig: Crusius, 1774).

43. Abraham Gottlob Werner, *Werner's Nomenclature of Colours, with Additions, Arranged So as to Render It Highly Useful to the Arts and Sciences, Particularly Zoology, Botany, Chemistry, Mineralogy, and Morbid Anatomy: Annexed to Which Are Examples Selected from Well-Known Objects in the Animal, Vegetable, and Mineral Kingdoms* (Edinburgh: William Blackwood, 1821).

44. Daniel Lewis, *The Feathery Tribe: Robert Ridgway and the Modern Study of Birds* (New Haven, CT: Yale University Press, 2012), chap. 7.

45. Martin Rudwick, *Bursting the Limits of Time: The Reconstruction of Geohistory in the Age of Revolution* (Chicago: University of Chicago Press, 2005), 545.

46. Wilhelm Zahn, *Ornamente aller klassischen Kunst-Epochen nach den Originalen in ihren eigenthümlichen Farben* (Berlin: Dietrich Reimer, 1849); Austen Henry Layard, *The Monuments of Nineveh* (London: J. Murray, 1849–1853).

47. *Trabalhos da Commissão Scientifica de Exploração* (Rio de Janeiro: Typographia universal de Laemmert, 1862). See also Renato Braga, *História da Comissão Científica de Exploração* (Fortaleza: Universitária do Ceará, 1962); M. Margaret Lopes, chap. 8 in this volume.

48. Andrew Szegedy-Maszak, "Introduction," in *Antiquity and Photography: Early Views of Ancient Mediterranean Sites*, ed. Claire L. Lyons et al. (Los Angeles: J. Paul Getty Museum, 2005), 9.

49. Baltasar Jaime Martínez Compañón, *Trujillo del Perú*, 9 vol., Real Biblioteca de Madrid (online access at "Trujillo del Perú," Real Biblioteca, accessed July 1, 2013, http://www.realbiblioteca.es).

50. Joanne Pillsbury and Lisa Trever, "The King, the Bishop, and the Creation of an American Antiquity," *Ñawpa Pacha* 29 (2008): 192–219. It should be noted, however, that the bishop's work was also very much ahead of its time in other respects; see Lisa Trever and Joanne Pillsbury, "Martínez Compañón and His Illustrated 'Museum,'" in *Collecting Across Cultures*, ed. Peter Mancall and Daniela Bleichmar

(Philadelphia: University of Pennsylvania Press, 2011), 236–53. See also Irina Podgorny on the importance of military engineers in eighteenth-century archaeology, "The Reliability of Ruins," *Journal of Spanish Cultural Studies* 8, no. 2 (2007): 213–33.

51. Schnapp, *Discovery of the Past*, 123.
52. Podgorny, "Silent and Alone," 544.
53. Gänger, *Relics of the Past*, chap. 1.
54. Gänger, "La mirada imperialista?," 87.
55. Gänger, *Relics of the Past*, chap. 1.
56. See letters 379 (1876) and 380 (1877) from Reiss to Raimondi in the collection of the Museo Raimondi in Lima; Villacorta, "Antonio Raimondi"; Gänger, *Relics of the Past*, chap. 1.
57. Brockmann and Stüttgen, *Tras las huellas*.
58. Reiss and Stübel, *Necropolis of Ancon*, 1:4. The volumes also include studies of crania by Rudolph Virchow, botanical specimens by Ludwig Wittmack, and faunal remains by Alfred Nehring.
59. Reiss and Stübel, *Necropolis of Ancon*, 1:4.
60. Daniela Bleichmar has referred to the stark, decontextualized "global white space" of botanical illustration, but here the intention seems less about excluding local specificity than it is about simplifying illustrations for comparative purposes; Bleichmar, *Visual Empire*, chap. 5.
61. See, for example, Bleichmar, *Visual Empire*, 67.
62. John Rowe, *Max Uhle, 1856–1944: A Memoir of the Father of Peruvian Archaeology* (Berkeley: University of California, 1954); David L. Browman and Douglas R. Givens, "Stratigraphic Excavation: The First 'New Archaeology,'" *American Anthropologist* 86, no. 1 (1996): 80–95. For recent studies on Max Uhle, see, among others, Peter Kaulicke et al., eds., *Max Uhle (1856–1944): Evaluciones de sus investigaciones y obras* (Lima: Fondo Editorial de la Pontificia Universidad Católica del Perú, 2010); and Kaulicke, ed., *Max Uhle y el Perú antiguo* (Lima: Fondo Editorial de la Pontificia Universidad Católica del Perú, 1998).
63. Letter of Alphons Stübel, February 26, 1875, cited in Carlson, "Reiss y Stübel en Ancón," 9. See also Susan Bergh, *Wari: Lords of the Ancient Andes* (New York: Thames and Hudson, 2012); and Margaret Young-Sánchez, *Textiles from Peru's Central Coast, 750–1100: The Reiss and Stübel Collection from Ancón* (Ann Arbor, MI: UMI Dissertation Services).
64. Rudwick, *Bursting the Limits*.
65. Ibid., 202.
66. Ibid., 187.
67. Reiss and Stübel, *Necropolis of Ancon*, 1:3.
68. Georges Cuvier, *Researches on Fossil Bones* (London: G. Henderson, 1810); cited in Rudwick, *Bursting the Limits*, frontispiece.
69. *New York Times*, Literary Notes, May 2, 1881. I am indebted to Natalia Majluf for discovering the print run.
70. Alphons Stübel remained in South America after Wilhelm Reiss left South America to return to Germany in 1877. Stübel eventually published various works with Max Uhle, including *Die Ruinenstaette von Tiahuanaco im Hochland des alten Peru: Eine kulturgeschichtliche Studie auf Grund selbstaendiger Aufnahmen* (Breslau:

Acher, 1892). For the later histories of Reiss and Stübel and the development of anthropology in Germany in particular, see Glenn Penny and Matt Bunzl, eds., *Worldly Provincialism: German Anthropology in the Age of Empire* (Ann Arbor: University of Michigan Press, 2003). See also Sandra Rebok, "La constitución de la investigación antropológica alemana a finales del siglo XIX: Actores y lugares del saber americanista," in *Los americanistas del siglo XIX: La construcción de una comunidad científica internacional*, ed. Leoncio López-Ocón, Jean-Pierre Chaumeil, and Ana Verde Casanova (Madrid: Iberoamericana, 2005), 213–44. Rebok recalls Reiss's introductory remarks at the 7th International Congress of Americanists in Berlin in 1888, where he stated that whereas Germany did not participate in the general discovery of America, it did participate in its "scientific discovery" (220); see also Gänger, "La mirada imperialista?" On the subject of collecting at Ancón, León de Cessac followed Reiss and Stübel at Ancón for the Trocadéro museum in Paris; see Margarita Díaz-Andreu, *A World History of Nineteenth-Century Archaeology: Nationalism, Colonialism, and the Past* (New York: Oxford University Press, 2007), 176. Stübel sold a second collection of South American archaeological material, owned partially by Reiss, to the Ethnology Museum of Leipzig in 1888. These collections were published as *Kultur und Industrie südamerikanischer Völker nach den im Besitze des Museums für Völkerkunde zu Leipzig befindlichen Sammlungen von A. Stübel, W. Reiss und B. Koppel*, ed. Max Uhle (Berlin: A. Asher, 1889–1890). These later volumes, in a smaller format, include many more images on a single page.

CHAPTER THREE

Place-Names and Indigenous Languages

Samuel Alexander Lafone Quevedo and British Antiquarian Methods in Nineteenth-Century Argentina

Máximo Farro

An object? Can a word, a locution, a breath-shred be endowed with all the properties—the material attributes—of an object?

Containing everything that might be found, eventually, within its sonorous outlines, can it be considered, indeed, as the object of objects, the "thing" preeminent?

—GUSTAF SOBIN, *LUMINOUS DEBRIS*[1]

One of the main lines of inquiry on indigenous languages of the Americas during the last third of the nineteenth century was related to the collection and systematization of manuscripts and printed sources that had been developed from the sixteenth century onward.[2] This constant preoccupation with obtaining new data for comparative studies took the form of critical editions of grammars and vocabularies that were originally composed by missionaries and officials from the Spanish crown.[3] Thus, an important part of the work consisted of collecting and reviewing data to make descriptions of grammatical structures and classifications of languages into families to the detriment of theoretical reflection.[4] In contrast to the research associated with the natural sciences, which were devoted to the study of language understood as a biological phenomenon, studies in indigenous languages of the Americas were circumscribed within the field of historical science, shaping a series of works dedicated to "linguistic ethnography," a field that reached its height especially in the last decade of the nineteenth century with the works of Daniel Garrison Brinton in the United States and Lucien Adam in France.[5]

It is within this general trend that we can place the work of Samuel Alexander Lafone Quevedo (1835–1920). Since the early 1880s he published critical editions of manuscripts and "rare books" that referred to those indigenous languages of South America in the Argentinean territory. A resident in Catamarca Province, northwestern Argentina, Lafone Quevedo gathered and compiled manuscript sources in local and national archives, recorded vocabularies from native informants, and reviewed information in libraries and manuscript collections of "Americanists" such as Bartolomé Mitre and Andrés Lamas.[6] They related mainly to the indigenous languages and dialects of that region and Chaco. With these materials he began to outline a classification scheme based on a specific grammatical feature associated with a particular form of agglutination that for him was proper to the Americas, such as pronominal particles and their form of articulation with both verbs and names. The collection of evidence to support this classification scheme involved a rigorous process of extracting, recording, and organizing data from a corpus of manuscripts and printed sources in order to make them a useful series for comparative work.[7] Lafone Quevedo collated documents from the sixteenth century onward in order to compile a regional toponymy of the Catamarca Province referring to the Cacan language spoken in northwest Argentina, especially in the Calchaquí valleys and partly in La Rioja, Santiago del Estero, and San Juan.[8] From the 1890s on he was devoted to the comparative study of the Chaco region and indigenous languages such as Lule, Vilela, and those belonging to the families Mataco-Mataguaya (Vejoz and Noctén) and Guaycurú (Mbayá, Abipón, Mocoví, and Toba).[9]

In the histories of the development of linguistic studies in Argentina, most of Lafone Quevedo's works, and also those by Bartolomé Mitre, are described generally within a teleological framework, such as belonging to the "pioneer stage,"[10] and encouraged only for the "non-theoretical and non-methodical" enthusiasm of passionate amateur collectors.[11] Nevertheless, these kinds of protagonists and their erudite practices deserve a more nuanced and unbiased attention on the part of historians. Recently, reviewing the implications and scope of Arnaldo Momigliano's seminal essay "Ancient History and the Antiquarian,"[12] Daniel Miller and Peter Burke pointed out that in order to research the connections between Renaissance antiquarian methods and practices and those of modern cultural sciences such as history, anthropology, ethnology, archaeology, and sociology, a balance must be achieved between the two ways of understanding these relationships. On the one hand, we must avoid teleological schemes, which show a single historical process marked by continuities, and reject specific differences and contingences—in this case between practices of the sixteenth century and the twentieth century. On the other hand, we must refine the approaches derived from Foucault's theory, which are more focused on the discontinuities and ruptures that usually tend to hide the aspects in common between them.[13] Taking this methodological advice, the aim of this chapter is to outline the connections between Lafone Quevedo's work and the methods and practices of the British antiquarian and local history traditions applied by him to the elucidation of Argentinean "linguistic ethnography." To do this, we focus on the evidence that emerges from the comparative analysis of his manuscript and working papers and the series of marks, underlines, scribbling, and annotations made in the margins of the books that form his vast personal library. I review briefly his training at Cambridge University, then note the methodological principles applied by Lafone Quevedo to collect and study the place-names of Catamarca, understood as "antiquities," namely, as material evidence of past peoples, principles which he drew from the chief works on philology, etymology, and ethnography developed in England at the time. In close connection with these latter principles, I address the ideas and practices Lafone Quevedo used to work with northwestern and Chaco indigenous languages. Most of these were deeply rooted in a tradition of research that emphasized the analogies between "nature" and "antiquities" through a set of concepts and methods that in the field of comparative philology and linguistics were conceived as following those of naturalists and antiquarians used for mounting, arranging, and classifying collections of natural history specimens and antiquities. Indeed, Lafone Quevedo was also one of the most prominent collectors of antiquities from northwest Argentina, and the study of the archaeology of the Calchaquí valleys was his other major field of study. Finally, in a brief digression, I suggest that Lafone Quevedo's internationally recognized skills for dealing with large sets of linguistic data could be related to the application of tacit knowledge derived from his daily practices. In our view, the subtle clues associated with note-taking and the reconstruction of reading practices,[14] the personal networks to draw and exchange information, and, finally, the process of collecting, organizing, and analyzing data illuminate some aspects and connections not explored in depth in the history of anthropology in Argentina.[15] This chapter also opens a dialogue with recent works on South American antiquarian practices that refer to the making of documents and book collections on "Americanist" issues by "erudite collectors"[16] and the development of numismatics collections in Argentina.[17]

Words and Places: Place-Names as Antiquities

Samuel Alexander Ernest Lafone Quevedo was a mining entrepreneur who lived in Catamarca as owner of the company Pilciao-Capillitas, at the time known as the "Catamarcan Mining Emporium,"[18] a sort of "El Dorado" that he occupied as a "lord of the manor" according to the testimony of an English observer.[19] His father, Samuel Fisher Lafone, belonged to an influential family of merchants connected since 1770 with the Liverpool leather trade and involved during the early nineteenth century in commercial traffic between the Rio de la Plata and England, with special emphasis on activities such as tanning, jerked-meat production, estate owning, mining, banking, and land speculations in Buenos Aires and Montevideo. As a result of these activities, Fisher Lafone had developed strong links with the leading business and elite social circles of the time, marrying María Quevedo y Alsina, the daughter of a prominent Spanish trader.[20]

Sent to England by his family in 1848, young Samuel Alexander studied first in Liverpool, and on May 13, 1854, he was admitted to St. John's College, Cambridge University, where he obtained a third class in the Classical Tripos in 1858 and his master of arts degree in 1863.[21] As a student in Cambridge, he made translations of prose and verse from Greek and Latin into English and vice versa and of entire passages of philosophers and rhetoricians such as Plato, Aristotle, Cicero, Lucretius, and Quintilian, and he wrote compositions on ancient history and classical philology.[22] In those years he experienced firsthand the growing development of regional societies devoted to antiquarian and natural history surveys through meetings and field excursions.[23] Once in Argentina at the beginning of the 1860s, he managed the family mining business in Catamarca. In his leisure time Samuel read works on South American history and, in the manner of antiquarians he had met during his formative years in England, he collected archaeological pieces, visited *antiguallas* (ruins), collected historical data in local archives, and made field excursions through the valleys with "father Lozano's work in hand."[24] He recorded testimonies and vocabularies from local inhabitants in order to study the historical changes in the toponymy of Catamarca and ancient Tucumán.[25] And he maintained a sustained interest in the methods of comparative philology, ethnology, and etymology, acquiring works by Robert Gordon Latham, Friedrich Max Müller, James Allan Picton, John Peile, and Walter William Skeat; in addition, Lafone Quevedo corresponded with the latter about the probable etymology of certain Spanish words.[26] Other branches of interest were British ecclesiastical history—mainly works on the general history and architecture of parish churches containing engravings, drawings, and plans—and works on classical and Biblical archaeology. Since his years in Cambridge, Lafone Quevedo was also acquainted with antiquarian methodologies applied to British local history from the sixteenth century onward that were based not only on philology and textual criticism but also on topography, fieldwork, and genealogical or heraldry studies. The methods devised by antiquarians for topographic regional studies were based on the close examination of place-names and surnames within a limited area of a district, establishing their historical associations with the landed properties in parishes or counties, the compilation of place-names series from legal documents, collections of ancient and modern maps, Anglo-Saxon charters—such as royal diplomas, royal writs, episcopal leases, and wills—poll surveys, ecclesiastical records, topographic charts, almanacs, chorographies produced by clerics, and glossaries based on knowledge obtained through oral tradition.[27]

In this context, toponymy was a fundamental source of knowledge about the ancient past, and place-names were conceived as inscriptions of names on the landscape, "the real archives of the annals of ancient nations,"[28] as durable, authentic, and reliable as those on ancient objects and ruins:

> Names have all some meaning when first imposed; and when a place is named for the first time, by any people, they apply to it some term—in early times generally descriptive of its natural peculiarities, or something else, on account of which it is remarkable, from their own language. When we find therefore, that the old names of natural objects and localities in a country belong, for the most part, to a particular language, we may conclude with certainty that a people speaking that language formerly occupied the country. Of this the names they have so impressed *are as sure a proof as if they had left a distinct record of their existence in words engraved on the rocks*. Such old names of places often long outlive both the people that bestowed them, and nearly all the material monuments of their occupancy. The language, as a vehicle of oral communication, may gradually be forgotten and be heard no

more where it was once in universal use, and the old topographical nomenclature may still remain unchanged.[29]

As Reverend Isaac Taylor eloquently expressed in his work *Words and Places,*

> The name of many an ancient city seems as if it were endowed with a sort of inherent and indestructible vitality: it is still uttered, unchanged in a single letter—*monumentum ære perennius*—while fragments of marble columns, or of sculptures in porphyry or granite, are seen strewing the site confusedly. . . . what has been affirmed by the botanist as to the floras of limited districts, may be said, with little abatement, concerning local names—that they survive the catastrophes which overthrow empires, and that they outlive devastations which are fatal to almost everything else.[30]

Thus, to acknowledge place-names or "geographical etymology" was essential to a broad understanding of the history, topography, and antiquities of a country. In cases where there was a scarcity of written sources, it was possible to collate data, and the researcher could also use maps that were read as historical "texts":

> The place-names of any land are the footmarks of the races which have inhabited it, and are numerous and important in proportion to the length of the stay and the numerical strength of each race. Thus the map supplies a clue to the history, and the history explains and confirms the hints of the map. While the latter gives us dates and details, leading incidents, and sketches of character, the former gives localities, preserves names of persons and forgotten episodes, and sometimes explains obscure allusions.[31]

Another auxiliary source of information in these traditions was the listings of surnames characteristic of certain British regions, such as those compiled in the works of Charles Wareing Bardsley and Arthur William Moore.[32] There was another connection between the research of place-names and antiquities that Lafone Quevedo was acquainted with. He closely followed newspapers and journals such as the *Times* and the *Saturday Review* and also acquired through the purchase of official publications the works on "biblical archaeology" supported by the British Palestine Exploration Fund since 1864, which were commanded in the field by lieutenants Claude Reignier Conder and Horatio H. Kitchener. Their research was published between 1871 and 1878, with a map issued in 1880 that included an area from Tyre to the Egyptian desert and from Jordan to the Mediterranean, with nine thousand Arabic place-names recorded.[33] The "biblical topography" was read and reconstructed using the textual framework offered by the Bible, a model of research Lafone Quevedo often eulogized in his manuscripts and published works.

Following Taylor, Lafone Quevedo understood place-names as "landmarks of History, Ethnology, Philology and many other sciences more" as they were linked to "all acts of more importance in the social and political life of man."[34] In fact, in his philological researches on the ancient names of the Catamarca region, he pursued Taylor's methodological advice on the principles or "canons" of the science of "onomatology." To illustrate most of the principles, in a manuscript titled "Capítulos de Filología Americana: Onomatología"[35] he made an extensive commentary on the works of Taylor taking local examples of the "Catamarcan Nomenclature." First, local names "are in no case arbitrary sounds" but always "ancient WORDS, or fragments of ancient words—each of them, in short, constituting the earliest chapter in the local history of the PLACES to which they severally refer." Second, in endeavoring to detect the meaning of a geographical name, "the first requisite is to discover the language from which the name has been derived," and then "the earliest documentary form of the name must be ascertained."[36] If no early form of the name can be discovered, "we must, guided by the analogy of similar names, endeavor to ascertain it by conjecture, bearing carefully in mind those well-known laws of phonetic change to which reference has already been made."[37] This having been done, "it remains to interpret the name which has been thus recovered or reconstructed," which implied a sound knowledge of the "ancient grammatical structure and the laws of composition which prevailed in the language in which the name is significant." Then Taylor stated that great aid "will be derived from the analogy of other names in the same neighborhood. A sort of epidemic seems to have prevailed in the nomenclature of certain districts."[38] Finally, having thus arrived at a probable interpretation of the name in question, the researcher must proceed to test the result: "if the name be topographic or descriptive, we must ascertain if it conforms to the physical features of the place; if, on the other hand, the name be historical in its character, we must satisfy ourselves as to the historic possibility of its bestowal."[39] Once established, this sort of "geographical etymology" would be very useful for the study of the ethnology of a given region, because

Ethnology is the science which derives the greatest aid from geographical etymology. The names which still remain upon our maps are able to supply us with traces of the history of nations that have left us no other memorials..., nations which once played a prominent part in the world's history, but which have bequeathed no written annals, which have constructed no monuments, whose language is dying or is dead, whose blood is becoming mingled with that of the other races. The knowledge of the history and the migrations of such tribes must be recovered from the study of the names of the places which they once inhabited, but which now know them no more—from the names of the hills which they fortified, of the rivers by which they dwelt, of the distant mountains upon which they gazed.[40]

Given the scarcity of a broad and unified corpus of written documents, and thus reliable historical data, place-names and surnames were essential to establish the ethnology of Catamarca by following Taylor's methodological principles and the ideas put into practice by Bardsley and Moore. With this in mind, from the early 1880s on, Lafone Quevedo had begun to collate data from various sources with the aim of editing a collection of local voices, a "Thesaurus," which he called *Tesoro de Catamarqueñismos*, composed mostly of place-names, surnames, and loose voices fundamental to "the elucidation of ethnological and linguistic history of the country."[41] These include national and provincial archives; public and private libraries; "rare" manuscript collections held by "Americanists" Andrés Lamas, Manuel R. Trelles, and Bartolomé Mitre; ancient and modern map collections; and legal document series held by the oldest families in the northwest region.[42] Then, in the archives of Catamarca and Buenos Aires, he systematized indigenous surnames from censuses known as "Empadronamientos de indios tributarios" taken by Spanish governors since the sixteenth century, and he made a record of changes in place-names from the "Actas capitulares," comparing it with the information extracted from *Relaciones geográficas de Indias: Perú*, compiled and published in four volumes by Marcos Jiménez de la Espada between 1881 and 1897, and the works of fathers Pedro Lozano and Nicolás del Techo. Another central source of information was the ancient series of "documents of demarcation" with which the owners of *mercedes* or *heredade* in the northwest credited his property titles, in a context characterized by an increasing number of legal disputes on land tenure that occurred throughout the nineteenth century. Lafone Quevedo stated that "these instruments" were "full of names now lost, while the maps, however great, must ignore the vast majority of names which, though lacking geographical or topographical importance, serve to define the ethno-linguistic influences."[43] All this information was collated with that contained in the ancient and modern cartography of the region: Lafone Quevedo used and copied maps and *croquis* (draft designs) taken from legal documents such as "mapas de deslindes," works of the Jesuits, the "crónicas de Indias," and modern maps published by Martin de Moussy in 1869 and Ludwig Brackebusch between 1889 and 1892 to observe changes in the location of indigenous groups in that region over time. He also made a collection of voices and phrases of the Cuzco language, which was the name that local inhabitants gave to Quechua, through interviews conducted in situ by him between 1884 and 1888 with creoles such as Teresa Hualcumay, Magdalena Gómez, and Rosa Cusillo.

By tabulating information thus obtained and by establishing the etymology of each word, he identified three main series that would correspond to the Quechua, Cacan, and Araucano languages. Examples of the second were place-names ending in *-ao* (Animanao), *-vil* (Yocavil), *-il* (Saujil), *-gasta* (Tinogasta), and indigenous surnames ending in *-ay* (Aballay). The last Araucanian language could be inferred in the names of hamlets and villages of Catamarca containing the Araucanian root *Co-*, denoting "water," as in Coneta and Conando, which attest to the possible existence of a primordial linguistic group that would have had in common the three languages. For Lafone Quevedo, this linguistic evidence, reinforced by the testimony of Fernando de Montesinos's work on ancient memorials of Peru, indicate the presence of a great pre-Inca nation that would have occupied the entire Andean region.

It was the fortuitous discovery of a word in a privately owned document that indicated to Lafone Quevedo that the Cacan language would not be "a more or less corrupted dialect of Quechua" but a different language. The collection of new evidence and the exercise of tabulating words, separating the roots that were undoubtedly Quechua from those that were not, led him to believe that the Cacan language would have chances of linguistic affiliation with those of indigenous groups of the eastern lowlands. This insight induced him to orient his investigations from inquiries into the place-names and topography of the region surrounding his place of residence to the study of Chaco indigenous languages.

The "Garden of Argentine Indigenous Languages"

In the late eighteenth century, a new research tradition in language studies began to be developed, characterized by data-oriented work aimed at collecting facts about languages for typological or historical reasons. Since then, there has been an increasing concern for the collection of linguistic data, both in the field and through the philological study of texts, and a growing interest in the detailed analysis of several languages.[44] In this context and in line with the factual and historical concerns of the nineteenth century, it was usual among philologists and linguists not only to refer to their own work but to resort to analogies with the methods, practices, and objects of natural history and antiquarianism. As part of a general movement that stressed analogies in the working methods between natural sciences and humanities,[45] the most pervasive rhetorical figures employed to illustrate linguistic ideas and practices were those related to botany, paleontology, geology, and archaeology.[46] From a practical point of view, it was possible to work with words as pieces of historical research in the manner of naturalists and antiquarians—collecting, sorting, arranging, and classifying vocabularies and crafting etymologies as if they were sets of natural history specimens or antiquities. As the philologist and former botanist William Dwight Whitney pointed out, there was no branch of historical study that was so like a physical science as linguistics, "none which deals with such an infinite multiplicity of separate facts, capable of being observed, recorded, turned over, estimated in their various relations." "A combination of articulate sounds forming a word," he argued, "is almost as objective an entity as a polyp or a fossil; it can be laid away on a sheet of paper, like a plant in a herbarium, for future leisurely examination."[47]

Lafone Quevedo often used in his works several of these figures of speech that linked language studies, nature, and antiquities, a close relationship that referred to specific ways of work related to certain theoretical ideas. One of them was the notion of the "Garden of Languages" to refer to the large number of Argentine indigenous languages and dialects that had long been considered intractable to classification according to the canons and methods devised by European philologists and linguists based only on textual criticism. Discussing the statements of Abel Hovelacque and Friedrich Max Müller about the state of the art in linguistic classification procedures and remembering the lessons taught by the Reverend John Stevens Henslow, Darwin's famous mentor, in his botany courses at Cambridge, Lafone Quevedo argued that though "philology depended on history," that is, on literature or documentary evidence,

> the science of language requires natural, not artificial facts to carry out or establish its principles. Very well-known and widely-read authors flatter themselves that we have left the Linnaean and reached the de Candolle stage of research, but it would seem to me as if this could hardly

be the case, for we are still classifying according to standards which depend mainly on Latin, Greek and Sanskrit models. I remember the late Professor Henslow warning us in his lectures against the "monsters" to be seen at a flower show, and surely literary dialects are "monsters," whereas the science of language should appeal to natural specimens untainted by the arts of schools and authors.[48]

Lafone Quevedo found evidence from various sources that many Argentinean indigenous languages and dialects, those "authentic natural flowers in the Garden of Languages,"[49] were characterized by mixtures and hybridization in their grammatical structures and mechanisms, as was noted by Wilhelm von Humboldt for other indigenous languages of the American continent. It is important to note here that in those years Lafone Quevedo began to outline a system of classification for the indigenous language families of South America based on a specific grammatical feature associated with a particular form of agglutination that for him was typical of the Americas, such as pronominal particles and their form of articulation both with the verbs and nouns. In his scheme, he proposed two "matrices grammars": a "Brazilian" or "Atlantic" group, which was characterized by prefixing the pronominal particles (e.g., "my-book") and another, the "Andean" or "Pacific," which was characterized by subfixing it (e.g., "Book-my(ne)"). The different Guaraní dialects and languages belonging to the Arawak-Maypure-Mojave family would be examples of the first group, geographically covering the space from the West Indies and Orinoco River to the Rio de la Plata basin and from the Atlantic to the slopes of the Andes. The Quechua, Aymara, and Araucanian, "the three central languages of the Andes" would be examples of the second group, comprising the Andean region "from Quito to the Straits of Magellan." Located between these two groups, he identified a series of languages and codialects of "nations" that he called the "middle group," enclosed between the Guaraní and Quechua and characterized by their use of two kinds of pronominal affixes of personal relationship (e.g., "My-Book-I"). Starting from the north, this third group included the Caribes and Maypures, the Chiquitos, and finally the "Mataco-Guaycuru nations" formed by the Mbayas, Lenguas, Payaguas, Abipones, Mocovies, and Toba, among others.[50] It is precisely this group of languages of the Chaco, "the natural specimens of the Garden of Argentinean indigenous languages" characterized by hybridization and mixture, to the in-depth study of which Lafone Quevedo thereafter devoted himself, grounded in the comparison of the articulation of pronominal particles as a primary classificatory feature.

Another idea applied by Lafone Quevedo was related to paleontology and archaeology: during his field excursions collecting Quechua vocabularies through interviews with local inhabitants, he recorded a series of "linguistic fossils," which he interpreted as "reliquias" (relics) of languages that had been spoken in the region since ancient times. Although the idea of relics remits clearly to his archaeological studies in the Calchaquí valleys, the concept of linguistic fossils also points to what Adolphe Pictet devised for the study of Indo-European languages. Pictet defined a sort of "linguistic paleontology" that, through lexical reconstructions, would know the center of origin and dispersal of a given language.[51] Closely tied to this was Friedrich Max Müller's idea of "biographies of words," a suggestive methodological assumption that linked comparative philology with antiquarian collecting practices. Likening language to a "museum," Müller delivered a series of recommendations to those readers who "really wish to arrange for themselves a small museum of words" in order to "show how words should be collected, how they should be cleaned and arranged, and how their migrations should be traced from century to century, or from country to country," pointing out that each word

> has its biography, beginning with its birth, or at least with its baptism. We may speak of its childhood, its youth, its manhood, and old age, nay, even of its death, and of its heirs and successors. The early chapters of these word-biographies are no doubt the most difficult and require very careful treatment; but, as in the lives of men and women, they are also the most important, and in the case of most words they often determine the whole of their subsequent career. In the earliest chapters we shall find that our authorities sometimes differ and are not always quite trustworthy; nay, there are many lives in which as yet the earliest chapters are entirely missing. But there are rich archives that still have to be ransacked, and every conscientious student, I believe, will find that, with proper care and judgment, his researches will be amply rewarded.[52]

Lafone Quevedo used this method in order to reconstruct the biography of words such as *macana* and *yapa*,[53] tracing their etymology to the Quechua language, showing their historical derivations and probable relationships with other languages, and stating that "the study of words in this way can provide us with a thousand points of ethno-linguistic, historical interest. There can be no science more sweeping than the biographies of words, as they carry us away with the impetus of their current. Whatever they may lack of the exact sciences, we shall overcome with our imagination, the obstacle to all popular etymology."[54]

To illustrate Lafone Quevedo's ways of handling evidence by coping with linguistic information he extracted from several sources, it is useful to briefly digress to relate another suggestive analogy with the aforementioned material dimension of practices and methods used for mounting and arranging collections of words. In this case it is not related to natural history and antiquarian surveys but to trade practices. Most of Lafone Quevedo's linguistic works were highly regarded at the time by scholars such as Lucien Adam and Daniel Brinton because of the thoroughness, clear organization, and methodical presentation of information in tables and his meticulous inquiry into the most diverse sources.[55] In this regard, I wish to emphasize here a point that probably influenced his skills in collecting and classifying evidence, and that is the application of tacit knowledge derived from business practices that constituted his main occupation until the early years of the twentieth century. As the eldest son of a family of active British merchants and entrepreneurs, Lafone Quevedo had been introduced early to the business world. Since his return from Cambridge to the Rio del la Plata in the early 1860s, he was in charge of the management of the family mining undertakings in Catamarca Province, carrying out the accounting business on a daily basis and sending remittances to banks in Buenos Aires, Montevideo, Liverpool, and London. He also managed the company as it significantly increased its number of employees and expanded not only geographically but also in terms of its investments, which soon extended to agriculture, livestock, and trade of overseas goods with Bolivia and northern Chile through the firm Lafone, Franco & Co.[56] It is worth mentioning here that the formal conventions of bookkeeping used in the world of trade are considered to have served as a model for note-taking and recording in scholarly pursuits since early modern times.[57] Moreover, as Mary Poovey has shown, the daily recording of trade movements and their organization in these books with double-entry tables (i.e., double-entry bookkeeping) was one of the first systems that privileged both the things in themselves (the objects and the money that merchants traded in) and the formal system of registration as a number, thus transforming the representations of those "things" into usable data.[58] As a system of writing, these double-entry tables had a broader epistemological effect that exceeded the narrow scope of operations of transcription and economic calculation, thereby providing an image of formal strictness and precision that eventually spread to all domains of knowledge. Lafone Quevedo himself attributed to this sort of "tabulation art" the most important findings and discoveries he had made related to the various mechanisms of agglutination of pronominal particles among the Chaco indigenous languages.

> [But] let us take the case of an agglutinating tongue. A priori we know it to be made up of various roots and particles with a more or less definite meaning. Let us then hunt them through all stocks and branches and *see what we get from tabulating the results of such investigations. What I have been able to learn as regards Mocoví, Abipón, etc. is mainly the outcome of tabulation.*[59]

For recording the Catamarca's place-names, Lafone Quevedo used the same sheets of paper employed for accounting purposes in his companies, with various columns, in order to write down not numbers, but the order of place-names by districts, with their orthographical corrections, a narrow column to record the probable language (e.g., "Q: Quechua"), and his translation into Spanish.

Final Remarks

Lafone Quevedo's philological and archaeological works have frequently been regarded as the by-products of a sympathetic approach toward his region of residence motivated mainly by physical proximity with respect to native populations and the remains of their ancestors embodied in archaeological objects, place-names, myths, and folklore. This sort of sensitive, essentialist approach to local issues by "the philologists" has long been imagined in opposition to the cold "naturalists" or savants residing in cosmopolitan Buenos Aires. However, a study of the methods and means of research into "local" issues should not be conceived in narrow ideologically driven frameworks that see an intrinsic connection between "local" history and some sort of essentialist "local knowledge." Such an approach is in danger of masking the less perceptible ties between methods and practices conceived in other contexts—in this case, to British antiquarian and local history traditions and comparative philological studies that resorted to metaphorical concepts linked to natural history and antiquarian practices and to how these were applied, adapted, and modified in order to survey Argentine linguistic ethnology. Moreover, the adoption of comparative philological concepts devised for the study of proto-Indo-European and Indo-European families of languages does not imply that Lafone

Quevedo completely subscribed to the hierarchical classifications of languages and peoples it promoted. Quite the contrary, in his works and his publications in the periodical press, he strongly defended and promoted the idea of the complexity of South American indigenous languages and the inadequacy of many of the theoretical models developed in Europe to study them. He seems to have taken and adapted a series of concepts linked to natural history, antiquarian, and philology traditions, mainly for their heuristic and evocative value, as working tools not only for the study of indigenous languages but also of northwestern Argentine archaeology, the other branch of study to which he was devoted as an important collector of antiquities. The reconstruction and description of Lafone Quevedo's methods and research practices—understood as cosmopolitan visions applied to local problems—drawn from his manuscripts and working papers, the correspondence, and the series of books in his personal library, which bear the visual traces of his reading habits, not only challenges previous assumptions based on teleological frameworks and an ideological bias but also shows us the set of mechanisms scholars relied on to construct their evidence and the subtle, almost invisible processes of reception and adaptation of methods devised in other research traditions to solve local ethnolinguistic, archaeological, and historical questions.

Acknowledgments

I am indebted to the editors of the volume—Stefanie Gänger, Phil Kohl, and Irina Podgorny—for helpful suggestions as well as corrections to the original version of the manuscript. I also owe thanks to the anonymous reviewers for the University of Arizona Press for the useful comments, especially the suggestion about the works of Gustaf Sobin, hitherto unknown to me.

Notes

1. Gustaf Sobin, *Luminous Debris: Reflecting on Vestige in Provence and Languedoc* (Berkeley: University of California Press, 1999), 112.
2. Sylvain Auroux and Francisco Queixalós, *Pour une histoire de la linguistique amérindienne en France* (Paris: AEA-CNRS, 1984).
3. Luis María Torres, introduction to *Catálogo razonado de la Sección Lenguas Americanas*, ed. Museo Mitre (Buenos Aires: Imprenta de Coni Hermanos, 1909), vii–xlii.

4. Sylvain Auroux, introduction to *Histoire des idées linguistiques*, vol. 3, *L'hégémonie du comparatisme*, ed. Sylvain Auroux (Brussels: Mardaga, 2000), 9–22; Piet Desmet, *La linguistique naturaliste en France (1867–1922)* (Leuven: Peeters, 1996), 451–52.

5. See Nélia Dias and Britta Rupp-Eisenreich, "Linguistique et anthropologie physique," in *Histoire des idées linguistiques*, vol. 3, *L'hégémonie du comparatisme*, ed. Sylvain Auroux (Brussels: Pierre Mardaga, 2000), 279–94.

6. See Pablo Buchbinder, "Vínculos privados, instituciones públicas y reglas profesionales en los orígenes de la historiografía argentina," *Boletín del Instituto de Historia Argentina y Americana "Dr. Emilio Ravignani*,*"* no. 13 (1996): 59–82; Máximo Farro, *La formación del Museo de La Plata: Coleccionistas, comerciantes, estudiosos y naturalistas viajeros a fines del siglo XIX* (Rosario: Prohistoria Ediciones, 2009).

7. For further discussion, see Máximo Farro, "Las lenguas indígenas argentinas como objeto de colección: Notas acerca de los estudios lingüísticos de Samuel A. Lafone Quevedo a fines del siglo XIX," *Revista de Indias* 73, no. 258 (2013): 525–52.

8. Samuel A. Lafone Quevedo, *Londres y Catamarca: Cartas a "La Nación", 1883–84 y 1885* (Buenos Aires: Imprenta y Librería de Mayo, 1888); *Tesoro de Catamarqueñismos: Nombres de lugar y apellidos indios con etimologías aisladas de la lengua Cacana* (Buenos Aires: Imprenta de Pablo Coni, 1898). This language was also known as *Kaká, Caca, Chaka, Catamarcana, Diaguita*, and *Calchaquí*. Ricardo Nardi, "El Kakán, lengua de los Diaguitas," *Sapiens*, no. 3 (1979): 1–33.

9. Samuel A. Lafone Quevedo, "Lenguas Argentinas: Grupo Mataco-Mataguayo del Chaco: Dialecto Vejoz: Vocabulario y Apuntes M.S. D'Orbigny," *Boletín del Instituto Geográfico Argentino* 17 (1896): 121–76; "Los indios Matacos y su lengua: Por el ingeniero Juan Pelleschi, con introducción por Samuel A. Lafone Quevedo M.A.," *Boletín del Instituto Geográfico Argentino* 17 (1896): 559–622; "Los indios Matacos y su lengua: Por el P. Joaquín Remedi Ord. Seraf. Misionero Apostólico, con Vocabularios," *Boletín del Instituto Geográfico Argentino* 17 (1896): 331–62.

10. Torres, introduction to *Catálogo razonado*; Fernando Márquez Miranda, "Las clasificaciones lingüísticas antes y después de la época de Mitre," *Ciencia e Investigación* 12, no. 2 (1956): 70–73.

11. Beatriz Bixio, "Lenguas indígenas del centro y norte de la República Argentina (siglos XVI–XVIII)," in *Historia Argentina Prehispánica*, ed. Eduardo E. Berberian and Axel E. Nielsen (Córdoba: Editorial Brujas, 2001), 878.

12. Arnaldo Momigliano, "Ancient History and the Antiquarian," *Journal of the Warburg and Courtauld Institutes* 13, no. 3/4 (1950): 285–315.

13. Peter N. Miller, introduction to *Momigliano and Antiquarianism: Foundations of the Modern Cultural Sciences*, ed. Peter N. Miller (Toronto: University of Toronto Press, 2007); Peter Burke, "From Antiquarianism to Anthropology," in *Momigliano and Antiquarianism*, 229–47.

14. On this subject, see Anne Blair, "Note Taking as an Art of Transmission," *Critical Inquiry* 31 (2004): 85–107; *Too Much to Know: Managing Scholarly Information Before the Modern Age* (New Haven, CT: Yale University Press, 2010).

15. See Máximo Farro, *La formación del Museo*; "Colecciones de cráneos, fotografías y manuscritos en el desarrollo de la antropología física y de la etnografía lingüística en la Argentina de fines del siglo XIX," in *Colecionismos, práticas de campo e representações*, ed. María Margaret Lopes and Alda Heizer (Campina

Grande: EDUEPB, 2011), 93–104; "Imágenes de cráneos, retratos antropológicos y tipologías raciales: Los usos de las primeras colecciones de fotografías del Museo de La Plata a fines del siglo XIX," in *Los secretos de Barba Azul: Fantasías y realidades de los archivos del Museo de La Plata*, ed. Tatiana Kelly and Irina Podgorny (Rosario: Prohistoria Ediciones, 2012), 69–104.

16. Horacio Crespo, "El erudito coleccionista y los orígenes del americanismo," in *Historia de los intelectuales en América Latina*, vol. 1, *La ciudad letrada, de la conquista al modernismo*, ed. Carlos Altamirano (Buenos Aires: Katz Editores, 2008), 290–311.

17. Diego Aufiero, "El Instituto Bonaerense de Numismática y Antigüedades y los estudios numismáticos en Buenos Aires en la década de 1870," *L'Ordinaire Latino-américain*, no. 212 (2010): 159–182.

18. Émil Hünicken, *Industria minera y metalúrgica en las provincias de La Rioja, Catamarca, Jujuy y Salta* (Buenos Aires: Imprenta de Juan A. Alsina, 1894).

19. Henry Charles Ross Johnson, *A Long Vacation in the Argentine Alps; or, Where to Settle in the River Plate States* (London: Richard Bentley, 1868).

20. Arnoldo Canclini, "Samuel F. Lafone: apuntes para su biografía," *Investigaciones y Ensayos*, no. 48 (1999): 123–61.

21. John Archibald Venn, *Alumni Cantabrigienses: A Biographical List of All Known Students, Graduates and Holders of Office at the University of Cambridge, from the Earliest Times to 1900*, pt. 2, 1752–1900, vol. 4 (Cambridge: Cambridge University Press, 1951).

22. Information drawn from copies of *The Cambridge University Calendar* for the years 1855–1869 and *Almanack and Register of the Cambridge University, 1853–1855*, both in his personal library. See also *The Student's Guide to the University of Cambridge* (Cambridge: Deighton and Bell, 1874); Edward Miller, *Portrait of a College: A History of the College of Saint John the Evangelist in Cambridge* (Cambridge: Cambridge University Press, 1961). For a detailed study of Cambridge University "Classical Tripos," see William Clark, *Academic Charisma and the Origins of the Research University* (Chicago: University of Chicago Press, 2006).

23. David Elliston Allen, *The Naturalist in Britain: A Social History* (London: Allen Lane, 1976); Ian Inkster and Jack Morrell, eds., *Metropolis and Province: Science in British culture, 1780–1850* (London: Hutchinson, 1983); Philippa Levine, *The Amateur and the Professional: Antiquarians, Historians and Archaeologists in Victorian Britain, 1838–1886* (Cambridge: Cambridge University Press, 1986); Simon Naylor, "Collecting Quoits: Field Cultures in the History of Cornish Antiquarianism," *Cultural Geographies* 10 (2003): 309–33; *Regionalizing Science: Placing Knowledges in Victorian England* (London: Pickering and Chatto, 2010).

24. The reference is to the work of Jesuit father Pedro Lozano, *Historia de la conquista del Paraguay, Río de la Plata y Tucumán* (Buenos Aires: Imprenta Popular, 1873–1875).

25. Lafone Quevedo, *Londres y Catamarca*.

26. Walter William Skeat to Samuel A. Lafone Quevedo, September 29, 1889, folder no. 138, manuscripts collection, Archivo Histórico del Museo de La Plata.

27. Martin Myrone and Lucy Peltz, eds., *Producing the Past: Aspects of Antiquarian Culture and Practice, 1700–1850* (London: Ashgate, 1999); Rosemary Sweet, *Antiquaries: The Discovery of the Past in Eighteenth-Century Britain* (London: Hambledon, 2004); Susan Pearce, ed., *Visions of Antiquity: The Society of Antiquaries of London*

1707–2007 (Oxford: Oxbow, 2007); Penny Fielding, *Scotland and the Fictions of Geography: North Britain, 1760–1830* (Cambridge: Cambridge University Press, 2008).

28. Hodder Westropp, *Handbook of Archaeology, Egyptian-Greek-Etruscan-Roman* (London: Bell and Dadly, 1867), 328.

29. Richard Morris, *The Etymology of Local Names: With a Short Introduction to the Relationship of Languages* (London: Judd and Glass, 1857), frontispiece (emphasis mine).

30. Isaac Taylor, *Words and Places: Etymological Illustrations of History, Ethnology and Geography* (London: Macmillan, 1864), 2.

31. Edmunds Flavell, *Traces of History in the Name of Places: With a Vocabulary of the Roots out of Which Names of Places in England and Wales Are Formed* (London: Longmans and Green, 1869), v–vi.

32. Charles Wareing Bardsley, *English Surnames: Their Sources and Significations* (London: Chatto and Windus, 1875); Arthur William Moore, *The Surnames and Place-Names of the Isle of Man* (London: Elliot Stock, 1890).

33. Claude R. Conder, Horatio Kitchener, and Edward Palmer, *The Survey of Western Palestine: Arabic and English Name Lists* (London: Committee of the Palestine Exploration Fund, 1881); Margarita Díaz-Andreu, *A World History of Nineteenth-Century Archaeology: Nationalism, Colonialism and the Past* (Oxford: Oxford University Press, 2007).

34. Samuel A. Lafone Quevedo, "Nomenclatura Indígena," *Revista Patriótica del Pasado Argentino* 3 (1890): 141–52.

35. Samuel A. Lafone Quevedo, MS 68, manuscripts collection, Archivo Histórico del Museo de La Plata.

36. Taylor, *Words and Places*, 476–77.

37. Samuel A. Lafone Quevedo, MS 68, manuscripts collection, Archivo Histórico del Museo de La Plata.

38. Taylor, *Words and Places*, 468.

39. Ibid.

40. Ibid., 40–41.

41. Lafone Quevedo, *Tesoro de Catamarqueñismos*, 19.

42. See Farro, "Las lenguas indígenas argentinas."

43. Lafone Quevedo, *Tesoro de Catamarqueñismos*, viii.

44. Anna Morpurgo Davis, *Nineteenth-Century Linguistics* (London: Longman Pearson, 1998), 24–58.

45. Krzysztof Pomian, *Collectors and Curiosities: Paris and Vienna, 1500–1800* (Cambridge: Polity, 1990). See also Martin J. S. Rudwick, "Transposed Concepts from the Human Sciences in the Early Work of Charles Lyell," in *Images of the Earth: Essays in the History of Environmental Sciences*, ed. Ludmilla Jordanova and Roy Porter (Chalfont St Giles: British Society for the History of Science, 1997), 77–92.

46. Jan Noordegraaf, "In the Shadow of the Language Garden," in *The Emergence of the Modern Language Sciences*, vol. 1, *Historiographical perspectives*, ed. Sheila Embelton, John E. Joseph, and Hans-Josef Niederehe (Philadelphia: John Benjamins, 1999), 13–25; Nathan Schlanger, "Series in Progress: Antiquities of Nature, Numismatics and Stone Implements in the Emergence of Prehistoric Archaeology," *History of Science* 48 (2010): 343–69.

47. William Dwight Whitney, *The Life and Growth of Language* (New York: Appleton, 1875), 311.

48. Samuel A. Lafone Quevedo, MS 34, Lafone Quevedo papers, Archivo Histórico del Museo de La Plata.

49. Samuel A. Lafone Quevedo, "Las lenguas argentinas y el Museo de La Plata," *La Nación* 23, no. 6774 (1892): 1–2.

50. Samuel A. Lafone Quevedo, "La Raza Americana de Brinton: Estudio crítico," *Boletín del Instituto Geográfico Argentino* 14 (1893): 505–28; "Progresos de la etnología en el Río de la Plata durante el año 1898," *Boletín del Instituto Geográfico Argentino* 20 (1899): 1–64.

51. Morpurgo Davis, *Nineteenth-Century Linguistics*, 175.

52. Friderich Max Müller, *Biographies of Words; or, the Home of the Aryas* (London: Longmans and Green, 1888), 4–5.

53. Samuel A. Lafone Quevedo, "The Words Yapa and Baqueano," *Standard*, Buenos Aires, June 23, July 2, 1893.

54. Samuel A. Lafone Quevedo, "Capítulos de filología argentina: La biografía de dos voces," MS 68, manuscripts collection, Archivo Histórico del Museo de La Plata.

55. On this aspect of Lafone Quevedo's work, see Farro, "Las lenguas indígenas argentinas."

56. Ross Johnson, *Long Vacation*; Hüniken, *Industria Minera y Metalúrgica*; Guillermo Furlong Cardiff, *Samuel A. Lafone Quevedo* (Buenos Aires: Ediciones Culturales Argentinas, 1964).

57. Blair, *Too Much to Know*.

58. Mary Poovey, *A History of the Modern Fact: Problems of Knowledge in the Sciences of Wealth and Society* (Chicago: University of Chicago Press, 1998), 29–91.

59. Samuel MS 34, Lafone Quevedo papers, Archivo Histórico del Museo de La Plata, (emphasis mine).

PART TWO

Settings

CHAPTER FOUR

Fraternal Curiosity

The Camacho Museum, Campeche, Mexico

Adam T. Sellen

This study analyzes the history of a cabinet of pre-Hispanic antiquities, natural specimens and historical artifacts, established in the first half of the nineteenth century in San Francisco de Campeche, a key port city in the state of Yucatán, Mexico.[1] Founded by the brothers Leandro and José María Camacho, Spanish priests with limited resources, their *museo* was the first of its kind in southeast Mexico and the first in the country to exhibit what would eventually be considered Mayan culture. Travelers passing through the port described the museum as an antiquarian's delight, a chaotic mélange that reflected both of the priests' intellectual breadth and inquisitive nature. A Scottish traveler opined that despite the richness of the objects on display, the priests themselves were the most interesting curiosities.[2]

My purpose in this paper is twofold: to reveal the various historical strands that gave meaning to the Camacho museum in the context of nineteenth-century Yucatán, and to understand the collecting practices of the priests by focusing on the history of the objects and how they arrived and then left the museum. To comprehend why the museum was so important at a particular moment in time, it is fundamental to reconstruct the biographies of the collectors and analyze the historical context in which they compiled the collection. This task is difficult because of the meager documentation available on the brothers and because the collection no longer exists as such. Dispersed when they died, the museum was disbanded into different holdings both in Mexico and overseas. With various travelers, the objects have traversed space and time, and their movements chart numerous histories about how they were discovered, acquired, collected, and exchanged.[3] Through this process, the objects generated, directly or indirectly, textual and visual documentation, such as correspondence, notes, catalogs, maps, and images. Although many authors have emphasized the imperialist character of these types of acquisitions,[4] the interest in material culture—particularly that from the region of Yucatán—was not only exploited by foreigners but also by Mexicans.

El Museo de los Hermanos Camacho

The Camacho brothers' museum was an obligatory visit for those who were passing through Campeche. The U.S. commander Matthew Calbraith Perry, for example, who between 1845 and 1847 headed the attack and siege on various coastal Mexican cities, brought his bellicose actions to a halt on December 7, 1847, to speak with José Cadenas, the military commander in Campeche. After the meeting, he rushed off to visit the home "of the dear *señores* Camacho, with the same idea that all foreigners go to visit them, to see their curious museum."[5] Thanks to these encounters and a few published accounts, we have some details about their collection. In this study I have relied on the works of four travelers: the American travel writer Benjamin Moore Norman, who briefly visited Campeche in 1841; the French naturalist Arturo Morelet and the Austrian Karl Bartolomeus Heller, who both resided in the city in 1847; and William Parish Robertson, from whom the richest testimony comes, an English trader who visited the port in 1849 and was the priests' greatest admirer.

Parish Robertson described the older brother, Leandro, as jovial, vigorous, plump, and obsessed with acquiring ancient artifacts and natural specimens. He was a student of phrenology, which supposedly enabled one to determine character and personality traits from reading the subtle ridges and valleys of the human skull, and for this purpose Leandro was said to have a large collection of crania. In physique and character his brother, José María, was almost a complete opposite: slender and softspoken.[6] A student of mechanics and the sciences, his technical ability was such that he had built his own printing press and copied a daguerreotype camera after examining it once. Various testimonies confirm that they collaborated closely in the museum, albeit with friendly antagonism: Leandro complained that his younger brother would ruin his ancient pots by using them to heat rabbit skin glue for his projects, while José María reproached his elder brother for using his fine tools to clean seashells.[7] Despite their sibling rivalry, they were inseparable.

We do not know exactly when Leandro José Camacho died. In February of 1849 Parish Robertson reported him alive, but a few months later a local newspaper announced an auction of books, religious articles, and personal effects that probably belonged to the priest,[8] suggesting that he could have passed away during the summer at the age of 62. His younger brother died in 1854 at the same age.[9]

The Camacho brothers formed their eclectic museum in a context that overlapped different traditions and erudite practices. The reforms carried out by the House of Bourbon in the eighteenth century renewed an interest in the Greco-Roman past and spawned a royal antiquarianism that documented the neoclassical style. By the beginning of the nineteenth century, Europe's age of archaeology had begun, and the past was a new frontier to be conquered not only by kings and princes but also by lesser mortals. The natural world formed part of the same outer limits, largely unknown, especially in regard to the exotic species of the New World that had not been fully classified and exploited. Thus, the priest's fervor to collect was tied to an interest in science and antiquarianism that focused on machines, ancient artifacts, and inscriptions from past cultures coupled with a desire to classify the natural world. A capacity to access important scholarly publications, as well as an ability to write and to draw, informed their collecting, ordering, and modeling. Parish Robertson mentioned that the pair had traveled all over Europe and were considered illustrious men of science.[10] It is probable, then, that they had knowledge of or had visited many of the grand museums and cabinets of the Old World and that these formed the intellectual and aesthetic bedrock for the religious brothers. Little more is known about their influences and motivations.

In the relative isolation of Yucatán, the fruits of the Enlightenment came slowly and unevenly, and new concepts, such as that of a museum, could be met with hostility. Pantaleón Barrera, writing for *El Registro Yucateco* in 1846, reported that the Camacho brothers encountered certain resistance in the populace toward their activities, and some people even believed that collecting strange objects was linked to sorcery.[11] Their dilapidated home, populated with stray cats and a mischievous monkey (the beginnings of a menagerie?), was packed to the rafters with artifacts and specimens and no doubt appeared otherworldly to some: Benjamin Moore Norman described it as a "necromancer's workshop."[12] Nonetheless Barrera, a local, was sympathetic to the acquisitive priests and compared them to the Spanish writer Enrique de Villena, who had been accused of witchcraft and had seen his library torched by an angry mob. Despite these medieval attitudes, the priests' modesty and good nature won over their detractors, and in time they became beloved characters. They could not have imagined at the outset that late in their lives their humble museum would soon be the source of political and nationalistic ambitions.

Justo Sierra O'Reilly and the Camacho Museum

The most fervent promoter of the Camacho Museum was the politician and writer Justo Sierra O'Reilly, a native son of Campeche who is considered the father of Yucatecan literature. In a series of articles published in two local journals, *El Museo Yucateco* (1841–1842) and later *El Registro Yucateco* (1845–1849), he proposed to use their museum as an instrument for creating a peninsular identity. Part of a grand project to create an autonomous region in Yucatán, he sought that the state and a group of close collaborators work toward the construction and administration of a collective memory that included museums, statues, archives, and publications with the aim to register information about the region and to fortify citizenry and social cohesion.[13] The museum fit into this scheme as a microcosm of what Sierra called "Yucatecan virtues," a diversity of historical, cultural, and geographic characteristics that exhibited in an appropriate way would drive its own political destiny.[14] The writer also had an interest in expanding the collections to reflect other relevant realities, and during a trip to the United States in 1848, he tore "brambles and small bushes" from the tomb of George Washington for the collection of his friends in Campeche.[15]

Sierra felt that if the state did not establish a locality for the museum, it could be lost or split up, and in an open critique of his countrymen, he lamented the lack of institutional support to acquire the holding. He argued that the priests, in all their generosity, would often give objects to passing travelers and were engaged in dismantling their legacy. He also warned that a French frigate under the command of a Monsieur Cosmao was poised to purchase the entire museum to enrich the museums of Paris.[16] True or not, the outside threat helped his case because foreign interest in the collection was evidence of its great worth. In the end, his calls fell on deaf ears: the separatist project failed, and the attempt to create an independent region was mired in the bloody caste war that lasted more than fifty years.

In 1849, when Leandro Camacho died, his brother José María, fragile in health and without his trusted companion, lost interest in the museum. In Mexico City the news of the collection's availability arrived, and the government commissioned Sierra, at the time a legislator in Congress, to acquire it for the Museo Nacional.[17] The exact date when this occurred is still unknown, as are the details about the negotiation, but there are a few references that help clarify details about the destination of the collection and when it was moved. In 1874 the geographer Antonio García Cubas commented on a museum that was probably the Camacho brothers'.

> The Ministerio de Fomento bought a beautiful yucatec museum, in which one can admire beautiful figures of ceramic that have been masterfully executed, and that reveal exactly the type that coincides with the inhabitants of India, China and Japan; but unfortunately this museum disappeared in the epoch of the French invasion. God willing it will be found useful to science![18]

Another reference is by Louis Toussaint Simon Doutrelaine, a colonel in the French army and collaborator in the Comission Scientifique du Mexique (1862–1893). In a study he sent to the French Minister of Public Instruction in 1865, he made it clear that the museum of the brothers Camacho was purchased by this ministry and was in the City of Mexico: "Today, the Ministro de Fomento [Orozco y Berra] is in possession of an interesting collection of chiapanec and yucatec antiquities that was formed in Campeche by the Camacho brothers, and that is well known in the world of American archaeology."[19]

The Mexican historian Manuel Orozco y Berra,[20] who held different positions during the administration of Maximilian I (1864–1867), also stated that the Ministerio de Fomento had acquired "a yucatec museum" and was to integrate it into the collections of the Museo Nacional and "other institutions" in Mexico City,[21] probably with the idea of accommodating the diverse collections.

There is no complete inventory list written by the brothers, only a few fragments on notes. While third parties have produced most of the references to the collection, there is sufficient data to sketch an idea of the museum that was in a permanent state of accessioning and deaccessioning objects.

The collection was organized in two rooms, one for the antiquities and another for the natural specimens.[22] Sierra, who knew the museum well, published a brief list of the museum's contents emphasizing the most interesting aspects. He also described it as having "no form nor consistency," perhaps in reference to the chaotic display of the collection.[23] In the list we can see three main divisions that correspond *grosso modo* to the two spaces the priests had designated for the museum:

[Historical objects]

Two paintings on canvas, each one two measuring two *varas* with the image of the Virgin. The king, Felipe II, gave them to the church of the Dulce Nombre de Jesús de Campeche.

A portrait of the Virrey Palafox, that is more than two hundred years old, and another of the vicar of Campeche, Diego Estafor.

An embroidered shoe of Juan de Palafox y Mendoza.

A lance of the Conquerors, in the shape and form that was used at that time.

[Archaeological objects]

A large collection of ceramic and stone idols, among which there are many that are noteworthy for their dimensions and for the variety of their postures and emblematic adornments.

A funeral urn that contains the remains of a man, and some figures of noteworthy antiquity dating back two thousand years.

A collection of vases, jugs, pitchers, and fonts of stone and ceramic, many of them decorated with hieroglyphs and with well preserved bright, clear colors.

A collection of lances, arrows, darts, and other instruments of war that were used by the ancient Indians. Almost all these instruments are of flint.

Another collection (in a poor state) of flutes and other ceramic musical instruments.

Another *id.* of earrings, beads, and adornments of burnished stone.

Another *id.* of sepulchral stones with various decorations and hieroglyphics.

Some loose pieces, without classification, from an exquisite construction.

A multitude of architectural fragments.

[Natural specimens]

A collection (and this is the most exquisite of the Camacho's museum) of seashells and thousands of mollusks from our coastlines.

Another mineral collection of gold, silver, iron, copper, antimony, and other metallic stones.

Another *id.* of different colored sands from our coastlines.

Another *id.* zoological (although quite small).

Another *id.* (also small) of the types of wood produced in the peninsula.[24]

The museum's incipient art gallery included various religious scenes and depictions of illustrious persons, such as the vicar Diego José de Estafor (?–1805), assistant pastor of the parish of Campeche and an important functionary in the structure of inquisitional Yucatán.[25] Of more significance is the portrait of Juan de Palafox Mendoza (1600–1659), Viceroy of New Spain and Bishop of Puebla. Educated in Salamanca, Spain, the beatified Palafox was a reformer of the laws of New Spain and a great defender of the Native Americans. A man of vast culture, in 1646, using his personal library of over 5,000 volumes, he founded the library of Puebla, today known as the Biblioteca Palafoxiana and considered to be the first public library in America. Immensely popular in his time, Palafox was immortalized in paintings and prints, and thousands of images circulated in New Spain, including Yucatán. In 1653 the Inquisition attempted to control his image by banning their production and seizing those that had already been distributed.[26] If, as Sierra remarked, the picture in the collection was "more than two hundred years old," it was a fortunate survivor. The Camacho brothers also possessed a very personal item of the viceroy: his shoe. Its whereabouts is unknown. Both objects reveal the special appreciation the priests felt toward the bishop, perhaps because he was an inspiration for their worldview.

The historical collection largely represented Mexico's colonial experience, but in Sierra's list there was no mention of artifacts that referenced the regional and ethnic conflicts that were occurring at the time, and the priests were not unaware of those events. Parish Robertson described a small box they owned that contained the charred remains of a man that had been burned alive by Indians at the beginning of the caste war. According to the Scot, Leandro Camacho had related in detail how this man was murdered, recounting the cruelties that the Maya were inflicting on the white population.[27] In the same vein, Morelet commented that the priests had shown him arrows stained with blood that were removed from the body of an Englishman who had perished while on his way through the Peten forest.[28]

The references to the archaeological pieces in Sierra's list are not sufficiently detailed to identify them using today's criteria, nor do we know how the priests interpreted them. The foreign travelers that visited the museum had a singular interest in the archaeology of the region, and they have left many testimonies on this aspect of the collection. Hubert Howe Bancroft, author of an extensive and widely distributed work on the autochthonous peoples of America, lamented that the artifacts from the Camacho museum had not been well described by the itinerant visitors, to the detriment of those unable to travel.[29] Perhaps he was right, but some of the descriptions give us a general idea of what types of objects were to be found on the museum's shelves and of the differing interpretations they received at that time.

Morelet was impressed with the ceramic figures that he described as "the expression of fact perfectly executed," referring no doubt to the so-called Jaina figurines, funerary sculptures from the region that portray individuals, often animated and with detailed dress, from the pre-Hispanic period. One object depicted a naked man with a belt who held in one hand a "lienzo" (linen) and in the other a double-edged stone. In front of this person there was a kneeling figure that he described as "resigned," and speculated that he might be a captive. Despite his enthusiasm for these figurines, the Frenchman felt that the state of the ancient arts in Yucatán was behind the times.[30]

Fortunately, there are some illustrations of this part of the collection. Benjamin Moore Norman, in his book on travels through Yucatán, mentioned that the Camacho brothers had given him many "antiquities" during his stay in Campeche. In the port city for only three days, without time to carry out excavations on his own, the artifacts he illustrates in his book are likely the same ones he obtained from the priests. Norman made a few feeble attempts to interpret the ceramic figures and emphasized their rarity in museums in the United States by comparing his modest collection with that of Joel R. Poinsett's, the former minister to Mexico, who had donated artifacts, largely from the area around Mexico City where he was stationed, to the American Philosophical Society in Philadelphia.

From the Camachos' collection Norman also acquired skeletal remains from the mounds on the island of Jaina, and he sent the fragments of four skeletons to be examined by Dr. Morton in the United States,[31] a Philadelphia doctor and author of the work *Crania americana; or, A Comparative View of the Skulls of Various Aboriginal Nations of North and South America* (1839). Of delicate health and unable to leave his home city, Morton compiled an impressive collection of bones from all over the world, relying on travelers who, in many cases, desecrated cemeteries. The doctor postulated that through the careful measuring of crania, it was possible to determine moral and cultural qualities about the individuals studied, but the remains from Jaina were in such a bad state of decomposition that he could only affirm that they were of great antiquity.

The brothers possessed a pair of very new objects for their time, two daguerreotypes taken by the Austrian Emmanuel von Friedrichsthal, the first photographer to have traversed the peninsula of Yucatán to document ruins with the new technique. He visited sites such as Chichén Itzá and Uxmal, but the only two images that have survived the passing of time are two that he gave to the fraternal priests in 1841 when he passed through the city and set up a portrait studio.[32] Five years later the brothers gave the daguerreotypes to the young Austrian botanist Karl Bartholomaeus Heller, who took them to Europe. They presently reside in the National Library of Vienna. One of the images depicts an ancient Mayan brazier with effigy that corresponds to the postclassic period. The photograph is the earliest known image of a pre-Hispanic Mayan artifact. Heller, impressed by the museum, frequented the Camachos' house, but lamented that he could not obtain more objects because, contrary to other testimonies, the priests would not part with them. The young traveler estimated that the collection had an incalculable value for science and feared it would be lost.[33]

Curiously, the famous American explorer John Lloyd Stephens did not visit the museum. Stephen's book *Incidents of Travel in Yucatan* generated an unprecedented interest in the antiquities of the region, and Justo Sierra O'Reilly translated the work into Spanish. Sierra maintained that many travelers to Yucatán had superficial opinions about his homeland and often arrived at erroneous conclusions, and while he admired Stephens, he did not hold back his criticisms of him in the notes and reproached him for not having visited the Camacho museum and learned more about ancient Mayan material culture.

> It is certainly surprisingly that Mr. Stephens had no knowledge of such exquisite and complex artifacts in wood, seashell, and coral, etcetera, of the ancient Indians of Yucatan, of which there are precious specimens in the museum of the Camacho priests in Campeche. All of these works were created without the use of metal instruments, and the priests can show any curious visitor the true instruments or chisels that were used to perfect them.[34]

Unlike Stephens, Sierra attributed the authorship of the pre-Hispanic monuments not to the ancestors of the Maya but rather to foreign invaders, depriving them of agency in their own history. When he marveled at the exquisite artifacts in the Camacho museum, he saw them as material evidence of Toltec tribes from distant lands.[35]

After the priests' deaths, some items from the collection appear to have stayed in the region. The Museo Yucateco, founded in Merida in 1871 by the priest Crescencio Carrillo y Ancona, had a relief carving in volcanic stone from the Camacho collection that is mentioned in the inventory list.[36] In 1882 the French explorer Désiré Charnay shipped to Paris a small effigy vessel from the ruins of Palenque that he had obtained in Campeche (fig. 4.1).[37]

An examination of the object in the Musée du quai Branly revealed a note in its interior written by Leandro Camacho: "Today, at six-thirty in the afternoon, I received from Mr. Francisco Lara y Sánchez this beautiful vase that was found in an excavation that was carried out in the ruins

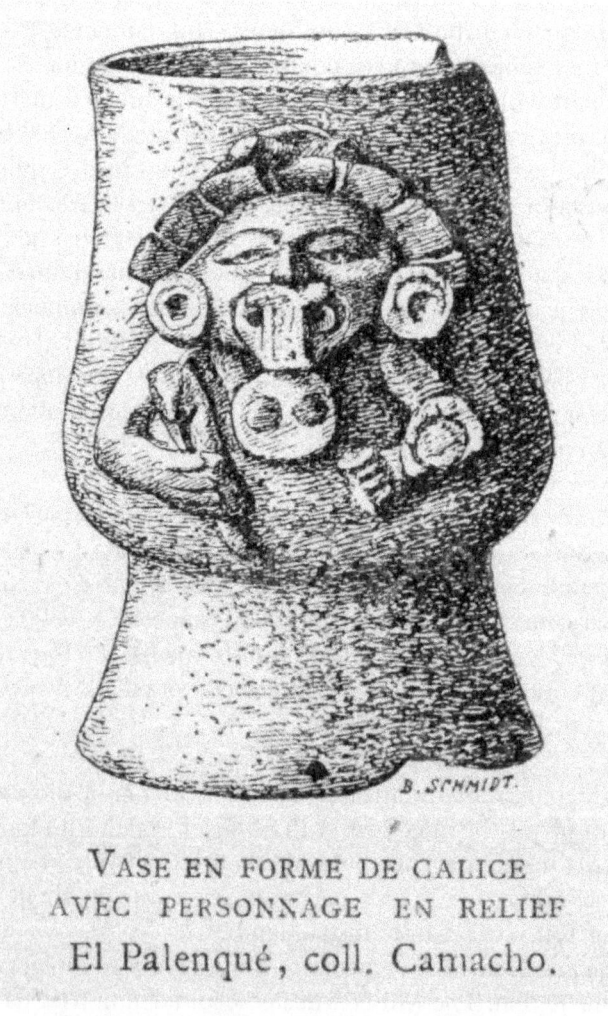

Figure 4.1. Effigy vessel from the Camacho collection. Drawing by Edward Seler. Image courtesy of the Seler Archive, Ibero American Institute, Berlin.

of the city of Palenque. He kindly gave it to me for my museum. Campeche, 26 May 1845. [signed] Presbyter, Leandro José Camacho."[38]

Colonel Doutrelaine reports a similar note that he found inside a small effigy vase that he was studying.

> Father Leandro Camacho certified the yucatec origin of this baked clay, and took care to place in its interior the curious label that I will copy in its entirety: "Today, at eight-fifteen in the morning, Friday, December 26th, 1845, coming from the chapel after mass, Benencia Molina, daughter of Ramón Molina and wife of Joaquin Molina, gave me this figure that was obtained from an excavation on the island of Jaina. This figure had been held by the parish priest of Holpelchen, Mr. N. Ortis."[39]

We do not know how many of these labels existed, but it is possible that each object had a note of this type, given that the priest—according to various testimonies—received many antiquities in the form of donations and gifts. The labels refer to the donor of the object as well as dates and events that situated the acquisition in time and space, a method of registration that differed from the more descriptive, object-centered inventories that existed around the same time.[40] The priests' labels show the role of the object as a mediator of interpersonal relations between the donor and the collector; rather than simply augment their museum, the acquisition enriched their social circle. In this sense the collection and its contours provided the Camacho brothers with an identity beyond their religious calling, one that united them with like-minded citizens, but upon their passing this aspect of the collection also perished.

In effect, when the collection was transported to the Museo Nacional in Mexico City, the identity between the museum and the brothers was erased. The holding acquired a new dimension, that of empirical evidence for the study of the history and behavior of the ancient Mexicans. Once in the Museo Nacional, Orozco y Berra described in detail a number of the artifacts that constituted the collection and attempted to find parallels with other cultural groups.

> A very fine figure in white clay, naked, with modeling worthy of a sculptor; wrapped around the waist is a Mayan-style loincloth, and covering the head a type of tall hat, with folds on the narrow brim like frills on a Spanish skirt; a similar hat can be seen in the paintings of Chichén [Itzá]. There are little altars identical to those of Copán, with three symbolic heads in a pyramid that appear to represent the trinity Maya, or

the *Trimurti* of the Hindu religion. Sitting figures with their legs crossed oriental style and their backs covered with a short cape the same length long as wide; these characters appear to be in tranquil contemplation in the same way as the saints or penitents that are so common in India. Other types that remind us of the cult of the phallus. Precious axe heads made from green rock from the polished stone age; thick beads with conical holes from remote times, or of ceramic, with complex designs. Vases of gray clay, cylindrical and with elegant forms, showing important persons in relief, hieroglyphic inscriptions, and tasteful adornments. Small seashells that are incised with the very finest of burins. Weapons are not abundant in this collection; this people had little propensity for conquest and did not stake out their territory with enemy tribes. They lived dedicated to the sweetness of peace.[41]

The idea that the ancient Mayan peoples were peaceful among themselves and with their neighbors was a notion that lasted almost a century among researchers despite the great corpus of evidence contradicting this position.[42] Orozco y Berra did not employ the word "Maya" to speak of this civilization because at that moment the link had not been conclusively established, but his comment regarding their pacifism is one of the earliest known. The archaeologist Ignacio Bernal felt that Orozco y Berra had overly "aesthetic" ideas and did not admire Mayan art because he had never seen it.[43] However, he knew of the sumptuary work of this "future" civilization thanks to the museum of the Camachos, and in this sense the priests contributed to making visible what was previously unknown.

Doutrelaine's Study

To date we have not been able to locate material that belonged to the Camacho collection among the objects in the Museo Nacional de Antropología de México (formally the Museo Nacional). Few museum inventories register their names, making the search for connections difficult, and over the years museum practice has comingled these collections with others and discarded the cataloging efforts of the original collector. Fortunately, the objects that Orozco y Berra referred to as belonging to the cult of the phallus were described in the only study of the collection that is known: an unpublished work in French recently discovered in the National Archives in Paris, titled *"Priapes et phallus,"* by Louis Toussaint Doutrelaine. This study forms part of a rich correspondence that Doutrelaine held with Victor Drury, a professor of history and the Minister of Public Instruction in France.[44] At that time the colonel, an energetic and erudite man, formed part of the President's Guard in the French occupying force of Mexico. After a few years he reached the rank of general and was a member of the board in the Ministry of Public Instruction that oversaw the missions to Mexico. He also collaborated in the first Congress of Americanists that was held in 1875 in Nancy, France.

In his study the colonel criticized the thesis of various authors, including that of Francisco Javier Clavijero, the Mexican Jesuit who was banished to Italy in 1767 after he was excommunicated from the order. In his well-known work *Historia antigua de México*, Clavijero had maintained that the religion of the ancient Mexicans could be characterized for its sexual modesty, contrary to that of ancient Greece, where gods such as Venus, Flora, Bacchus, and Priape were adored. Doutrelaine, on the other hand, believed in the existence of "shameful and scandalous" practices among the ancient Mexicans and accused Clavijero of exaggerating their prudish nature and questioned the veracity of his sources, namely Sahagún and Torquemada, Franciscan chroniclers of the sixteenth century. In his arguments in favor of the cult of the phallus, the French colonel used various Aztec legends and interpretations of the goddess Tonatiuh-Nanahuatzin, mentioned by the Italian collector Lorenzo Boturini and the Nahautl scholar Fausto Galicia Chimalpopoca. But the strongest evidence, he felt, were several ceramic figures in the Camacho collection[45] — seven artifacts, consisting of whistles and small effigy vessels from the island of Jaina and outlying regions — that were drawn by him and included in his study (fig. 4.2).[46]

Five of the figures had zoomorphic and anthropomorphic characteristics that show genitalia, while two of the objects are amorphic whistles. The study did not manage to convince Orozco y Berra, however, but at the end of his letter to Drury he magnanimously included the historian's dissent: "I do not believe the cult of the phallus had a public; they had their vices and indecencies, such is the fruit of shameful people, but the public institutions were quite severe."[47] According to Keen, Orozco y Berra often preferred to ignore unsavory cultural aspects that did not fit his idea of the "noble Aztec," such as cannibalism.[48] The research by Doutrelaine, analyzing antiquities as historical documents, shows how antiquarians and Americanists were working in concert, employing written records and the opinions of illustrious historians, and analyzing the mounting empirical evidence, such as the artifacts in private collections and museums.

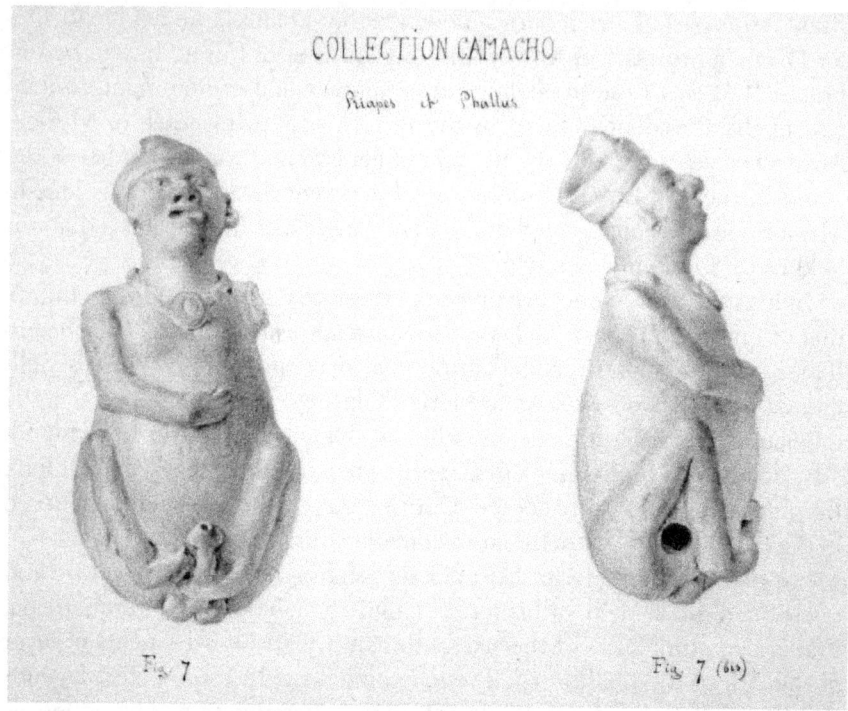

Figure 4.2. Figurines in the Camacho collection drawn by Doutrelaine. Image courtesy of Archives nationales, Pierrefitte-Sur-Seine, Paris, Exploration scientifique du Mexique, dépêche no. 51, F/17/2914/3, plate 1.

The Cabinet of Natural History

According to Sierra the most exquisite part of the Camacho museum was that dedicated to natural history: seashells from the coasts, a sampling of sand from the different beaches, specimens of different types of woods from the region, a collection of metallic minerals, and a zoological cabinet. Parish Robertson described the shell collection in some detail, indicating that in their free time the priests had made canoe trips up and down the coast and received many gifts of conches and shells from "poor fishermen and grateful Indians."[49] The shells, which occupied half a room, were arranged "picturesquely" in a grotto-like fashion, similar perhaps to European displays such as Grotto Hall in Sanssouci's New Palace near Potsdam, Germany. On the walls and shelves they placed dissected fish, beetles, and other objects in a style that resembles Renaissance cabinets. The dialogue between art and nature was a common theme among collectors of this era and earlier periods, and in particular there were direct connections between the grotto and the cabinet proposed by Italian collectors, where the bedrock was carved out to serve as the spaces for the collections and extensions of the gardens.[50]

We do not know exactly how they classified this collection, but a book from their library provides a few clues. In 1849, a little while after the death of Leandro, the sale of some of their personal belongings was announced in the newspaper and included books.[51] According to the list they had works published in Spanish: *Compendio de la historia romana* (1822) by the Irish writer Oliver Goldsmith; *El derecho de gentes* (1834) by the Swiss philosopher Emerich de Vattel; and *Lecciones elementales de la historia natural de los animales* (1834) by the French naturalist Georges Cuvier. This last work was largely an instruction manual on methods for classifying the natural world, from mollusks to mammals. Therefore, we know that the priests had the basic tools of the time to organize their collection. In his book Cuvier summarized the courses given at the École Centrale du Pantheon in Paris, and he combined different systems: for mollusks he had based his classification on his own observations and those of Lamarck, in what referred to the genus and subgenus of the species. For mammals he combined his system with that of Stors and Saint-Hilarie; and for birds he relied on Linnaeus and Buffon.[52] As it occurred in the Paris Museum of Natural History and in Cuvier's book, the Camacho brothers probably relied on more than one system of classification to organize their collection.

Conclusions

The collection of the Camacho brothers left Campeche sometime after the death of the younger sibling, leaving the region without a museum that Justo Sierra O'Reilly so desired. In this vacuum another collector came forth, Florentino Gimeno Echevarría, a Spanish merchant who arrived in the port city in 1847 and lived there for more than three decades. He amassed an impressive collection of archaeological artifacts that he kept in his clothing store, reportedly among the rolls of fabric. At his death, Gimeno's collection numbered more than twelve thousand objects as evidenced by his handwritten catalog. For each object he carefully measured, described, and organized it according to type and function, and in the extensive notes he also attempted to interpret the materials he possessed.[53]

When Gimeno sold his collection to the Ethnographic Museum in Berlin in 1878 (the same year as his death), Campeche again was deprived of a museum.[54] (It was not until 1892, under the government of Leocadio Preve, that one was established.[55]) Despite the insistence of some citizens, few believed in the necessity of establishing a museum with public funds. Private collections were the norm, and these were managed for what they were: individual property, restrained by specific heritage laws, but mostly controlled by their owners and the dynamics of inheritance and commerce. For this reason, the Camacho brothers interchanged objects with friends and associates, and Gimeno's collection was sold internationally to whoever made the best offer.

There is a possibility that Gimeno obtained part of the Camacho collection when the brothers passed away, because according to a newspaper article in Merida, he had known them well.

> Mr. Gimeno, aficionado of archaeology since the time of the Camacho priests and who had collaborated with them when he was younger, has dedicated all his time and sacrificed his interests to this field, bringing together over the course of many years a collection that scientific travelers qualify as without equal in the world.[56]

From the information we have at our disposal, Gimeno made a conscious decision to exclude from his collection much of the botanical and historical specimens that were part of the Camacho's original cabinet and amassed exclusively archaeological artifacts. His move away from the concept of the cabinet of curiosity—with its rich if chaotic blend of antiquities—constitutes an important shift in nineteenth-century collecting practices that were becoming increasingly more focused and specialized. His mentors, the Camacho brothers, were formed in a different tradition that retrieved, displayed, and organized natural specimens and other material evidences without standardized methods, drawing instead on practices that were familiar and at hand. While we have noted that there is some evidence they organized parts of their collection according to botanical classifications used widely in Europe, other concerns, such as aesthetics, may also have influenced the overall appearance of the display. When Doutrelaine wrote his study on the archaeological objects with phallic representations, had these already been grouped together by the brothers, or was it a classification of his own making? Without more concrete evidence—such as a photograph, an engraving, or a detailed description of how the museum displayed the objects—we will always be driven to speculation on this point.

Finally, the Camacho brothers took a very personalized approach to their collection: each object represented a link with the person who had donated, gifted, or somehow transferred the material into their hands. In this sense they may have seen their museum as a collection of relationships, beginning with the fraternal bond that inspired their profound curiosity about the world and that no doubt gave them countless hours of pleasure.

Notes

1. In 1863 the state of Yucatán was officially divided, establishing Campeche as a separate state.
2. William Parish Robertson, *A Visit to Mexico by the West India Island, Yucatan and United States, with Observations and Adventures on the Way* (London: Simpkin, Marshall, 1853), 164.
3. Amiria J. M. Henare, *Museums, Anthropology and Imperial Exchange* (Cambridge: Cambridge University Press, 2005), 3.
4. This argument can be followed in Robert D. Aguirre, *Informal Empire: Mexico and Central America in Victorian Culture* (Minneapolis: University of Minnesota Press, 2005), xxiv.
5. "Crónica de la península," *La Revista Yucateca* 1 (1847): 224.
6. This brother wrote a humorous description of himself that was published posthumously: "José María Camacho," *El Campechano* (1861), 25–27, reprinted in its entirety in Adam Sellen, "Los padres Camacho y su museo," *Península* 5, no. 1 (2010): 67–70.
7. Robertson, *Visit to Mexico*, 206.
8. "De venta," *El Fénix*, July 20, 1849.
9. Entierros parroquiales, no. 619, Archivo Diocesano de Campeche. The author wishes to thank Arturo Taracena for this information.
10. Robertson, *Visit to Mexico*, 200.
11. Pantaleón Barrera, "Hospicio de pobres," *El Registro Yucateco* 4 (1846): 151–155.
12. Benjamin Moore Norman, *Rambles in Yucatán: Including a Visit to the Remarkable Ruins of Chi-Chen, Kabah, Zayi, Uxmal, &c.* (New York: J. and H. G. Langley, 1843), 222.
13. Arturo Taracena Arriolla, *De la nostalgia por la memoria a la memoria nostálgica: La prensa literaria y la construcción del regionalismo yucateco en el siglo XIX* (Mérida: UNAM, 2010), 35–36.
14. Terry Rugeley, *Rebellion Now and Forever: Mayas, Hispanics, and Caste War Violence in Yucatán, 1800–1880* (Stanford, CA: Stanford University Press, 2009), 333–35.
15. Justo Sierra O'Reilly, "Mount-Vernon (Un fragmento de mi viaje)," *Miscelánea instructiva y amena* (1849), 1:328.
16. Justo Sierra O'Reilly, "Teogonía de los antiguos," *El Museo Yucateco* 1 (1841): 57n1.
17. "Sobre que el diputado don Justo Sierra pase a Campeche para adquirir antigüedades indígenas para el Museo Nacional," July 5, 1852, Archivo General de la Nación, Gobernación, box 411, file 1, pp. 12–15. The author would like to thank Miruna Achim for this information.

18. Antonio García Cubas, "Ensayo de un estudio comparativo entre las pirámides egipcias y mexicanas," in *Escritos diversos de 1870 a 1874* (Mexico City: Imprenta de Ignacio Escalante, 1874), 328n23.

19. "Le Ministre du Fomento, á Mexico, est possesseur aujourd'hui de l'intéressante collection d'antiquités yucatèques et chiapanèques, qui a été formée à Campeche par les frères Camacho, et qui est bien connue dans le monde des archéologues américains," Doutrelaine to Duruy, August 18, 1865, Archives nationales (site de Paris), Exploration scientifique du Mexique, dépêche no. 51, F/17/2914/3, f. 1 (my translation).

20. He was a member of the Scientific Commision in Mexico—a delegation formed by the representatives of France's scientific community and local Mexican contributors—the subsecretary for the Ministerio de Fomento, and the director of the Museo Nacional. In Antonia Pi-Suñer Llorens, *México en el Diccionario Universal de Historia y de Geografía*, vol. 3, *La contribución de Manuel Orozco y Berra* (Mexico City: UNAM, 2004), xxv.

21. Manuel Orozco y Berra, *Historia antigua y de la Conquista de México*, vol. 2 (1880; Mexico City: Editorial Porrúa, 1960), 336.

22. Robertson, *Visit to Mexico*, 203.

23. Justo Sierra O'Reilly, "El Museo de Los Padres Camacho, Segundo Artículo," *El Registro Yucateco* 1 (1845): 374.

24. Ibid., 374–75 (my translation).

25. Pedro Miranda Ojeda, "Las comisarías del Santo Oficio y funcionarios en la estructura inquisitorial de Yucatán, 1571–1820," *Desacatos* 25 (2007): 186.

26. Ricardo Fernández García, "Alegórica y Emblemática Entorno al Retrato del Virrey Don Juan de Palafox," in *Emblemática Aurea: La emblemática en el arte y la literatura del Siglo de Oro*, ed. R. Zafra and J. J. Azanza (Madrid: Akal, 2000), 163.

27. Robertson, *Visit to Mexico*, 204–5.

28. Arthur Morelet, *Viaje a América Central (Yucatán y Guatemala)* (1857; repr., Guatemala City: Academia de Geografía e Historia de Guatemala, 1999), 41.

29. Hubert Howe Bancroft, *The Native Races of the Pacific States of North America*, vol. 4, *Antiquities* (London: D. Appelton, 1875), 265n100.

30. Morelet, *Viaje a América Central*, 40–41.

31. Norman, *Rambles in Yucatán*, 214–17, 222.

32. Arturo Taracena Arriola and Adam Sellen, "Emmanuel von Friedrichsthal: Su encuentro con las ruinas yucatecas y el debate sobre el origen de la civilización maya," *Península* 1, no. 2 (2006): 55–56.

33. Karl Bartholomaeus Heller, *Viajes por México en los años 1845–1848*, translation and introduction by Elsa Cecilia Frost (1853; repr., Mexico City: Banco de México, 1987), 197.

34. John L. Stephens, *Viaje a Yucatán, 1841–1842*, illustrations by Frederick Catherwood, introduction by José Ortiz Monasterio, and translation by Justo Sierra O'Reilly (Mexico City: Fondo de Cultura Económica, 2003), 110n3 (my translation).

35. See Justo Sierra O'Reilly, *Los indios de Yucatán: Consideraciones históricas sobre la influencia del elemento indígena en la organización del país* (Mérida: C. Menéndez, 1954); John F. Chuchiak, "Los intelectuales, los indios y la prensa, el periodismo polémico de Justo Sierra O'Reilly," *Saastun. Revista de Cultura Maya* no. 2 (1997): 3.

36. Centro de apoyo a la investigación histórica de Yucatán, Libro 190, Documentos del Museo Yucateco, 1870–1885, p. 2, no. 12.

37. Ernest Theodore Hamy, *Galerie Américaine du Musée d'Ethnographie du Trocadéro* (Paris: Ernest Leroux 1897), 48.

38. Note discovered inside the ceramic effigy vessel cat. 82.17.84, Musée du quai Branly (my transcription and translation).

39. Doutrelaine a Duruy, August 18, 1865, Archives nationales (site de Paris), Exploration scientifique du Mexique, dépêche no. 51, F/17/2914/3, p. 7.

40. Cf. the detailed inventory list of Florentino Gimeno, a Spanish merchant and collector who lived thirty years in Campeche. In Lynneth S. Lowe and Adam Sellen, "Una pasión por la antigüedad: La colección arqueológica de Don Florentino Gimeno en Campeche durante el siglo XIX," *Estudios de Cultura Maya* 36 (2010): 148–49.

41. Orozco y Berra, *Historia Antigua*, 358–59 (my translation).

42. David Webster, "The Mystique of the Ancient Maya," in *Archaeological Fantasies: How Pseudoarchaeology Misrepresents the Past and Misleads the Public*, ed. Garrett G. Fagan (London: Routledge, 2006), 142–44.

43. Ignacio Bernal, *Historia de la arqueología en México* (Mexico City: Editorial Porrúa, 1992), 97.

44. Armelle Le Goff and Nadia Prévost-Urkidi, "Commission de l'exploration scientifique du Mexique (1862–1893)," 2009, Paris, Archives nationales de France, pp. 3–4.

45. Doutrelaine had attributed these figures to the Aztecs, given that at this time the concept of the ancient Maya had not been explored.

46. Apparently Doutrelaine had asked the commission's draftsman, Eugéne Leon Méhédin, to copy the figures, but he was busy at the site of San Juan Teotihuacan.

47. Doutrelaine a Duruy, August 18, 1865, Archives nationales (site de Paris), Exploration scientifique du Mexique, dépêche no. 51, F/17/2914/3, p. 12 (my translation).

48. Benjamin Keen, *The Aztec Image in Western Thought* (New Brunswick, NJ: Rutgers University Press, 1971), 416–17.

49. Robertson, *Visit to Mexico*, 203–4.

50. Arthur MacGregor, *Curiosity and Enlightenment* (New Haven, CT: Yale University Press, 2007), 37.

51. "De venta," *El Fénix*, July 20, 1849.

52. Georges Cuvier, "Prefacio," *Lecciones elementales de la historia natural de los animales*, vol. 1, trans. José Garriga y Baucés (Valencia: Cabrerizo, 1834), vi–xiv.

53. Lowe and Sellen, "Una pasión por la antigüedad," 169.

54. Ibid., 148–49.

55. This museum was called Pedro Baranda and was located in the Instituto Campechano. Georgina Quiñoz Flores and Elia Guadalupe Salavarría Pedrero, *Estado de Campeche: Informes de Gobierno 1862–1910* (Campeche: CONACULTA/PACMYC, 2003), 205.

56. "Bibliotecas públicas y museo," *La Revista de Mérida*, April 2, 1871.

CHAPTER FIVE

The Many Natures of Antiquities
Ana María Centeno and Her Cabinet of Curiosities, Peru, ca. 1832–1874

Stefanie Gänger

The European and North American travelers and Peruvian visitors who entered Ana María Centeno de Romainville's (1817–1874) private collection by the 1850s were struck by the many and diverse things the affluent Peruvian lady—the daughter of a former high-ranking colonial official and wife of the Frenchman Pierre de Romainville[1]—had brought together in her Cuzco mansion. One felt as if in a bazaar, one visitor said, because the things in Centeno's collection were "spread all over the place, unsystematically, often one on top of the other, almost impossible to tell apart."[2] Visitors stumbled over almost one thousand "antiquities": clay pots, vessels, plates, and whistles; some wooden jars and figures; almost three hundred stone antiquities; over two hundred precious metal plates, adornments, and jewelry; woven tunics made of fine fabrics; and a mummy, wrapped up in cloth. In the midst of her antiquities, Centeno had placed almost one hundred dissected birds: *pariguanas*, thrushes, toucans, and hummingbirds, mainly from the southern Andes. Centeno also displayed snakes, toads, and reptiles; strange or "enormous spiders"; a "white, enormous, and very curious worm," as the 1876 catalog of her collection— authored by or on the authority of Centeno's heirs, her sons Eduardo and Adolfo Romainville[3]—described it; animal fetuses; and "rare" or "strange" fish, all "preserved in [bottles of] alcohol."[4] Among the amphibians, snakes, and antiquities were over one hundred and forty minerals, including hyaline quartz crystals from the Alps, laminar graphite from England, native sulfur in limestone from Sicily, steatite from China, copper from Siberia, and silver, marble, and coal from the Cuzco area.[5] The collection also contained precious stones—rubies, emeralds, lapis lazuli, and ancient Roman mosaics with gems[6]—and over three hundred "very curious" shells "of an infinite variety of shapes, colors, and sizes": mother-of-pearl, corals, and *pututo* conch shells.[7] Centeno also displayed a dozen "Spanish antiquities from the Conquest," including swords, richly decorated daggers, sugar bowls, embroidered silk stockings, and a painted missionaries' cross.[8] There were also copies of Spanish and French religious paintings.[9] Centeno's numismatic collection contained North and Latin American, European, Japanese, Chinese, and Ottoman coins and commemorative medals.[10] She owned cast statuettes "representing types of clothing that are disappearing and that are original to the country"—a "drunken Indian," a water carrier, or a lady wearing the traditional *saya*. Centeno also possessed "natural phenomena and curiosities in alcohol": a chicken with three feet, several human fetuses—some days, others months old—various miscarriages of sheep—one of them "curious because there are two young [*crias*] conjoined at the neck," another one "with two heads and six legs"—different species of tapeworms extracted from human bodies, almost two hundred butterflies "of all shapes and colors, eye-catching and rare," and a hundred insects—beetles, botflies, and salamanders—"of all classes, sizes, and colors from the Cuzco valleys."[11] Centeno also owned "natural petrifactions, phenomena, and curiosities related to mineralogy": thirteen onyx "of different shapes and colors" found underneath the city walls of Jerusalem, stones taken from a basin in the Papal Basilica of Saint Paul in Rome, a stone from Napoleon's grave on St. Helena, an aluminum pencil, several petrifactions discovered in animal stomachs, "a petrified shell, a fossil stone, very curious."[12] Centeno had likewise crammed her rooms with things from "the savages of the Paucartambo, Santa Ana, Marcapata, and Lares valleys," the Amazon lowlands to the east of Cuzco: their wooden bows and arrows, feather adornments, painted pots, studs that perforated their lower lips, and truncheons.[13] Centeno owned Chinese porcelain jars and cups—some bearing elaborate drawings—Japanese porcelain plates, a Japanese figurine, and Sèvres porcelain cups.[14] Centeno's "diverse curiosities" also included Chinese ivory fans, an ivory box containing billiard balls, and Chinese embroidered silk dresses, painted elephant tusks, "a crystal glass flattened but unbroken in the Arequipa earthquake," gilded coconuts, a piece from Francisco Pizarro's cape, an albino's hair, "a curious flower that grows only in the highest snow-covered peaks of the cordillera," and the skeleton of a fetus "dissected with remarkable curiosity."[15]

Like many other private, provincial and miscellaneous collections, Centeno's cabinet has not received any attention from historians of museums, science, or collecting in nineteenth-century Latin America. In the context of a long-standing historiographical focus on nineteenth-century public, national museums and exhibitions and on specific types of collectibles— usually either pre-Columbian antiquities or natural specimens[16]— collections such as Centeno's have fallen "between the cracks" of scholars' attention.[17] And indeed, Centeno's heterogeneous and perplexing assemblage bringing American antiquities together with a wide range of things— from European handicraft to natural specimens, from personal keepsakes to Chinese utensils—a century after collecting had supposedly become public, specialized, and "naturalized," had allegedly begun to focus on useful specimens and had theoretically moved from the puzzling juxtaposition of apparently disconnected things to a lesson in order and taxonomy, may seem an untimely, even undue endeavor.[18] In this article I look back on the collection and inquire into its owner's meaning in forming it over the space of decades, with all the effort and expense it must have cost her and all the thought she—a cosmopolitan, well-educated lady—must have given to it. I argue that rather than questioning Centeno's ability to follow up on her time's conventions for collecting—rather than disregarding the collection as an anomaly, that is—we ought to reappraise whether collecting at the mid-nineteenth century really was public and specialized, "disciplined" and "naturalized," in Spanish America and beyond, whether collectors really held these conventions to be self-evident. Centeno's cabinet, I claim, is not only worthy of being looked back on for its own, jumbled sake but also because it may shed light on practices and discourses, on venues and sites for the collecting of American antiquities we have been too precipitate to disregard—on the variety of reasons for which and the diversity of settings where antiquities could still be collected, considered, and marveled at long into the nineteenth century.

Though it was to fall into oblivion after the 1920s, Centeno's collection was well known among her contemporaries, mainly through the reports of some of her visitors.[19] Centeno's early biographers, writing in the decades immediately following her death, almost invariably sought to apologetically make Centeno's collection and person comply with what they assumed were the epistemic and social conventions of their time or those held by their European counterparts. Many imputed to her the wish to order and catalog her "bazaar"-like, miscellaneous collection. She had spoken of having shelves constructed and of recording the details she kept in her memory in a catalog, wrote the Lima journalist Ricardo Dávalos y

Lissón in 1875. Centeno had not "dared to classify" because she had died before she believed she had collected enough, he wrote.[20] Her museum had remained "but a depository"; one needed not "look in it for the effect of it in its entirety, but only that of [its] details."[21] Other early biographers expressed their admiration of the antiquities in Centeno's collection and passed the fetuses, bones, and chickens over in silence. The Cuzco writer Clorinda Matto de Turner, who became an active member of the city's literary circles following the mid-1870s—around or shortly after the time of Centeno's death—praised Centeno's collection of "Peruvian antiquities" in 1878, and in 1924, the writer Elvira García y García lauded Centeno's "historical-archaeological museum in which one could follow the history of Peru through its different epochs";[22] both implied a national and a disciplinary—archaeological—narrative neither Centeno herself nor the 1876 catalog ever suggested. Other early biographers compared Centeno's salon with the leading French Enlightenment parlors—that of Madame Geoffrin in particular—partly, at least, to accommodate Centeno's erudition and social prominence in a legitimate sphere for a female. Centeno's private museum indeed served as a meeting ground for learned and polite society; it attracted and brought together upper-class Cuzqueños and the European and North American travelers who visited Cuzco following independence. We have testimonies from contemporaries that she was a considerable intellectual presence in the eyes of her visitors from Peru and abroad; an educated woman and a prolific reader, many found her conversation about the objects in her collection informed and valuable.[23] And yet, Centeno was not, or at least not solely or primarily, a charming *salonnière*, just as she was no archaeologist avant la lettre and no disciplined, taxonomic collector, frustrated in her endeavor at "ordering" her collection only by a want of time and material.

Centeno's collection was, in many ways, an assembly of dissimilar and disparate things. Centeno's "antiquities" were mostly Incan and from the Cuzco area, but the sculptured ceramics in the collection—in the shape of human heads, birds, wildcats, or foodstuffs—are associated today mostly with Peru's north coast, a space with a long-lived tradition of sculptured ceramics, stirrup bottles, and other closed forms depicting fauna, flora, and humans.[24] The collection catalog singled out those antiquities that were particularly "curious" in their making and their choice of subject: "a toad made of *champi*, very curious," "a stone idol, very curious, a very fine piece, polished, representing an Indian with his imperial crown," or a "very curious stone, picturing the intestines of an animal."[25] The catalog still accentuated the exhibits' dissimilarity—each of them rare and singular—their diversity and abundance. Centeno's butterflies were "of all shapes and colors, eye-catching and rare," her insects "of all classes, sizes, and colors," and she had chosen those birds that were notable and "very beautiful" in their "varied colors," strange and "funny," or "rare as a species."[26] Contemporaries relate that Centeno "learned to dissect" and prepare birds for conservation and display:[27] and, indeed, her birds were mounted in true-to-life fashion to draw attention to their peculiar hunting or nesting habits—some of the birds of prey in Centeno's collection were "in the posture of devouring a little bird"; some of the partridges and ducks were "brooding eggs."[28] She was perhaps a reader of the manuals of taxidermy that were circulating in the early nineteenth century, instructing the naturalist how to empty an animal's stomach, detach its skin, or fabricate artificial eyes.[29] Centeno's snakes, fish, and reptiles were remarkable and "curious" in their "enormous" size, their "rare" or "strange" aspect. Centeno had placed miniscule shells from Cuzco in glass bottles because they appeared even more "curious in their variety." She chose her shells because they were delicately curled or beautifully colored, and a pink coral because she appears to have believed it was "much sought after, fashionable these days."[30] Placed among Centeno's "diverse curiosities," her Chinese porcelain, worked ivories, and silk dresses seem to have retained their century-old association with the exotic and the strange in the eyes of their Andean beholders.[31] Centeno's three-legged chicken, the sheep with two heads, and conjoined twins, in turn, imply that Centeno was fascinated by monstrous birth and deformities—humans and animals trespassing on the norms of nature. Albino hair, the "curious flower" blossoming only in snow and ice, or the "crystal glass flattened but unbroken" in an earthquake breached—like monsters—boundaries and subverted categories.[32] The Amazon lowlands remained uncharted and mysterious land even to Cuzqueños into the 1840s and beyond; its "savage" inhabitants and their material culture embodied what was uncivilized and strange to upper-class Cuzqueños of Centeno's generation.[33] The things in Centeno's collection were dissimilar and disparate in many aspects, but they were remarkably consistent and uniform in another: animals and humans, flowers and grave goods, birds and billiard balls shared one similarity, one common ground: they were in one way or another "curious" things—rare and exotic, outlandish and diverse, wondrous and strange.

The traces of Centeno's own voice that have come down to us verify what the material composition of the collection and the descriptions in the catalog suggest: that Centeno's purpose was not to be an orderly collector of her fatherland's antiquities but the owner of a collection of curiosities. Centeno herself told Dávalos y Lissón upon his visit to the museum in the early 1870s that her "intention was to form a museum of curiosities rather than one of antiquities; and there was no [curiosity] she would not have if she could."[34] In the historiography, curiosity and wonder as a "sensibility" are largely associated with sixteenth- and seventeenth-century Europe.[35] Centeno's express wish to collect curiosities by the mid-nineteenth century, however, was not an isolated or unseasonable one even though it might appear so in the light of Foucault's "epistemes." The transition from a fascination with the extreme to an interest in the typical, from delighting in the world's strange offerings to an attempt to master and control its diversity, was rather more gradual and brittle than scholars have hitherto assumed. Curiosity has a long history that stretches back to the Middle Ages but also one that reaches, as historians are gradually realizing, into at least the early nineteenth century. Centeno's collection was not too different from the composition of many early- and mid-nineteenth-century public and private museums in Manchester, London, or Berlin; in Mexico City, Lima, and Buenos Aires; in Washington or Paris—collections that continued to display the rare or the dissimilar rather than the typical, to juxtapose specimens pertaining to the realms of nature and art rather than follow disciplinary bounds, and to display their objects in unruly assortments rather than glass-fronted cases.[36] As historians have shown for the Mexican National Museum and for Buenos Aires's Public Museum in the decades following independence, many museums at the time were not even intended as museums portraying a linear and unique national ancestry or a condensed vision of a nation's territory and its assets. Its makers preferred mineralogical collections or stuffed birds from distant places over local antiquities; they would amass art, medals, and "curious" *naturalia* because they were consciously aspiring to create a "cabinet of curiosities," a collection that would convey an image of the owner as cosmopolitan and in touch with the world's diversity.[37] Ideas about the museum as a lesson in order and taxonomy with a focus on natural and useful—rather than curious—specimens were circulating in the early 1800s along the veins of scientific and intellectual networks. Whether or not and, above all, in what way men and women all over the world wished and were able to respond to these changes, however, differed vastly from context to context. Collections such as Centeno's are a testament to the fragility, contingency, and relativity of epistemic shifts and epochs, and they compel us to reconsider the association of the ideal of curiosity, of human sensations such as wonder and marvel, and of the cabinet with the early modern period; moreover, they require that we either revise the chronology, terminology, and premises that ground the history of science and collecting or that we recognize they are applicable only to some of many places and people in this immeasurable and diverse world.

Throughout its long history, curiosity has been culturally and historically contingent—it has adopted distinct forms and comprehended different objects as time went by. Centeno was, like others before her, responding to the particular cues and fashions of her time, to her readings, and to her visitors' reactions to her collection. Centeno's curiosity focused on objects that attracted inquisitiveness in the early and mid-nineteenth century: fossils (associated then with extinct species and symbols of a newly discovered truly temporal history of the earth),[38] "pink corals, fashionable these days" (as the catalog explains), Chinese porcelain (just then taken up by antiquarian connoisseurs all over Europe as the material embodiment of an ancient and highly advanced civilization),[39] and dissected bodies (at a time when taxidermy was a fashionable pastime for the educated). When visitors asked Centeno for her meaning in bringing together so diverse a collection, she told them her objective was to "please and appeal to the foreigners and the enlightened men, but also men and women from the provinces, who prefer European curiosities over Indian antiquities."[40] Centeno indeed appears to have modeled her collection on her audience's divergent tastes and visual habits because different things "pleased" and astounded different beholders. Centeno's pre-Columbian antiquities, which outnumbered the remainder of Centeno's collection by two thirds, would not have been astonishing or rare to Centeno and Cuzco's upper circles in the same way they were for French or North American visitors. By midcentury, virtually every member of the local elite in the former capital of the Incan Empire owned a collection or at least some scattered Incan antiquities openly on display in their private mansions.[41] To European travelers in the 1840s, entering a world that had been largely closed off to non-Spaniards before the country's independence, however, Peru's antiquities were known only in glimpses from royal collections and some few European travelers' accounts and atlases.[42] Pre-Columbian and in particular Incan antiquities were easily acquired in early republican Cuzco; they could be excavated and purchased, or contemporary pieces, akin in Cuzqueños' eyes to pre-Columbian "antiquities," could be taken from Andean herders or peasants at comparatively little expense—but, it will seem, with considerable effect on Centeno's foreign visitors.[43] Paintings, stockings, daggers, and sugar bowls from the early colonial period likewise appealed to foreigners unfamiliar with that material culture, while in the writings of Lima or Cuzco observers, the boundary separating the collection from the mansion's colonial decor blurred when it came to Spanish and Flemish paintings, images of the Virgin Mary, and Goblin carpets.[44] The production of cast statuettes and other early *costumbrismo* art—human types on the verge of extinction, "disappearing," on the way to becoming rare and "exotic"—mainly responded to foreign demand that was in turn closely intertwined with Enlightenment encyclopedic costume books and travel accounts.[45] Worked ivories, Chinese porcelain, Alpine minerals, or aluminum pencils, on the other hand, would have been a "curious" sight for the "men and women from the provinces" Centeno mentions but perhaps less so for her nineteenth-century European and North American visitors. Following the late eighteenth century, Cuzco had become an isolated place: with the segregation of Upper and Lower Peru, the economic axis connecting Lima with Potosí dissolved, and the collapse of that commercial circuit marginalized the region from trade routes and the republican economy.[46] Centeno was a wealthy woman, one of the precious few in Cuzco who had the cosmopolitan connections and the means to acquire things from all over the world in the early nineteenth century. Several of the things in her collection had come a long, arduous, and costly way: Chinese porcelain, ivories, and silk had reached colonial Cuzco from Asia via the Manila Galleons for centuries—via the port of Acapulco in Mexico, from whence Chinese goods were transshipped to Peru and transported from Lima overland to Cuzco.[47] Her minerals from Sicily, England, China, or Siberia and the petrifactions and stones from Jerusalem or St. Helena may have reached her through one of Cuzco's foreign merchant houses.[48] Perhaps, as in the case of the French porcelain, they may have found their way into her belongings through her family's networks; Centeno's husband shared his wife's passion for collecting.[49] Centeno was well aware of an emerging archaeological, historical, and ethnographic interest in Cuzco's past and present among Europeans and Peruvians in her time, and she responded to it. She catered, however, in the same way to those Cuzqueños' tastes whose visual habits longed for what was unheard-of, outlandish, cosmopolitan, or extraordinary in their eyes. The conflation of American "Indians" with the continent's nature in museums of natural history has come to be viewed critically in recent years,[50] and historians have shown many instances, particularly in North America, in which practices and discourses that establish a connection between American indigeneity and nature make sense of ethnic hierarchies or sociopolitical structures. If we take Centeno's wish to "please" seriously, however, her antiquities—like other *artificialia*, Flemish paintings, embroidered stockings, and Chinese porcelain—belonged, intrinsically and essentially, with nature and its marvels under the shared rubric of the curious, of what pleased and interested men and women of her time.

Centeno's curiosity was neither the medieval period's sinful lusting after forbidden knowledge nor the seventeenth century's pious appreciation of the divine order nor the pleasure in novelty and consumption of the eighteenth century, even though it retained these times' fascination for strange worlds and precise observation, for inquisitiveness and anything novel that could challenge existing knowledge.[51] Centeno's curiosity was a deeply modern and contemporary sensibility, and so were its objects.

According to her biographers, Centeno began to collect when she was still a teenage girl, perhaps as early as 1832.[52] By that time, and even into the second half of the century, there was neither in Paris nor in Philadelphia nor in Cuzco a self-evident set of practices for the retrieval, collecting and display of the material evidence of America's pre-Columbian societies or a set of discourses for their study or even their description and depiction. Little of what would come to constitute Peru's antiquities in the decades around 1900 was settled by the midcentury, though some of it had been suggested or implied: the pieces' association with the Peruvian nation-state was by no means undisputed, the monetary value attributed to them was as yet minimal, their right to occupy separate archaeological museums or separate departments was rarely ever called for, and even their ability to contribute to the understanding of a past that distinguished periods and places was in no way self-evident as yet.[53] Thus for Centeno—unlike her biographers writing but a few years later—as she was forming her collection over the 1840s, 1850s, and 1860s, there was no reason why pre-Columbian objects' value and sense should not derive from their newness to European observers or their grotesque and picturesque choice of subject or their ability to focus, like three-legged chickens or flattened glasses, their observers' attention on diverse and fascinating forms.[54] Historians of science have argued for some time that that the history and development of archaeology, like that of other disciplines, was not linear but involved multiple coexisting strands— possibilities and practices coalescing and "growing back on themselves."[55] Centeno's collection, though it was premised on its owner's awareness of and significantly fed into an emergent "archaeological" interest, was no "collection of Peruvian antiquities." It was a self-consciously miscellaneous collection of curiosities of which some happened to be antiquities.

Coda

When Ana María Centeno passed away in 1874, leaving all her possessions to her two sons Eduardo and Adolfo Romainville, her museum parlor remained open to the public for some years. It was only in 1887 that

Centeno's sons decided to sell part of their mother's collection to the Berlin Ethnological Museum. The Berlin buyers were interested primarily in the pre-Columbian antiquities; only Centeno's cast statuettes were allowed to accompany her ancient jugs, jewelry, and pots.[56] The items that remained in her museum—the malformed chicken, the steatite from China, the gilded coconut, and the tapeworm—were forced to stay behind their former companions. We do not know what Centeno's heirs chose to do with them. It was common practice in Cuzco for other collectors to buy a collection or parts of it after its owner's demise, but by the late 1870s "curiosities" were as little *en vogue* among the younger generation of Cuzco collectors as they were with the collection's Berlin buyers, both interested primarily in Andean man-made material culture. The collections that came into being in Cuzco following Centeno's death in the 1870s—at the hands of men such as Emilio Montes, Miguel Garcés, or José Lucas Caparó Muñiz—were antiquarian study collections of Incan antiquities that increased in number as the city of Cuzco became reimagined as the "living archaeological museum" of the Incan past it remains to this day.[57] Perhaps some of Centeno's curiosities were disposed of or put to new uses: her Spanish paintings to decorate walls, the Chinese porcelain perhaps to be useful again, and the white, enormous worm locked away in some drawer and taken out occasionally to scare Centeno's grandchildren out of their wits. What is for certain, however, is that the malformed chicken and the ancient jug, the Japanese porcelain and the two-headed sheep, the snow flower and the thrush, could never in their lives be together again.

Acknowledgments

I thank Kristin Jansen, librarian at the Ethnology Institute of the University of Göttingen, for supplying me with a copy of the catalog of Centeno's collection. I would also like to thank Manuela Fischer and the staff of the Berlin Museum of Ethnology for granting me access to the museum's archives and storage rooms. My particular thanks go to Irina Podgorny and Miruna Achim for commenting on previous drafts of this paper and for suggesting some of its main ideas to me.

Notes

1. Centeno's father was the administrator of Cuzco's mint in the colonial period, the Casa de la Moneda. José Tamayo Herrera and Eduardo Zegarra Balcázar, *Conversaciones: Las elites cuzqueñas* (Cuzco: Instituto Nacional de Cultura, 2008), 70.

2. Ricardo Dávalos y Lissón, "El Museo de la Señora Centeno," *El Correo del Perú*, September 5, 1875.

3. "Testamento de la Señora Doña María Ana Centeno, Cuzco, 15 de Julio." No author of the catalog is mentioned in the publication, but because the collection was still in the family's possession in 1876, the catalog must have been authored either by or on the authority of Centeno's sons. Centeno's visitors relate that their hostess shared her ideas and stories about the pieces in her salon with her guests, and we may assume that Centeno's sons were familiar with their mother's accounts. Ephraim George Squier, *Peru: Incidents of Travel and Exploration in the Land of the Incas* (London: Macmillan, 1877), 456.

4. The animals preserved in alcohol are listed as numbers 1024–58. *Catálogo del Museo de la señora Centeno* (Lima: Merced, 1876).

5. Ibid., catalog entries 1077–1218, listed "mineralogy."

6. Ibid., catalog entries 1219–26.

7. Ibid., catalog entries 1291–1304.

8. Ibid. The sixth section—"Spanish Antiquities from the conquest and others"— includes the catalog entries 927–38.

9. Ibid. The canvases are listed in the catalog entries 1305–24.

10. Ibid. The contents of the numismatic collection are listed in the catalog entries 1430–90.

11. Ibid. The section "natural phenomena and curiosities in alcohol" contains the catalog entries 1059–76.

12. Ibid. The catalog entries pertaining to "natural petrifactions, phenomena, and curiosities related to mineralogy" include numbers 1227–48.

13. Ibid. The "dresses, adornments, arrows, utensils from the savages of the Paucartambo, Santa Ana, Marcapata, and Lares valleys" are recorded in the catalog entries 1249–90.

14. Ibid. Centeno's Asian porcelain is cataloged in section twelve of the catalog, numbers 1346–60, 1363–66.

15. Ibid. The "curiosities" are all listed in section number thirteen, in catalog entries 1367–1413.

16. Most histories of collecting in Latin America in the nineteenth century, including my own, focus on specific types of collectibles—usually either pre-Columbian antiquities or natural specimens. Stefanie Gänger, "Disjunctive Circles: Modern Intellectual Culture in Cuzco and the Incan Antiquities, c. 1877–1921," *Modern Intellectual History* 10, no. 2 (2013): 399–414; Elizabeth A. Williams, "Art and Artifact at the Trocadero: Ars Americana and the Primitivist Revolution," in *Objects and Others: Essays on Museums and Material Culture*, ed. George W. Stocking Jr. (Madison: University of Wisconsin Press, 1985).

17. In contrast to private collections, Latin American national and public museums, in particular those of the Southern Cone, have been studied in-depth in recent years. For a comprehensive survey of the literature on natural history museums, see Maria Margaret Lopes and Irina Podgorny, "The Shaping of Latin American Museums of Natural History, 1850–1890," *Osiris* 15 (2001): 108–18.

18. As Paula de Vos points out, these ideas have hardened in recent years under the influence of histories of collecting based on Michel Foucault's conceptions of "epistemes" (Michel Foucault, *The Order of Things: An Archaeology of Knowledge*

[New York: Pantheon, 1971]) and European ideas about nature and taxonomy applied to the development of museums. These assumptions run through a number of works, including Susan M. Pearce, *On Collecting: An Investigation into Collecting in the European Tradition* (London: Routledge, 1995); and Thomas DaCosta Kaufmann, *The Mastery of Nature: Aspects of Art, Science, and Humanism in the Renaissance* (Princeton, NJ: Princeton University Press, 1993); all cited in Paula de Vos, "The Rare, the Singular, and the Extraordinary: Natural History and the Collection of Curiosities in the Spanish Empire," in *Science in the Spanish and Portuguese Empires, 1500–1800*, ed. Daniela Bleichmar (Stanford, CA: Stanford University Press, 2009), 275, 405.

19. For Squier's visit and account, see Squier, *Peru*, 456. The German traveler Brühl also commented on Centeno's museum in a passage that bears close resemblance to Squier's account of his visit. Gustav Brühl, *Die Culturvölker Alt-Americas* (Cincinnati, OH: Benziger Brothers, 1875–1887), 126. Francis de Castelnau published a widely read travelogue in which he refers to Centeno's museum, but by the name of her husband; Francis de Castelnau, *Expédition dans les parties centrales de l'Amérique du Sud, de Rio de Janeiro a Lima, et de Lima au Para: Exécutée par ordre du gouvernement français pendant les années 1843 a 1847* (Paris: B. Bertrand, 1851), 4:244.

20. Dávalos y Lissón, "El Museo de la Señora Centeno."

21. Ibid., 291.

22. Elvira García y García, "Ana María Zenteno," in *La mujer peruana a través de los siglos* (Lima: Imprenta Americana, 1924), 254. Mark Thurner has examined the making of this "textbook trinity"; Mark Thurner, "Peruvian Genealogies of History and Nation," in *After Spanish Rule: Postcolonial Predicaments of the Americas*, ed. Mark Thurner and Andrés Guerrero (Durham, NC: Duke University Press, 2003), 165.

23. Centeno shared her own ideas about the pieces in her salon: García y García, "Ana María Zenteno," 254. See also Squier, *Peru*, 456. Steven Shapin makes a similar case for the sister of Robert Boyle, Lady Ranelagh: Steven Shapin, *A Social History of Truth: Civility and Science in Seventeenth-Century England* (Chicago: University of Chicago Press, 1994), 371.

24. Karen Olsen Bruhns, *Ancient South America*, Cambridge World Archaeology (Cambridge: Cambridge University Press, 1994), 131.

25. *Catálogo del Museo de la señora Centeno* (Lima: Merced, 1876), entries 798, 799, and 813.

26. Ibid., entries 955, 1961, and 1015.

27. Miruna Achim, "Setenta pájaros africanos por antigüedades mexicanas: Canjes de objetos y la formación del Museo Nacional de México (1825–1867)," *L'Ordinaire Latino-américain* 212 (2010): 8.

28. García y García, "Ana María Zenteno," 118. The "dissected birds" are listed in *Catálogo del Museo de la señora Centeno* (Lima: Merced, 1876), entries 939–1017.

29. On the circulation of manuals in Mexico, see Achim, "Setenta pájaros africanos," 8. On how natural history—as it emerged over the sixteenth, seventeenth, and eighteenth centuries as an elite interest—expanded to a much broader public by the nineteenth century in Europe and North America, see Nicholas Jardine and Emma Spary, "The Natures of Cultural History," in *Cultures of Natural History*, ed. Nicholas Jardine, Emma Spary, and James A. Secord (Cambridge: Cambridge University Press,

1996); and Margaret Welch, *The Book of Nature: Natural History in the United States, 1825–1875* (Boston: Northeastern University Press, 1998).

30. *Catálogo del Museo de la señora Centeno* (Lima: Merced, 1876), entries 1296, 1300, 1304.

31. On the Chinese ivory industry and export, see Martha Chaiklin, "Ivory in World History: Early Modern Trade in Context," *History Compass* 8, no. 6 (2010): 537. The worked ivories are listed in *Catálogo del Museo de la señora Centeno* (Lima: Merced, 1876), entries 1374–77, and the silk dresses as numbers 1396 and 1397. On Chinese export ceramics and exoticism, see David L. Porter, "Monstrous Beauty: Eighteenth-Century Fashion and the Aesthetics of the Chinese Taste," *Eighteenth-Century Studies* 35, no. 3 (2002): 399.

32. See chap. 5 in Lorraine Daston and Katherine Park, *Wonders and the Order of Nature, 1150–1750* (New York: Zone Books, 1998).

33. On the history of Cuzco's relationship with the Amazon in the nineteenth century, see Núria Sala i Vila, "Cusco y su proyección en el Oriente amazónico, 1800–1929," in *Fronteras, colonización y mano de obra indígena, Amazonía Andina (siglos XIX–XX): La construcción del espacio socio-económico amazónico en Ecuador, Perú y Bolivia (1792–1948)*, ed. Pilar García Jordán (Lima: PUCP Fondo Editorial, 1998).

34. Dávalos y Lissón's report on his visit to Ana María Centeno's collection was first published in 1875; Ricardo Dávalos y Lissón, "Las reliquias del pasado," in *Artículos literarios*, ed. Ricardo Dávalos y Lissón (Lima: Gil, 1914), 123; Dávalos y Lissón, "El Museo de la Señora Centeno."

35. For some of the most prominent works on cabinets of curiosity, see Krzysztof Pomian, *Collectors and Curiosities: Paris and Venice, 1500–1800* (Cambridge: Polity Press, 1990); John Elsner and Roger Cardinal, "Introduction," in *The Cultures of Collecting*, ed. John Elsner and Roger Cardinal (London: Reaktion, 1994); Daston and Park, *Wonders and the Order of Nature*.

36. In nineteenth-century Berlin, for instance, the idea of the "rare" persisted in the idea of "scarcity"—the rare, the odd, the old—as a category for selecting artifacts and designating their value. Glenn H. Penny, *Objects of Culture: Ethnology and Ethnographic Museums in Imperial Germany* (Chapel Hill: University of North Carolina Press, 2002), 80. For the remnants of curiosity in the Smithsonian Institution, see Douglas Cole, *Captured Heritage: The Scramble for Northwest Coast Artifacts* (Seattle: University of Washington Press, 1985). See also Barbara Benedict, *Curiosity: A Cultural History of Early Modern Inquiry* (Chicago University of Chicago Press, 2001); and Samuel J. M. M. Alberti, *Nature and Culture: Objects, Disciplines and the Manchester Museum* (Manchester: Manchester University Press, 2009), 16. The Spanish crown, as Paula de Vos has shown, sought to augment rather than diminish its collection of curiosities during the second half of the eighteenth century. In contrast to northern Europe, where science experienced a shift from curiosity to utility in natural history collecting, the Spanish crown pursued an empirical and utilitarian research program as early as the late fifteenth century only to shift to the collection of curiosities on a significant scale at the beginning of the eighteenth century; Vos, "The Rare, the Singular." On the Manchester Museum, see Alberti, *Nature and Culture*, chap.1.

37. Achim, "Setenta pájaros africanos." On Buenos Aires, see Irina Podgorny and Maria Margaret Lopes, *El desierto en una vitrina: Museos e historia natural en la Argentina, 1810–1890* (Mexico City: LIMUSA, 2008).

38. On the history of fossil collecting, see Martin J. S. Rudwick, *The Meaning of Fossils: Episodes in the History of Palaeontology*, 2nd ed. (Chicago: University of Chicago Press, 1976); Martin J. S. Rudwick, "Minerals, Strata and Fossils," in *Cultures of Natural History*, ed. Nicholas Jardine, James A. Secord, and Emma Spary (Cambridge: Cambridge University Press, 1996).

39. Clare Le Corbeiller and Alice Cooney Frelinghuysen, "Chinese Export Porcelain," *The Metropolitan Museum of Art Bulletin*, n.s., 60, no. 3 (2003): 60. On the aesthetic perception of Chinese porcelain, see Porter, "Monstrous Beauty," 399.

40. Daston and Park, *Wonders and the Order of Nature*, 267.

41. Note, e.g., the Frenchman Castelnau's descriptions of the ancient artefacts Cuzco families kept in their homes: Castelnau, *Expédition*, 4:244.

42. For a survey of travel accounts and archaeology in Latin America, see Jorge Cañizares-Esguerra, "Travel Accounts," in *Guide to Documentary Sources for Andean Studies, 1530–1900*, ed. Joanne Pillsbury (Norman: University of Oklahoma Press, 2008).

43. Stefanie Gänger, *Relics of the Past: The Collecting and Study of Pre-Columbian Antiquities in Peru and Chile, 1837–1911*, Oxford Studies in the History of Archaeology (Oxford: Oxford University Press, 2014), chap. 1, 2.

44. Dávalos perceived paintings, porcelain, tapestries, and Catholic images as part of the decor in what was to him a Spanish-style colonial mansion. Dávalos y Lissón, "El Museo de la Señora Centeno," 290. The 1876 catalog, on the other hand, listed the same things as part of the collection.

45. Peruvian types, as Natalia Majluf observes, appeared in the earliest Spanish costume collection by Juan de la Cruz Cano y Olmedilla; see Juan de la Cruz Cano y Olmedilla, *Colección de trajes de España* (1777). Natalia Majluf, *Reproducing Nations: Types and Costumes in Asia and Latin America, ca. 1800–1860* (New York: Americas Society, 2006), 29.

46. Natalia Majluf, "De la rebelión al museo: genealogías y retratos de los incas, 1781–1900," in *Los Incas, Reyes del Perú*, ed. Thomas Cummins (Lima: Banco de Crédito, 2005), 79, 258, 305; Javier Flores Espinoza, "La añoranza del pasado: Justo Sahuaraura Inca y sus Recuerdos de la monarquía peruana," in *Recuerdos de la monarquía peruana o bosquejo de la historia de los Incas* (Lima: Umbral, 2001).

47. For a useful survey of the history of the Manila Galleons trade, see "Introduction," in *European Entry into the Pacific: Spain and the Acapulco-Manila Galleons*, ed. Dennis O. Flynn, Arturo Giráldez, and James Sobredo, *The Pacific World: Lands, Peoples and History of the Pacific, 1500–1900*, vol. 4 (Ashgate: Variorum, 2001).

48. César Lomellini, "Ces. Lomellini y Ca. Importadores—Exportadores: Casa fundada en 1886," *El Comercio* (Cuzco), July 12, 1898. On European merchants in Cuzco, see Magnus Mörner, *Notas sobre el comercio y los comerciantes del Cuzco desde fines de la colonia hasta 1930* (Lima: IEP, 1979), 15.

49. Centeno's husband was in the habit of showing the family's antiquities to his fellow countrymen on their visits to Cuzco. Castelnau, for instance, speaks of ancient artifacts he was shown by his compatriot M. Romainville; Castelnau, *Expédition*, 4:244. The cups are listed in *Catálogo del Museo de la señora Centeno* (Lima: Merced, 1876), entries 1361, 1362. The Sino-centered monopoly on porcelain was broken in the early eighteenth century by researchers in Meissen and duplicated by Sèvres in France; Robert Finlay, *The Pilgrim Art: Cultures of Porcelain in World History* (Berkeley: University of California Press, 2010), 9.

50. David Hurst Thomas, *Skull Wars: Kennewick Man, Archaeology and the Battle for Native American Identity* (New York: Basic Books, 2000), 119.

51. On the distinct expressions of curiosity in the early modern period, see James Delbourgo, "Slavery in the Cabinet of Curiosities: Hans Sloane's Atlantic World" (2007), http://www.britishmuseum.org/research/research_news/hans_sloanes_atlantic _world.aspx; Daston and Park, *Wonders and the Order of Nature*; Benedict, *Curiosity*.

52. García y García, "Ana María Zenteno," 255.

53. On the indeterminacy of pre-Columbian objects' value, political association, status as evidence, and manner of display around the mid-nineteenth century see, e.g., Gänger, *Relics of the Past*; Miruna Achim, "Colecciones de papel: hacia una ciencia de las antigüedades mexicanas en el siglo XIX" (2013); Williams, "Art and Artifact at the Trocadero"; George W. Stocking Jr., "Essays on Museums and Material Culture," in *Objects and Others: Essays on Museums and Material Culture*, ed. George W. Stocking Jr. (Madison: University of Wisconsin Press, 1985). See also the introduction in this volume.

54. Lynn L. Merrill, *The Romance of Victorian Natural History* (New York: Oxford University Press, 1989), 5.

55. Tim Murray and Christopher Evans, eds., *Histories of Archaeology: A Reader in the History of Archaeology* (Oxford: Oxford University Press, 2008), 3.

56. For the correspondence between the Ethnological Museum in Berlin and Centeno's heirs in relation to the transaction, see Adolfo Romainville, "Carta a Adolf Bastian, Lima, 24 de Septiembre."

57. On the collection of José Lucas Caparó Muñiz, see Armando Guevara Gil, "La contribución de José Lucas Caparó Muñiz a la formación del Museo Arqueológico de la Universidad del Cuzco," *Boletín del Instituto Riva-Agüero*, no. 24 (1997): 167–226." On Emilio Montes, see Brian S. Bauer, *Avances en arqueología andina* (Cuzco: CBC, 1992), 30, 114. On Cuzco collectors, see Gänger, *Relics of the Past*, chap. 1.

CHAPTER SIX

From Lake Titicaca to Guatemala

The Travels of Joseph Charles Manó and His Wife of Unknown Name

Irina Podgorny

In April 1886, at the Caribbean seaport of Colón, a man, accompanied by his wife, stepped aboard the *Saint-Simon,* on the point of starting to France. Whether he had gained the confidence of his fellow travelers, we do not know: seven days later he died. By April 30, several scientific journals announced that Mr. Joseph Charles Manó had passed away at the age of fifty-five. The obituaries mourned over this French archaeologist and engineer, who in the last ten years of his life had made various journeys in Spanish America for scientific purposes, working as a geologist in Ecuador, Colombia, and Guatemala. Associated with the Panama Channel Company, he had contributed as well to the geologic study of the Isthmus.[1]

His wife, known just as "Madame Manó," soon thereafter wrote to the Société de Géographie in Paris to ask what to do with the collections that they had amassed on their journeys.[2] The geographers hesitated: they had first heard of the Manós just a few years before when, late in 1884, Joseph Charles had requested to be accepted as a member of the society. In a long letter sent from Panama accompanied by his photograph, he presented himself as a traveler in pursuit of the path of South America's earliest civilizations, summarizing his and his wife's travels. According to him, in 1872 they had traversed the Chaco following the Pilcomayo River, from Villa Occidental (Paraguay) to Ciudad Rodrigo (Bolivia). In 1873, they returned to Paraguay from Chile after a stay at the Magellan Strait and La

125

Plata River. Then they traveled in the Paraguayan "highlands" and visited the ancient Jesuit missions of the Alto Paraguay. In 1874 they went up the Paraguay River and crossed the Chaco at 19° southern latitude. After visiting Lake Titicaca and the Highlands of Sorata in Bolivia (1875), they moved on to Peru, Ecuador, Colombia, Central America, and Mexico (fig 6.1).[3]

Little was known of the Manós' earlier life. When he asked to be admitted into the Société de Géographie, Manó claimed he had been born in

Figure 6.1. Itineraries of J. C. Manó. Map drawn by Samanta Faiad, Museo de La Plata. Itinerary 1, 1872: Asunción, Paraguay, via the Pilcomayo River to Villa Occidental (Villa Hayes) and Villa Rodrigo (Caiza-Yacuiba, Bolivia). Itinerary 2, 1872–1873: Chile to Paraguay via the Magellan Strait (till now, there were no records of this travel). Itinerary 3, 1873: Maracayu and Amambay mountain ranges to the Hills of Villarica, visiting the Jesuit missions. Itinerary 4, 1874: Asunción, Paraguay, to Corumbá, Brazil, and from there to Santa Cruz de la Sierra, Bolivia. Itinerary 5, 1875–1877: Santa Cruz to Cochabamba via the Piray River, and Cochabamba to Lake Titicaca up to La Paz. Itinerary 6, 1877–1880: Peru to Guayaquil, Ecuador, and Pasto and Cali, Colombia. Itinerary 7, 1881–1882: Bogotá to La Guajira, Rioacha, Villanueva, and Barrancas. Itinerary 8, 1883: Guatemala: Huehuetenango, Quiché, Alta Verapaz and Baja Verapaz, and Salinas de Magdalena. Itinerary 9, 1884–1886: Panamá Canal zone to Colón and Carúpano.

continental France. On other occasions, apparently when he had reason to wish to be identified with the Americas, he said he was a French Caribbean.[4] A man with the ability to please his interlocutors, he was gifted with the talent of anticipating what others wished to hear. Thanks to this ability to live up to expectations, he discovered that the words "coal," "railroad," "ancient civilizations," and "museum collection," opened the doors of government officials, private entrepreneurs, and learned societies located on both sides of the Atlantic, along the Pacific, and finally around the Caribbean. In every city the Manós visited, he offered his services as a writer and as a scientific expert. He succeeded: Manó advised several Spanish American national governments on issues such as education, railroad construction, and official scientific expeditions, writing extensive reports on the geology and the antiquities of Spanish America.[5]

But once one starts reconstructing the travels of Manó and his wife, it becomes clear that he was a freelance propagandist, a journalist who took on the role of a traveling naturalist in order to sell projects and collections of antiquities to Spanish Americans and Europeans alike.[6] Con men such as Manó, far from being a single case, abound in the literature and history—as well as in police records—of Europe and both Americas, speaking both the same language as their interlocutors and, as Joshua D. Bellin phrased it, taking "the Indian cure."[7] Paraphrasing the famous first lines of Karl Marx's *The Eighteenth Brumaire of Louis Bonaparte*, one can say that Manó, although not a great personage, appeared in history more than twice.

Manó is not an example of the success of European travelers in impressing Latin American elites, as a simplistic reading might suggest; rather, he confronts us with the specificity of nineteenth century con men, characters that, in fact, make their appearance throughout history and across continents since medieval and early modern times. Published just a couple of years after the expression "confidence man" was ushered into American vocabulary,[8] Marx's essay dealt with the characters and personages created by the late eighteenth and early nineteenth centuries' bourgeois revolutions and counterrevolutions. No doubt in Europe and the Americas these changes led to the loss of stable, hierarchical relationships in the social, political, and economic spheres, providing opportunities for people to reinvent themselves, their lives, and their pasts. For many authors, this created a context of a "crisis of social identity," where the culture of imposture—as represented by the old phenomena of con men—now generated social anxiety. For Marx, disguise is what defines the social relationships of his era. What this essay argues is that nineteenth-century con men took what Karl Marx analyzed in his *Eighteenth Brumaire* to a different level and how historical circumstances allowed "characters of grotesque mediocrity" to play the hero's part. Manó, in this sense, allows us to show how the trade in natural objects and antiquities was one element of the strategies of disguise and propaganda.

Throughout the nineteenth century, the scientific study of nature was promoted as a means to solve the conflicting character of literature and politics: the description of nature should provide a common basis, an uncontested reality that could serve to create consensus and a neutral ground on which societies could build their futures.[9] This chapter, by tackling some stations of the Manós' itineraries—in particular the travels and sojourns in Paraguay, Bolivia, and Colombia—shows that the description of nature and the study of antiquities, truth, and falsehood proved to be just as unstable as politics were.

Paraguay

The first records of Manó's itineraries in South America lead us to Asunción del Paraguay early in the 1870s, when the war against Brazil, Argentina, and Uruguay had just come to an end. Employed as propagandist by the government of Paraguay, he became the secretary of the so-called Italian Scientific and Medico-Chirurgical Commission, presided over by a man who called himself Commendatore Guido Bennati, an Italian charlatan who, in the late 1860s, started traveling in South America with his family, his remedies, and a collection of natural history.[10] Together, they traveled in Bolivia, after which Bennati went back to Argentina while the Manós moved on to the north of the continent.

In 1870, Asunción, the capital city of Paraguay, was still occupied by the Brazilian army and was in an uproar after the devastating consequences of the Paraguayan War. Argentina and the Brazilian Empire were disputing control over the territories of the ancient missions, the Chaco, and the Upper Paraguay River, and the city itself witnessed several political riots and the arrival of French adventurers who wanted to profit from these years of chaos. One of them was José Carlos Manó.[11] Up to now, little is known about how and when Manó and his wife arrived in Paraguay. In December 1871, Manó took on the position of secretary of the congress during the term of President Jovellanos, and, from 1872, he was a member of the newly established Consejo de Instrucción Pública.[12] If we believe Manó's own accounts, in 1874 they traveled between Asunción and Tarija

(Bolivia), following the course of the Pilcomayo River, territory controlled by Tobas and Chiriguanos. They were accompanied by "the Negro of Jamaica Jean Guyon," who died in Villa Rodrigo (Bolivia), two Bolivian gauchos, and a young Guaycuru Indian, who was going to accompany them as far as Guatemala.[13] Back in Asunción, they found the city even more troubled than before their departure. Manó, however, managed to obtain the patronage of a French trader of Yerba Mate and of the minister Emilio Gill, brother of the then current Paraguayan president, whom, apparently, Manó had met in Paris in 1865. Emilio Gill proposed that Manó direct *La Patria*, a newspaper to support the government, a task he accepted in March 1874, "taking into account that Gill's policy was about reconciliation and progress."[14] When he was directing the newspaper, "two Italian physicians accompanied by a band of followers arrived in Asunción. They prepared a trip to Bolivia, crossing the hills of Chiquitos, around 6 degrees farther north than the route of the River Pilcomayo." It was the so-called Medico-Chirurgical Scientific Italian Commission, presided over by Commendatore Bennati.

The Italian Commission, as was common among traveling dentists, surgeons, and photographers at that time, announced its arrival in the newspapers and promoted the services and a series of gifts they offered to the Paraguayan people and government. Among those gifts were the fragments of the skeleton of *Megatherium* that had been discovered in the surroundings of Asunción, the remains of that formidable fossil mammal that would come to constitute the iconic animal of South American prehistoric times for decades.[15] In January 1875, President Gill accepted for the nation the gift presented to create Paraguay's national museum—a museum that, however, never was inaugurated.[16] It is probable that when Bennati took the advertisement to be published in *La Patria*, he met its editor, discovering that they shared strategies and common interests. Bennati invited Manó to join the expedition, covering his travel expenses. Manó, in exchange, had to record geological and botanical observations.[17] Together they navigated the Upper Paraguay River up to the Brazilian fluvial port of Corumbá, a connecting link with Mato Grosso and the Amazon Basin, which, with the opening of the Paraguay River after the war, had become strategically important for international trade.

Manó and Bennati traveled and at the same time created a network of itinerant individuals: exiles, émigrés, disappointed European politicians, anarchists, republicans, revolutionaries, and adventurers or pretenders who traveled throughout the Continent trying to survive by selling their skills to those who were willing to pay for them. The press, their writings, and the supposedly neutral rhetoric of science, nature, and progress represented the tools that assured their survival in the New World. During their stay in Paraguay, members of the commission collected fossils as well as ethnographic objects, such as mates, bowls, arrows and bows, remains found on the battlefields of the Paraguayan War, and textiles made by Paraguayan women.[18] These objects would be exhibited at different stations along the itinerary as a museum of the three kingdoms of South American nature. Where did they learn to collect and to exhibit fossils, stones, and ethnographic objects? How did they know that even amid the uproar of permanent political revolt a fossil skeleton would serve to gain esteem and the favors of local people and politicians? What we know is that Bennati, in Europe, had done what all charlatans and medicine men had done since medieval times: sell balms and ointments—framing his sales with music and theatrical performances—at the fairs and in the marketplace, all the while claiming they were the inventions of people presented as natives from Africa, the Americas, or Asia. It was in South America where he changed his sales strategy, replacing the theater with a traveling museum of natural history that included, as in Europe and the United States, an association with the "indigenous." Whereas other medicine men alleged that they had lived among the natives and had been introduced by them into the secret healing powers of the Americas' nature,[19] Bennati not only hired "Inca women" as receptionists of his museum, he renamed his old balsams with "indigenous" names, pretending that he had found them during his archaeological excavations in Bolivia. Manó's reliance on indigeneity is evidence not only of the survival of the "genre of Christian piety that placed the best hope of salvation in the poor and ordinary people" but also of the general awareness that this trope worked as marketing strategy all over the bourgeois world.[20] From Arcona to Lille, from London to New York, from Philadelphia to New Orleans or Buenos Aires, traveling medicine and con men learned from each other at the marketplace: they replicated strategies and moved forward, bringing with them what they had seen at the fairs they just left behind. Bennati had certainly witnessed in Italy and France the seasonal fair spectacles arriving and departing with their automats, wax figures, "native" acrobats, and collections of antiquities and wonders. Furthermore, in the 1850s, when Bennati started his activities as charlatan, traveling popular museums and ethnographic spectacles began to proliferate in Europe and the Americas, sharing the space of the marketplace and the foyers of theaters with the traveling medicine men.[21] In the case of Bennati, we also know that he arrived in Argentina when the first national exhibition of industrial and natural products was being organized and that several provincial governments, where he was acting as traveling doctor, commissioned him to collect samples of local nature and to attend—as their representative—the national exhibition in Córdoba. He wrote reports and even gave speeches in Italian on behalf of progress, applauded by an audience of educated gentlemen who, although they might not have understood a single word of what he said, were eager to greet the enthusiasm Bennati displayed for the future of the country.[22] Most probably, the experience of the exhibition and the instructions regarding what and how to collect taught him which kind of objects were most valued by governments and politicians and that the gathering of industry and nature promised to be worthy of his attention here, there, and everywhere along the road he knew he was forced to pursue.

Bolivia

The commission arrived in 1875 in Santa Cruz de la Sierra and subsequently continued to other Bolivian cities—Cochabamba, La Paz, Sucre, Potosí, Tarija.[23] In every single city they visited, they were involved in conflicts with different local actors who sought to demonstrate that the commission was a fraud and that none of its members actually was what they pretended to be.[24] Despite these allegations, the Italian commission moved freely in the cities' scientific and literary circles, accepted and welcomed by several members of the political factions and some members of the Catholic clergy, who dispensed them honors and patronized their initiatives in the fields of public health and science.

The commission exhibited its collections in Santa Cruz and undertook some excursions to the Inca ruins existing nearby as a means to demonstrate their interest in all the manifestations of local nature and culture. From Santa Cruz de la Sierra, two publications by the Italian Commission appeared: *Relación del viaje de la Comisión Científica Médico-Quirúrgica Italiana por el norte del Gran Chaco y el Sud de la Provincia de Chiquitos* and *El naturalismo positivo en la medicina* (1875); in Cochabamba they published *Compendio de los trabajos ejecutados en este trayecto* and *Diplomas i documentos de honor de Europa y América que adorna el nombre del ilustre comendador Dr. Guido Bennati* (1876).[25] While "Diplomas and documents" is a transcription of testimonies called to witness the veracity of the titles of Bennati as a doctor of medicine, the second and the fourth are travel descriptions, and the third is a compendium of ideas on the most modern methods in medicine. These publications described what the members of the commission encountered on their itineraries: fauna, flora, mineral resources, ruins, and natives. They also proposed a plan of action for the local government and the elites for how to improve the economic situation of those lands by means of new roads and the encouragement of industry and commerce. Probably written by Manó, an expert in the art of propaganda, these pamphlets were printed on low-budget paper with very dense typography and in the printing offices of the newspapers in which the commission worked or those owned by its protectors.

In November 1876, the commission arrived in La Paz, allegedly after having completed "the scientific study of the material resulting from their travels with regards to hygiene, climatology, botany, mineralogy, geology, zoology, industry, and commerce of the Argentinean, Paraguayan, and Uruguayan Republics."[26] They wanted to "publish the most exact work on its ethnography and the systems of mountains and rivers, questions absolutely related to the problem of hygiene." They promised to publish a "Descriptive history of the Republic of Bolivia," imitating the propagandistically minded publications advertising natural resources that had allowed other Spanish American countries to successfully attract European migration. This work would be integrated in three quarto volumes of more than four hundred pages. They were in fact calling for a subscription and also for the provision of data, information, and objects.[27]

In La Paz, the commission installed its offices and museum in a house located in the main square of the city. While the cabinet of Dr. Bennati opened from 7 to 11 a.m., the museum opened from 1 to 4 p.m., displaying curiosities and the diversity and richness of the natural kingdoms and the arts of South America.[28] The museum was a medium to exhibit the commission's collection but also to enrich it further: Manó and his companions offered a monetary compensation for plants, fruits, fossils, petrifactions, furniture, books in all languages or in Spanish from the time of the conquistadores, animals, minerals, artifacts, and everything related to the arts and the nature of these regions. The museum was indeed the center of a medical-commercial enterprise. They were not the first—nor would they be the last—to exchange healing for antiquities and food: the literature abounds in similar cases, such as John Lloyd Stephens in Central America and many others, traveling and trading in medicines, medical instruments, and collections bringing together antiquities and natural specimens. In the case of Bennati, healing was performed in the same space of the museum, which, at the same time, exhibited the local medical and industrial products he and his companions had collected on their travels.

Nature and antiquities were not separated from industry: in one and the same room, the Italian Commission kept the secrets to remedy the pain of the world. The museum attracted not only potential patients to the medical cabinet but also artifacts and books to be resold on a market that would carry them to other places and people. The museum also allowed them to procure documents, materials, and paragons for the format and style of writing about the topics they had supposedly investigated in the field. The books taught them how to classify what they had, how to arrange the objects, and also the language appropriate to describe nature and civilizations.

In November 1876, the newspaper *La Reforma* of La Paz published the account of a four-month excursion of the Italian Commission to Lake Titicaca and the ruins of Tiahuanaco. They were obliged, they said, to the Bolivian government for "the help and support given to science" as well as the collaboration of the local authorities in the Titicaca regions, including the priest of the parish of Tiahuanaco and the officials from the Peruvian side of the lake. They presented the results of these explorations, explaining that the craniological and archaeological observations showed "that Tiahuanaco had been the cradle and center of origin of the civilization of the Americas, which irradiated from the shores of the Titicaca to all the continent."[29] In a tomb opened by a previous excavation they observed the coexistence of two different human types: one representing a higher organization, similar to the pre-Aztec skulls and the other representing a lower race, probably enslaved by the first, similar to the skulls of the higher families of apes.[30] Given that Manó wrote these lines once he was already in Colombia, it is difficult to ascertain when he made these "observations." In 1878, Paul Broca was analyzing three skulls sent to the School of Anthropology in Paris by another traveler from Tiahuanaco that displayed two kinds of artificial deformation. Broca classified them as belonging to two different human types; Paul Topinard compared the stone implements from Bolivia to the tools found in Patagonia, suggesting there might have been some past relationship,[31] ideas that the Italian Commission had already promoted in 1876.

In La Paz, Manó broke with Bennati and returned to journalism. In March 1877, he became associated with Eloy Perillán y Buxó, a Spanish anarchist and antimonarchist, director of the newspaper *El Inca*. Perillán y Buxó had to leave Spain and go into exile in 1874 because of his provocative writings. Since then he was traveling—also with his wife—in South America.[32] He declared himself "member of no academy, honorary fellow everywhere, and active fellow at home."[33] Perillán y Buxó—like Bennati and Manó—both mocked and profited from the tastes, impostures, and consumption habits of the petite bourgeoisie of Europe and the Americas. Aware of the importance that government officials and the urban bourgeoisie attached to academic titles, collections, and scientific rhetoric, they sought to gratify these expectations. Throughout their itineraries the written word, the formation of museums, and the affirmation of their own scientific expertise combined with the foundation of newspapers and the offering of their services to the political factions of the troubled South American republics. Manó and Perillán y Buxó opened a new periodical, *El Ferrocarril* (the railroad),[34] a name that was not adopted by chance: a symbol of speed and progress, the railroad was connected to the power of science and technology. In March 1877, they announced that they were collecting archaeological pieces to be dispatched and published in

Figure 6.2. Gateway of Akapana (or Gate of the Sun), Tiwanaku, from "Recuerdos de Bolivia," in *La Ilustración Española y Americana* 43 (November 1877), 316. © CSIC, Centro de Ciencias Humanas y Sociales, Biblioteca Tomás Navarro Tomás, Madrid. This is a very well-known image attributed to German photographer Georges B. von Grumbkow and described as a portrait of German geologist Alphons Stübel in Tiwanaku. However, recent research has proven that the man in the picture is M. Bernardi, the travel companion of French traveler Théodore Ber (see Natalia Majluf, *Registros del territorio: Las primeras décadas de la fotografía, 1860–1880* [Lima: Museo de Arte de Lima, 1997]; Pascal Riviale and Christophe Galinon, *Une vie dans les Andes: Le journal de Théodore Ber (1864–1896)* [Paris: Ginkgo, 2013]).

La Ilustración Española y Americana, an illustrated journal from Madrid.³⁵ Offering to pay for contributions, they obtained "mummies, Incan pottery, medals, arrows, photographs of ruins and Indian types, idols."³⁶ On November 22, 1877, *La Ilustración* published "an engraving with five peculiar views of the Bolivian Republic, based on direct photographs sent by an old correspondent of our periodical." These "souvenirs of Bolivia," sent by "Mr. P. y B.," showed vistas that probably portrayed the visit of the Italian Commission to the ruins and village of Tiwanaku (figs. 6.2, 6.3).³⁷

However, the museum and the group's archaeological pursuits were buried in the turmoil of Bolivian politics. Manó, Bennati, and Perillán y

Figure 6.3. Church at Tiahuanaco, Bolivia. Stones taken from ruins of ancient structures and members of the Commission(?), from "Recuerdos de Bolivia," in *La Ilustración Española y Americana* 43 (November 1877), 316. © CSIC, Centro de Ciencias Humanas y Sociales, Biblioteca Tomás Navarro Tomás, Madrid.

Buxó wrote in favor of their political patrons in their newspapers. In so doing, they got protection but became vulnerable as soon as their patrons fell from grace. Manó and Bennati's itineraries were propelled by the conflicts in which they were involved, even though they would account for their frequent departures as preconceived plans to survey the natural resources of the places they visited. Manó ended up explaining that his itinerary had been designed to follow the exodus of civilization from south to north, from Bolivia to Palenque, in Chiapas, to see with his own eyes the sites portrayed in the images published in works by Dupaix, Brasseur de Beaubourg, and Stephens, well-known authors of travels and reports on Mexican antiquities, quoted and revisited by all those who wanted to study the history of civilization in the Americas.[38]

Colombia

While Bennati, going south, appointed new secretaries for his Italian Commission, Manó was going to participate—this time as archaeologist, geologist, and director—in two other scientific commissions, one in Colombia, the second in Guatemala. There are almost no traces of Manó's presence in Peru; the references to Ecuador are also obscure: he only mentions once that he was appointed professor of geology in Guayaquil. Undoubtedly he arrived in southern Colombia coming from Ecuador, because his first stop there was Pasto, in Nariño.[39] In August 1880 Manó was in Cali, the capital of the Cauca region, writing for *El Ferrocarril de Cali* on education and on American ethnology, the very same articles that he was later going to republish in the *Anales de la instrucción Pública*.[40] From Cali, Manó wrote to Juan Montalvo, the politically liberal Ecuadorian writer, on the stupidity and evilness of Ignacio Veintimilla, the self-proclaimed president of Ecuador—hated by Montalvo—and the conflict he had had with him regarding the railroad to Yaguachi (Guayas).[41] From Cali he also sent a letter on the natural resources of Central America to *Le Courrier des États-Unis*, a French newspaper published in New York that was read all over the Americas and Europe at the time. Reviewed also in Bogotá,[42] Cali local politicians and journalists introduced Manó to the intellectual circles there, which, in turn, started promoting him as a French traveling naturalist. As liberal politician and senator Narciso González Lineros—doctor in medicine, editor of *La Reforma* de Bogotá, and expert in education—was proposing to organize a Colombian Scientific Commission to explore the natural resources of the country, the name of Manó was suggested as the naturalist to be in charge of such a mission. Law 59, passed on June 11, 1881, established a permanent commission devoted to the study of the three kingdoms of nature in the whole territory of the republic, comprising all the subjects related to botany, geology, mineralogy, zoology, geography, and archaeology.[43] The commission, according to that law, was to be directed by a man who would oversee the general work. Next to the director, the commission was going to be made up of two Colombian professional naturalists, a draftsman, a secretary to the editor, and six students of the school of natural sciences of the national university to be selected by the government.

The commission's purpose was to arrange two identical collections; one to be dispatched to the exposition that was going to take place in New York in 1883,[44] and the other to be exhibited in a museum space that was to be opened in Bogotá by the president's office. For that purpose, the naturalists had to collect and classify all the plants, rocks, minerals, stone implements, specimens of pottery, or any other material that could help the progress of natural studies and enlighten ethnological questions related to universal history and, in particular, the history of Colombia. These collections had to be done under the supervision of the director. Whereas the draftsman had to take an image of every object and keep records of them in a special inventory book under his supervision until they were given to the government, the secretary had to keep the records of the observations, events, and of "all that could be transcendental for the civilization of the country." The reports by the commission should refer to all that was observed along their travels, from natives to ruins, rivers and trees, objects, drawings, plans, antiquities, and transactions. They all had to be forwarded monthly to the national government and the Colombian museum. Finally, the congress ended up proposing for the position of director the name of José Carlos Manó, who was then considered "an eminent geologist, a man with the brain of a savant, and the heart of a philanthropist." The writer Jorge Isaacs was appointed secretary. The literary circles celebrated the presence of Isaacs: his extraordinary poetic and descriptive talents and his love of nature were going to produce pages that would be comparable to the best pages of *Maria*,[45] his successful novel. The commission departed for the Magdalena River, which was then being canalized and had its own body of experts surveying the territory and publishing reports about its resources.[46] The reports signed either by Isaacs or Manó were published in the *Anales de la Instrucción Pública*.[47] Following the instructions of Law 59, they appeared on a monthly basis between February and July 1882.

Jorge Isaacs and Manó broke up very soon thereafter and did not go together on the planned scientific expedition.[48] In reality, Isaac's style of working was not too different from Manó's: they combined the act of traveling with the glossing of existing reports and already published materials and the assertion of some facts obtained from local informants, such as "there was coal" or "the local population uses certain trees for this and that." Whereas Isaacs was celebrated for his prose, by the end of the year 1882, the Society of Medicine and Natural Sciences of Bogotá evaluated the reports written by Manó, and in 1883 they published in the *Revista Médica* the disappointing results: Manó's observations could not be taken seriously, his reports "added" very little; rather, they collected truisms or condensed what others had written in the past. Manó, as they said, was more a traveler than a naturalist: the government and the nation had been victims of "thoughtless resolutions."[49]

This case in fact reveals the background of the laws and initiatives that proliferated everywhere in South America regarding the study of nature and antiquities. Law 59 was a proposal where everything seemed to be planned, where the will to control the objects, the inventories, and the drawings was more than evident. Scientists appear as mere employees of a state that sets the rules and the timing of reporting, how and what to observe, and for whom and what to collect. However, for many years it would remain difficult to differentiate between a writer, a journalist, and a traveler on the one hand and an expert in geology or in archaeology on the other. The nomination of scientific experts was connected with lobbies, networks, and literary circles. The cases of Manó and Bennati show how permeable these lobbies were. We agree with Colombian historians that there was a circle of scientific experts that evaluated the results of Manó's travels and concluded that they were a hoax; however, the effect was that far from controlling the territory, the actions promoted in the name of science introduced more doubts into the supposedly neutral territory of nature. Demonstrating their connection with politics, they showed that factions also dealt in influences and favors in the sciences.

Manó moved on once more, this time to Guatemala, where the government, after checking his credentials, hired him as a geologist to map deposits, analyze and classify samples, and train assistants in practical geology. He soon published three reports on his geological excursions,[50] but his contract was canceled after only a few months. Apparently government officials lost interest when Manó failed to produce innovative results in the most promising areas of Huehuetenango.[51] In the meantime, Manó had been accepted as a corresponding member by the Société de Géographie in Paris, to which he dispatched observations and collections. When he and his wife embarked on the trip on which he was going to die, he had already spent some time working for French engineers in Panama.

Concluding Remarks

Manó and his wife arrived in cities without a history attached except for the stories they themselves told and his talent and skills to interact with the local societies. Either on canoes, ships, mules, horses, wagons, the backs of local people, or simply on foot, they traversed countries and continents. The scandals, rumors, and allegations they always left behind. The case of Manó poses a kind of paradox for the history of knowledge: Manó's endeavors were possible because his fame as an impostor did not propagate far beyond the cities where he had been. The news on him from Ecuador never reached Colombia; his Colombian reputation did not prevent the government of Guatemala from hiring him as geological inspector.[52] Helped by the regional fragmentation of the Americas, Manó, with his library and his writing skills, reinvented himself on every stop of his long journey.

However, these territories were not completely disconnected. To be sure, as the itineraries of Manó prove, things, people, and knowledge did circulate. Manó, as well as the local newspapers, were aware of and published the latest news in the world of science and inventions. His writings abound in quotations from contemporary writings published in other parts of the world and in the most diverse fields, such as medicine, anthropology, geography, education, literature, and archaeology. One can say that Manó, beyond all his intentions, was shaped by a series of discourses and practices that circulated on both sides of the Atlantic; in particular, the importance of the study of Americas' nature and its antiquities. From Argentina to Guatemala, from Asunción to Paris and New York, from La Paz to Cali, Manó filled the newspapers with his travel reports and ideas.

Manó was an impostor, but he was neither uneducated nor ignorant. His opinions were discussed not only by his contemporaries but also by ours. Does it mean that they were true? For the readers, at least, they seemed to be true. Manó did pretend that he was devoted to the study of nature, railroads, and antiquities, because he was aware that there was a growing demand and interest in those subjects. Manó and his partner Bennati followed but one maxim: "when in Rome do as the Romans do." In that sense, Manó, Bennati, and Perillán y Buxó were probably much better observers of reality than their enemies tried to prove: they knew what they wanted to buy. On the other hand, what Manó wrote was not totally false: they had been in the places they described and he had read about those places. On the road, they became aware of what had been written and with which topics people liked to be deceived. Nature and antiquities were just two of them. Crossing regions plagued by conflicts and at the borders of the new national states, they collected objects and things not collected before; they gained new insights into objects unknown in the metropolitan museums or in collections. Whereas Manó's itinerary had really happened, for the historians it still remains invisible because of the dispersion of sources and the historiographical disconnections. Thus, Manó is a kind of puzzle that still has to be resolved by crossing territorial boundaries and scientific disciplines. Not only are the sources and documents spread in different repositories all along the road: treated as a subject related to national projects or local concerns, Manó teaches us historians that unless we want to be deceived by the creations of the nineteenth century, we have to pay attention to the transnational character of confidence men and their topics.

Acknowledgments

This paper is based on research done at the National Libraries of Medicine (Washington, DC), the National Libraries of France, Bolivia, Paraguay, and Argentina, and the Biblioteca Luis Angel Arango (Bogotá). It is part of Proyecto Investigación Plurianual-CONICET 0116 and was finished while on a fellowship at Internationales Kolleg für Kulturtechnikforschung und Medienphilosophie, Weimar. It owes much to the help of Carlos Podgorny, Susana García, Camilo Quintero, Daniel Delachaux, Alejandro Martínez, Paula Peña, María Isabel Martínez Navarrete, Marie-Noëlle Bourguet, Samanta Faiad, Pascal Riviale, Natalia Majluf, and Julia Tarsten.

Notes

1. *Proceedings of the Royal Geographical Society and Monthly Record of Geography* 8 (1886): 598; *Comptes rendus des séances de la Société de Géographie et de la Commission centrale* (1886): 357–58.

2. "Mme. Manó to the Société de Géographie," *Comptes rendus des séances de la Société de géographie et de la Commission centrale* (1886): 358.

3. J. Ch. Manó to the Secrétaire Général de la Société de Géographie, Panama, December 1, 1884, IFN-8452968, Bibliothèque nationale de France.

4. To the Société de Géographie, he said he was born in Bordeaux, in the parish of Saint Seurin, on May 11, 1835. In Colombia, many authors considered him to be from Algeria. See "J. C. Manó to Juan Montalvo, Cali, April 23, 1880," in *Montalvo en su epistolario: 362 cartas íntimas y cartas sobre asuntos públicos y literarios entre Juan Montalvo y grandes personalidades del Ecuador, América, España y Europa*, ed. Roberto Agramonte (Río Piedras: Universidad de Puerto Rico, 1982), 180.

5. I. Podgorny, "Coleccionistas de arena: La Comisión Médico Quirúrgica Italiana en el altiplano boliviano, 1875–1877," *Antípoda* 11 (2010): 165–88; and *Los viajes en Bolivia de la Comisión Médico-Científico Quirúrgica Italiana* (Santa Cruz de la Sierra, Bolivia: Fundación Nova, 2011).

6. Cf. Guillermo Francovich, *La filosofía en Bolivia* (Buenos Aires: Losada, 1945); Carl Henrik Langebaek Rueda, *Arqueología colombiana: Ciencia, pasado y exclusión* (Bogotá: Inst. Colombiano para el Desarrollo de la Ciencia y la Tecnología F. J. de Caldas, 2003); Arturo A. Roig, "Estudios sobre el positivismo argentino: Mendoza y los visitantes positivistas," *Revista de la Junta de Estudios Históricos de Mendoza*, vol. 3 (1966): 245–69; Diana Obregón, "El sentimiento de nación en la literatura médica y naturalista de finales del siglo XIX en Colombia," *Anuario Colombiano de Historia Social y de la Cultura* 16/17 (1990): 141–61.

7. Joshua David Bellin, "Taking the Indian Cure: Thoreau, Indian Medicine, and the Performance of American Culture," *New England Quarterly* 79, no. 1 (2006): 3–36.

8. In 1849, the American Press popularized the term "confidence man" to describe the deceptions of William Thompson. See Karen Halttunen, *Confidence Men and Painted Women: A Study of Middle-Class Culture in America, 1830–1870* (New Haven, CT: Yale University Press, 1982); I. Podgorny, *Charlatanes, Crónicas de remedios incurables* (Buenos Aires: Eterna Cadencia, 2012).

9. See Claude Blanckaert, *Le Muséum au premier siècle de son histoire* (Paris: Muséum National d'Histoire Naturelle, 1997); I. Podgorny and Margaret Lopes, *El Desierto en una vitrina: Museos e Historia Natural en la Argentina* (Mexico City: Limusa, 2008).

10. I. Podgorny, *Viajes en Bolivia*; "Travelling Museums and Itinerant Collections in Nineteenth-Century Latin America," *Museum History Journal* 6, no. 2 (2013): 127–46; *El sendero del tiempo y de las causas accidentales: Los espacios de la prehistoria en la Argentina, 1850–1910* (Rosario: Prohistoria, 2009).

11. Harris Gaylord Warren, "Brazil's Paraguayan Policy, 1869–1876," *The Americas* 28, no. 4 (1972): 388–406; *Paraguay and the Triple Alliance: The Postwar Decade, 1869–1878* (Austin: Institute of Latin American Studies, University of Texas at Austin, 1978); "Journalism in Asunción under the Allies and the Colorados, 1869–1904," *The Americas* 39, no. 4, (1983): 483–98. See also Fernando Casablanca, *Mis Memorias* (Asunción: AGR, 2009).

12. *Rejistro oficial del gobierno provisorio de la República del Paraguay* (Asunción: El Pueblo, 1871), 39, 124; Cecilio Báez, *Resumen de la historia del Paraguay desde la época de la conquista hasta el año 1880: Seguido de la historia particular de la instrucción pública desde el gobierno de Domingo Martínez de Irala hasta nuestros días* (Asunción: Talleres Nacionales, 1910).

13. Manó to Monsieur Dabry de Thiersant, Chargé d'affaires de France à Guatemala, Guatemala, November 18, 1882, Carton MA-Maron, 742–763, Société de Géographie, Cartes et plans, Bibliothèque national de France. All the information provided hereafter refers to this manuscript; quotations from all foreign-language sources are in my translation.

14. Beatriz González de Bosio, *Periodismo escrito paraguayo, 1845–2001: De la afición a la profesión* (Asunción: Intercontinental, 2001), 119.

15. Martin J. S. Rudwick, *Scenes from the Deep Times: Early Pictorial Representations of the Prehistoric World* (Chicago: University of Chicago Press, 1992); and also I. Podgorny, "Fossil Dealers, the Practices of Comparative Anatomy, and British Diplomacy in Latin America," *British Journal for the History of Science* 46, no. 4 (2013): 647–74.

16. "Decreto de creación de un museo nacional," *Colección legislativa de la república del Paraguay*, ed. Fernando Viera (Asunción: Graus, 1896), 84.

17. Guido Benatti, "Al Señor Viviani: Encargado de la legación italiana en Lima," *El Pueblo Constituyente* (Cochabamba), September 1876.

18. *Museo Científico Sud-Americano de Arqueología, Antropología, Paleontolojía y en general de todo lo concerniente a los tres reinos de la naturaleza por el Dr. D. Guido Benatti* (Buenos Aires: Tipografía La Famiglia Italiana, 1883).

19. Bellin, "Taking the Indian cure."

20. Harold Cook, *Matters of Exchange: Commerce, Medicine, and Science in the Dutch Golden Age* (New Haven, CT: Yale University Press, 2007), 34. See also Bellin's discussion of the "Indian cure" as part of a desire for unmediated access to the real and the belief that the "Red man, in his unique communion with nature, possessed knowledge of its curative powers unrevealed to civilized man" (Bellin, "Taking the Indian Cure," 5–7, 10).

21. Podgorny, "Travelling Museums"; James W. Cook, *The Art of Deception: Playing with Fraud in the Age of Barnum* (Cambridge, MA: Harvard University Press, 2001); S. Qureshi, *Peoples on Parade: Exhibitions, Empire, and Anthropology in Nineteenth-Century Britain* (Chicago: University of Chicago Press, 2011).

22. I. Podgorny, "'La industria y laboriosidad de la República': Guido Bennati y las muestras de San Luis, Mendoza y La Rioja en la Exposición Nacional de Córdoba," in *Argentina en exposición: Ferias y exhibiciones durante los siglos XIX y XX*, ed. Andrea Lluch and Silvia Di Liscia (Madrid-Sevilla: Consejo Superior de Investigaciones Científicas, 2009), 21–59.

23. Podgorny, *Viajes en Bolivia*.

24. Podgorny, "Coleccionistas de Arena."

25. Podgorny, *Viajes en Bolivia*.

26. *El Titicaca*, November 9, 1876.

27. "Historia descriptiva de Bolivia," *La Reforma*, November 15, 1876.

28. "Museo," *La Reforma*, December 16, 1876. For a description of the museum, see Podgorny, *El sendero*.

29. La Comisión Italiana, "Escursion a Tiaguanaco y al lago Titicaca," *La Reforma*, November, 1876.

30. Manó to Dabry de Thiersant.

31. Paul Broca, "Sur des crânes et des objets d'industrie provenant des fouilles de M. Ber à Tiahuanaco (Perou)," *Bulletins de la Société d'anthropologie de Paris* 3rd ser., 1 (1878): 230–35.

32. Luis Monguió, "Una desconocida novela hispano-peruana sobre la Guerra del Pacífico," *Revista Hispánica Moderna* 35, no. 3 (1969): 248–54; Pedro Gómez Aparicio, *Historia del periodismo español: De la Revolución de Septiembre al desastre colonial* (Madrid: Editora Nacional, 1971).

33. Eloy Perillán Buxó, *Almanaque de la Broma para 1884* (Madrid: Imprenta del Universo, 1883).

34. Gustavo Torrico Landa y Cristóbal Kolkichuima P'ankara, *La imprenta y el periodismo en Bolivia* (La Paz: Fondo Ed. de los Diputados, 2004).

35. "Museo Boliviano," *El Ferrocarril*, March 7, 1877.

36. "Museo Boliviano," *El Ferrocarril*, March 14, 1877.

37. In a recent book, Pascal Riviale noted that these pictures were given or sold to Manó or Bennati by Georges B. von Grumbkow, a German photographer, or by French explorer Théodore Ber, who had commissioned Grumbkow to take pictures in Tiwanaku. See Pascal Riviale and Christophe Galinon, *Une vie dans les Andes: Le journal de Théodore Ber (1864–1896)* (Paris: Ginkgo, 2013); Natalia Majluf, *Registros del territorio : Las primeras décadas de la fotografía, 1860–1880* (Lima: Museo de Arte de Lima, 1997).

38. R. Tripp Evans, *Romancing the Maya: Mexican Antiquity in the American Imagination, 1820–1915* (Austin: University of Texas Press, 2004). See Achim, chap. 1, and Sellen, chap. 4.

39. Sergio Elías Ortiz, "Viaje de estudio del doctor José Carlos Manó por el sur de Colombia," *Centro de Cultura Nariñense* (1969): 17–21.

40. *El Ferrocarril de Cali*: "La enseñanza en Cali," August 6, 1880; "Cartas," September 3, 1880; "Carta de José Carlos Manó sobre etnología Americana," September 24, 1880; "Apuntes de etnología Americana," November 5, 1880; "Continuación de los apuntes de etnología Americana," November 19, 1880; "Justicia," December 24, 1880; "El jesuita Juan de Velasco," January 28, February 4, 11, 1881; José Carlos Manó, "Del lago Titicaca a Bogotá: Apuntes de etnología prehistórica," *Anales de la Instrucción Pública en los Estados Unidos de Colombia* (1881): 35–42, 117–25, 268–75.

41. Even though they never met, Manó's comments on Montalvo's *Catilinarias* accompanied every edition of this work. Manó compared Montalvo to Jean de La Bruyère, the French moralist from the seventeenth century. See Agramonte, *Montalvo en su epistolario*.

42. *Bulletin de la Société Belge de Géographie* 5 (1881): 576; Adriano Paéz, "Conversaciones semanales: Una poetisa y un sabio," *La Pluma: Periódico Literario*, Bogotá, August 20, 1881.

43. Accessed January 10, 2011, http://www.unesco.org/culture/natlaws/media/pdf/colombia/colombia_ley_59_11_06_1881_spa_orof.pdf.

44. Probably it refers to Boston's American Exhibition of the Products, Arts, and Manufactures of Foreign Nations; cf. Charles B. Norton, *Official Catalogue Foreign Exhibition* (Boston, 1883), 432.

45. Adriano Paéz, "Comisión Científica Colombiana," *La Pluma*, September 6, 1881.

46. *Anales de la canalización del Magdalena* (Bogotá, 1882).

47. *Anales de la instrucción pública en los Estados Unidos de Colombia* (1882): Jorge Isaacs, "Comisión Científica Colombiana," "Las hulleras de Aracayaca,"

363–68; José Carlos Manó, "Yacimientos hulleros de las provincias de Padilla, Santa Marta y a Goagiras (Estado del Magdalena)," 4–12; "Comisión Científica Colombiana: Estudio de los tres reinos en el territorio de la república: Segundo informe oficial," 85–111; "Comisión Científica Colombiana: Estudio de los tres reinos en el territorio de la república," 415–44.

48. Camilo Domínguez, "Prólogo," in Jorge Isaacs, *Obras completas: Estudio sobre las tribus indígenas del Estado del Magdalena: Exploraciones* (Bogotá: Universidad Externado de Colombia, 2005), xvii–xviii.

49. "Informe del Secretario de la Sociedad de Medicina y Ciencias Naturales de Bogotá, leído en la sesión solemne anual que celebró esta corporación el día 27 de febrero de 1884, en el salón de grados de la Universidad Nacional," *Papel Periódico Ilustrado* 62 (1884): 224; Obregón, "El sentimiento de nación."

50. *Cuenca geológica y mineralógica del departamento de Huehuetenango: Primer informe presentado a la Secretaria de Fomento por José Carlos Manó, comisionado por el Supremo Gobierno para estudiar la República de Guatemala; Segundo informe presentado a la Secretaría de Fomento: Cuencas geolgicas y mineralógicas de los departamentos del Quiché, Baja Verapaz y sud de la Alta Verapaz; Tercer informe presentado a la Secretaría de Fomento: Salinas de Magdalena* (Guatemala City: El Progreso, 1883). These reports were reissued by the Sociedad de Geografía e Historia de Guatemala in 1940.

51. David McCreery, *Development and the State in Reforma Guatemala 1871–1885* (Athens, OH: Ohio University, Center for International Studies, Latin American Program, 1983), 59.

52. Paradoxically, the same problem still exists in contemporary historiography, where transnational characters such as Manó are studied only in connection with the local or national context.

CHAPTER SEVEN

Visualizing Culture and Nature

William Taylor's Murals in the Hall of Northwest Coast Indians, American Museum of Natural History

Susan Roy

It would not be surprising if a distinct type of mural decoration grew out of the work done in the American Museum of Natural History. The painters working there are surrounded by objects of the past, not as they are represented in art, but as they are discovered and preserved for precise study, and their special concern is to place these objects in a natural environment. They have as much of nature as can persist through the disintegration process of time to suggest color and form, and many contrasts and resemblances.
—"A NEW TYPE OF MURAL PAINTING," *NATURAL HISTORY* (1918)[1]

I would be very glad if you would give us the privilege of selling fish—I don't know why the white people won't allow us to fish on their river. We have claims to this river ever since the Indians were made. The Government or the Fishery Inspectors did not bring the fish into the rivers after they came into the country—The salmon were here even before we were—We claim the salmon ourselves and it should not have anything to do with the whites—We were here before they were and we claim all the fish.... When this earth was made and this river with salmon in it and the forests with deer in it and all that we use, they were made for us to use and everything that was in it.
—TESTIMONY OF TSESHAHT SPOKESPERSON MR. BILL TO THE ROYAL COMMISSION ON INDIAN AFFAIRS, 1914[2]

In 1914, Mr. Bill, of the Tseshaht Nation on Vancouver Island, made an emotional plea to the Royal Commission on Indian Affairs for the province of British Columbia about his community's aboriginal rights to their fisheries, lands, and waters.[3] In similar settings across the province, aboriginal leaders and spokespersons passionately argued for the security of their traditional territories in light of intense settler encroachment and restrictive resource legislation that made fishing and hunting illegal and threatened the chiefly prestige economies of the Pacific Northwest. Settler society generally viewed nature as sublime landscapes to be contemplated or as lands and natural resources—including timber, minerals, and fish—to be extracted and developed. In their testimonies to the commission, which was established to resolve land issues in the province, aboriginal leaders spoke to a deep connection to their territories—the lands and resources over which a community held jurisdiction according to customary legal systems—as an integrated physical, temporal, economic, and spiritual land- and waterscape. Territory comprised much more than resources to be exploited and included the histories, songs, stories, and memories animating relationships with the natural world and linking people to deceased ancestors and spiritual beings and to the unborn generations of the future.[4] "Nature"—including the forests and fisheries—was a central site of conflict among indigenous communities and settler society at the turn of the century in British Columbia.

Around the same time as these proceedings, in New York City, artist William S. Taylor produced a set of murals to adorn the four walls of the Hall of Northwest Coast Indians in the American Museum of Natural History (AMNH), which displayed cultural objects collected by Franz Boas and his colleagues during the museum's Jesup North Pacific Expedition (1897–1902), from George T. Emmon's substantial Tlingit collection, and from other acquisitions. Between 1909 and 1926, the museum commissioned Taylor to produce the series depicting the themes of aboriginal industry, ceremony, war, and peace. The murals were applauded in museum circles and by spectators alike. As the press reported on the new artistic contributions, "This idea of museum decoration is capable of further development, and without a doubt will also gain in popularity as artists of distinction are drawn into the work and encouraged to place as much stress upon the aesthetic as upon its archaeological side."[5] Drawing on the conventions of natural history painting, Taylor's murals provided a contextual, naturalized, and romanticized backdrop to the material culture exhibits of the Northwest Coast hall. This paper examines the political and economic circumstances surrounding this mural project and Taylor's work in the context both of these assertions of aboriginal sovereignty and of the varied and convergent expressions of indigenous associations with nature, especially in relation to the fisheries and forestry industries. This historic moment was a critical time in the formation of North American ethnography and museum-based representations of culture and nature. It was also a critical time in the history of indigenous peoples' assertions of rights to the lands and resources of their territorial homelands—rights based on complex political relationships of their communities to history, culture, and nature.

In 1909, the AMNH's new president, Henry Fairfield Osborn, sent Taylor and archaeologist Harlan I. Smith to Washington State, British Columbia, and Alaska to photograph and sketch indigenous peoples and local landscapes in preparation for the first set of murals depicting Indian industries.[6] Smith believed it best that Taylor visit the region in person, "to get thoroughly soaked with the feeling and color of the northwest."[7] Taylor was a well-known artist and member of the National Society of Mural Painters. He was an instructor of mural painting and composition at the Pratt Institute in Brooklyn and later a professor of art at Brown University. In addition to painting the murals in the Northwest Coast hall (fig. 7.1), in the late 1920s, Taylor produced three murals depicting the progression of Western civilization for the J. P. Morgan Memorial Hall of the museum. Smith, who accompanied Taylor as his supervisor, had worked under the direction of Boas as archaeologist for the Jesup expedition from 1897 to 1899, during which he excavated shell middens and burial grounds, photographed individuals, and collected objects and carvings at villages along the Pacific Northwest. Following his trip with Taylor, in 1911 Smith left

Figure 7.1. William Taylor, detail of the mural *Warfare*, ca. 1922–1926. Photograph by Amir Gavriely, 2011.

the museum to become the archaeologist with the Geological Survey of Canada.[8]

Over a three-month period in the spring and summer of 1909, the two men traveled from Seattle to Skagway and along the coast, visiting indigenous villages, local sites, and cannery towns. In the fall, Smith returned to New York and left Taylor to continue his research in Haida and Nuu-chah-nulth territories. Taylor made preliminary sketches of landscapes, vegetation, and "Indians in their artificial and natural environments." Smith took more than three hundred photographs "of all phases in Indian life," purchased additional photographic prints illustrating ethnological conditions, resumed the archaeological reconnaissance he had begun on the Jesup expedition, and collected cultural objects, houseposts, and totem poles not already represented in the museum's collections.[9] Taylor's research collaboration with the archaeologist was meant to secure scientific reproduction in the murals of indigenous material culture, cultural practice, physicality and gesture, and the specific visual characteristics of the Northwest Coast landscape while allowing him independence in artistic treatment.[10] In Wrangell, Taylor wrote, "I made color notes valuable to my work, but it was not until I reached the Great Glacier on the Stickine River that I caught the spirit of Alaska. Having waited two days for the dense fog to rise, I at last beheld a beautiful glacier partly covered with snow converging toward a small river of ice at the junction of the mountains. The scene partly in sunlight gave me the first inspiration for the Tlingit decoration."[11]

Henry Fairfield Osborn, who had replaced Morris Ketchum Jesup as museum president in 1908, commissioned the paintings in an effort to complete the anthropological exhibits of the hall begun during Boas's time at the museum. Under Boas's direction, the museum had sponsored the ambitious Jesup North Pacific Expedition to investigate the biological, cultural, and linguistic relationships that might have existed between indigenous peoples of Northeastern Asia and the Northwest Coast. Through this work, the museum amassed one of the largest collections of Northwest Coast cultural objects in the world. Unlike Jesup, Osborn, a vertebrate paleontologist, was not supportive of anthropology, judging it to be "merely opinion, or the gossip of the natives [and] many years away from being a science." In his view, "Mr. Jesup and the Museum spent far too much money on anthropology."[12] Instead, Osborn emphasized the museum's public education role through outreach to New York City's school children and in service of the assimilation of new immigrants to American society.[13] Efforts were also made toward "decluttering" the Northwest

Coast hall. Curator Clark Wissler removed the archaeological cases located in the hall's central aisle and built a spectacular "life-group" that, once placed in a massive canoe, was meant to illustrate the "physique, garb, and action" of a group of Tlingit arriving at a potlatch.[14] Much like the habitat dioramas of their natural history counterparts, life groups were full-scale sculptural representations of indigenous peoples that were meant to replicate the wonder of an intimate, personal viewing of authentic Indians engaged in a ceremonial or economic activity, the action conveniently frozen in time.[15] However, life groups were extremely expensive to build, leading Osborn to prefer murals as "a cheaper means of putting 'life' into the displays."[16] Murals provided the effect of the landscapes from which the objects had come, and they freed museum space: they were flat, "like tapestries," but had enough relief and depth to lend reality to the scenes depicted. The positioning of the paintings, framed by "weathered old totem poles, canoes and other symbols of Indian art" ensured, according to museum commentators, that the "simple out-of-door life of the people with the true local color" was presented without interference from the modern architecture usually found in institutional or museum settings.[17] Just as in Taylor's painting *Weaving a Blanket*, in which the Great Glacier on the Stikine River provided the environmental context and inspiration for the cultural production of the Chilkat blanket, murals could "vitalize an exhibit by setting forth the life and the country that the exhibit represents."[18] Taylor strove to incorporate cultural objects on display in the hall into his canvases "to enhance the educational value of the exhibit in unusual degree."[19]

Aside from these alterations to the hall, the collection retained the geographical emphasis and local historical categorization that Boas had intended during his tenure at the museum (1896–1905). Boas, whose theories and methods dominated ethnographic research from the late 1900s to the mid-twentieth century, was concerned with reconstructing local indigenous cultures before major social, economic, and political shifts brought about cultural change and inevitable "assimilation." Challenging museum representations of world cultures as a series of evolutionary stages from primitive to civilized, Boas presented culture in terms of localized historical and cultural considerations: his culture-area approach to museum displays grouped cultural objects to represent visually a bounded cultural group such as the "Bella Coola" (Nuxalk) or the "Nootka" (Nuu-chah-nulth) and their representative artistic styles, ceremonial practices, and local economies. This emphasis on cultural relativism challenged the typological organization that dominated the U.S. National Museum in the late nineteenth century. Here, curator O. T. Mason emphasized evolutionary schemes that described the development of technologies, so that objects of the same kind (e.g., pottery, basketry, tools) were placed together despite community origin. While curator William Holmes later incorporated regional arrangements in the exhibits, the museum never completely abandoned its developmental schemes.[20] George Dorsey, of the Chicago Field Museum, praised the AMNH's exhibit: "It was evident that the objects on exhibition were neither placed there with the idea of their beauty nor was their arrangement such as to present primarily a beautiful picture, but rather one felt that as one passed from the exhibit of one tribe to that of another that the dominating features of each culture were so presented that they were apparent. . . . The collections revealed so far as possible the influence of environment both geographical and historical as the culture of one tribe upon that of another."[21] While recognizing some differences among these groups, the organization of such culture areas in the metropolitan museum contributed to the broader categorization of the Northwest Coast as a distinct landscape and as a distinct group for anthropological research.

Between 1910 and 1926, Taylor produced nineteen murals depicting indigenous life and landscapes of the Pacific Northwest. In keeping with Boas's theories and under the advisement of Smith, George T. Emmons, and other museum curators, Taylor aimed to portray historical scenes and authentic environments. Taylor's paintings depicted seven tribes of the Northwest Coast, the same tribes that had been organized and contained in the museum's display cabinets: the Tlingit, of Alaska; the Haida, of Haida Gwaii; the Tsimshian, of the Nass and Skeena rivers; the Bella Coola (Nuxalk), between the Burke and Dean channels; the Kwakiutl (Kwakwaka'wakw), on the northeast end of Vancouver Island; the Nootka (Nuu-chah-nulth), on the west coast of Vancouver Island; and the Coast Salish, of southern coastal British Columbia and Washington State around Puget Sound. While details of Taylor's and Smith's tour of the specific communities from which the museum's images and objects came can be found in its archives, in the displays, the AMNH did not provide many details about these originating communities—whether it was the Songhees reserve in Victoria, the Tlingit village of Kluckwan, the eulachon fisheries of the Chilkat River, or at other villages or sites. Instead, objects and photographs obtained through on-site negotiations were subsumed within the regional identities of Coast Salish, Bella Coola, or Tlingit, for example, and the even larger "Northwest Coast," thereby reinforcing these tribal and culture-area categories.

Crucial to this history are museum discourses that also considered "nature" and "culture" in conjunction, made visual through the emerging aesthetics of natural history painting as both an artistic and a scientific endeavor. In its exhibits, the museum brought exotic, remote, and distant "natures" to the museum's publics. Natural history museums (and not fine art museums) collected and displayed indigenous or tribal cultural objects. In New York City, two major cultural institutions that physically straddled Central Park divided the material objects of "nature" and "culture": the AMNH displayed nature and the Metropolitan Museum of Art exhibited European and Western fine art. This art-artefact divide was based on the premise that Western art merited aesthetic and isolated intellectual contemplation while "artifacts" or tribal objects were produced by less progressive societies and lacked depth of meaning. Therefore, they required further contextual cultural explanation.[22]

Nature was not only the background for indigenous material culture collections; the museum also wanted to show how nature had formed these cultures. Just as animal habitat dioramas required meticulously researched and constructed natural contexts, it would be difficult to understand Northwest Coast cultural objects without reference to the coastal landscapes from which those objects came: the cedar forests, smoky fires, mountain ranges, and majestic glaciers of the north. "Mountain mists and steam-clouds are gracious mediums for invoking the ideal," wrote one museum reviewer.[23] Taylor stressed the work involved in getting the color right: "To obtain the data for the second or Haida decoration, I went to Masset, Queen Charlotte Islands, but in all the twelve days spent there, I had a few hours of sunshine in which to make sketches and so gather in the materials I had located. There were days of waiting and watching in the rain. When an opening came in the clouds I had to cover a hasty two miles along the sand beach to catch on canvas the brilliancy of color displays—gaining often severe drenching as an additional reward."[24] The positioning of indigenous material culture in the natural history museum also reified the notion that aboriginal peoples were inherently aligned with "nature" and had innate artistic capability (all of Taylor's murals depict aboriginal people outside). One commentator noted, "One finds himself picking out the various items that signify a development of love of beauty in this primitive race; speculating on the fact that the grandeur of the country has its concomitant in the earnestness of its people; and seeing in the pose and expression of certain of the figures evidence that mind and spirit, here as in all primitive races, have developed with the training of eye and hand."[25] But this was a narrow sense of the natural world and indigenous culture, one that did not take notice of contemporary indigenous dispossession from those same landscapes or of indigenous cultural innovations in the context of contemporary political life and the new industrial economy of the late nineteenth and early twentieth century.

The murals depicted the indigenous homeland as an idealized, naturalized, ethnographic past, an imagined ethnographic moment just before sustained contact with European outsiders. However, as anthropologist Aldona Jonaitis points out, Taylor did not actually witness the idyllic scenes he painted back at the museum, because by 1909, most aboriginal peoples he encountered lived in "Christian" homes, wore tailored clothing, and participated as wage laborers in the industrial economy. And as a museum writer of the time observed, "Most of the old industries had disappeared however—as had also the old costumes—so that with all effort these mural paintings have to be largely restorations."[26] Taylor's paintings of traditionally clothed (or partially clothed) people in front of communal cedar plank houses were, as Jonaitis notes, "competent reconstructions" based on "scenes the artist observed, on old archival photographs, on information from library texts, and on artifacts from the American Museum collection."[27]

William Taylor organized indigenous activity into two distinct sets of practice: "industry" and "ceremony." Running along one side of the hall, the murals depicted "Industrial Arts"—house and canoe building, salmon fishing, and basket and blanket making, for example. Reminiscent of cultural-diffusion explanations of cultural change (that change among aboriginal peoples came about through interactions with other groups and not internal innovation), Taylor's aim was to illustrate the long-standing commercial relationships among the various indigenous communities on the coast:

> I am trying to show . . . that the trading among the tribes of the northwestern coast was mainly through the products of their own industry. The Tlingit exchanged their Chilcat blankets for Haida canoes. The Haida traded their canoes for eulachon grease of the Tsimshian. The Bella-Coola, who were the bread makers, exchanged their bread with the neighboring tribes. Thus through all the coast tribes we find distribution of industrial products going on, and to-day the results of this commerce are evident, for in the extreme south one finds the work of the tribe living farthest north, and vice versa.[28]

This emphasis on interconnectedness contributed to the formation of the Northwest Coast as a cultural region deserving of anthropological attention, yet it also challenged the notion of regional containment by pointing to well-established patterns of mobility and travel and the centrality of commerce and trade to indigenous cultures and economic systems.

Taylor's second set of paintings depicted so-called ceremonial activities, such as the potlatch, the first salmon ceremony, a betrothal, ceremonial dog eating, and a dancing shaman. The murals separated commerce and industry from culture, a distinction also reflected in colonial resource management regimes but not one made by aboriginal peoples themselves. For example, the Northwest Coast "potlatch," categorized by Taylor as "ceremony," refers to a range of ceremonial, political, and economic institutions that cemented relationships and responsibilities, prestige and wealth, and rights and prerogatives. Furthermore, hunters, gatherers, and fishers needed ritual and cultural knowledge to locate and obtain resources as well as the appropriate kin connections to access resource sites and trading networks. Such knowledge and oral traditions, including songs, chants, and affiliations with spiritual and nonhuman beings, are not components of most Western economic models, and Taylor's categorization of the first salmon ceremony as a ceremonial canvas, for example, reflects this division. Furthermore, the Canadian state has historically viewed fishing for food and commerce as two separate and distinct practices. By the late nineteenth century, the state's containment of aboriginal fisheries to a "food fishery" and prohibitions against selling fish had drastically eroded aboriginal peoples' access to their fisheries.[29] As pointed out at the opening of this chapter by Tseshaht leader Mr. Bill (who demanded "the privilege of selling fish"), indigenous communities did not make a rigid divide between industry and ceremony or subsistence and commerce but participated in large regional networks of relations and alliances throughout and beyond their territories. However, by the early twentieth century in British Columbia, aboriginal communities were subject to intense state assimilation policies, including the criminalization, through the Indian Act's "potlatch ban," of ceremonial activity; the state-funded and church-managed Indian residential school system; the establishment of small Indian reserves at a limited number of locations; and restrictive management of hunting and fishing economies. In Washington and Alaska, aboriginal communities also faced unrelenting dispossession and colonization directed at their economies, cultures, and political systems. In the early 1900s in the Chilkat-Tlingit village of Kluckwan, which Smith and Taylor visited, the Bureau of Indian Affairs constructed an Indian school, and children were sent to boarding schools as far away as Kansas.[30]

As a result of these policies, at the time of Taylor and Smith's 1909 research trip, much of the ceremonial or commercial activity depicted by Taylor had been outlawed, and aboriginal peoples were facing increased dispossession of their territories and resources. Importantly, aboriginal communities were also engaged in active political assertions of their aboriginal rights aimed at challenging or circumventing such state interventions and based on indigenous systems of law and cultural conventions that persisted despite colonialism's challenges. In the mode of salvage ethnography or reconstruction, the murals masked reference to indigenous creative adaptation and innovation emerging from these negotiations with state power, missionary activity, settler encroachment, and the industrial economy.

Colonial Policy and Aboriginal Industries on the Northwest Coast

In British Columbia during the second half of the nineteenth century, the colonial state established small and scattered Indian reserves at some of the places where aboriginal peoples lived, fished, and interred their ancestors. As legal scholar Douglas Harris has revealed, many of these small plots of land were located so that communities could maintain their traditional fisheries: Indian reserves were bridges to the water and to land processing sites. For example, the Douglas Treaties of 1850–1854 recognized aboriginal peoples' right to "fish as formerly," and various Indian reserve commissions working between 1876 and 1910 established over 750 reserves with an explicit connection to fishing. The province's Indian reserve geography was premised on the state's view that aboriginal communities required access to their fisheries, an admission that was in itself a recognition of the right to fish. Over time, however, aboriginal peoples were denied control of the fisheries through increasingly discriminatory legal regimes that prioritized industrial capital, commercial operators, and sport fishers, so that by the early twentieth century, the deeply rooted connection between land and fish was unraveling.[31] Regulatory regimes that prioritized nonaboriginal fishing and limited aboriginal fisheries to a food fishery alone wrested control of the fisheries from indigenous peoples and undermined a highly successful fish-based economy.

Taylor recognized the centrality of the fisheries to Northwest Coast communities by choosing fish processing and ceremony as subjects in a number of his murals. *The First Salmon Ceremony* (which he categorized as a ceremony distinct from industry) depicts an intergenerational Coast Salish family: a woman processes a single salmon while a man looks on cradling in his arms a second fish. In 1996, Siyémches te Yeqwyeqwi:ws (Chief Frank Malloway, of Yakweakwioose, on the Lower Fraser River, Coast Salish territory, British Columbia) explained the relevance of the ceremony, in which the first spring salmon was given away to ensure "good luck" or a productive fishery for the remainder of the season. Siyémches described these events as small, private family affairs linking people to the landscape and reasserting and reproducing long-standing connections to and responsibility for environmental stewardship. The first salmon ceremony was (and is) part of an integrated governing system of resource management, linking the human world with a spiritual waterscape inhabited by benevolent, supernatural "people":

> One of the *shxwlá:m* [Indian Doctors] had a dream that the creator was sending something up the river and told him to go down to the river and scoop their dip nets, and it was the salmon. They told them how to respect the salmon and thank the ones that sent the salmon. The salmon people from out in the ocean, you pray to them and thank them for what they sent. He used the word children. I don't hear it often but he used the word children. The salmon people sent their children up to you so you'd have something different to eat that gives you better energy [than meat obtained from hunting]. . . . You have to just thank them; take the bones and send them back after you have eaten the first salmon. He said if you didn't do it you weren't showing your respect for the salmon people and they would quit sending their children out to you.[32]

In another fisheries-themed mural, Taylor painted the Tsimshian eulachon fisheries of the north, where the small oily fish (also known as "candle fish" because they were so rich in fat that they could be lit on one end and burned like a candle) was rendered into eulachon grease. It was appropriate that Taylor chose eulachon rendering as his subject. Before the arrival of Europeans, the two most important trade items on the northern plateau between the Rocky Mountains and the Coast Range were eulachon oil and dentaliam shells. In early spring, great quantities of eulachon arrived in coastal rivers at a time when food supplies were diminishing. "So welcome were these finger-sized fish that the Nisga'a called them the 'little saviours,'" observes historian John Lutz.[33] Fisheries, including salmon and eulachon, were essential to the Coast Salish of southern coastal British Columbia as well as to the cultures and economies of northern indigenous communities.

Indigenous fishing practices were not limited to small-scale, family-based processing, as depicted in Taylor's paintings such as *Salmon Fishing*. Since the late nineteenth century, aboriginal families had taken advantage of new opportunities for work in salmon canneries located on the Fraser River and at Rivers Inlet, where they worked as commercial fishers and, despite restrictions, sold fish and other products to nonaboriginal markets. During the summer fisheries, villages all along the coast emptied as entire families traveled to the canneries. In 1882, the Indian agent on southern Vancouver Island reported that the villages under his jurisdiction were deserted during the fishing season.[34] Because of this concentration, canneries and other sites of the industrial economy became convenient locations for anthropological research. In June 1909, Smith photographed a Nuu-chah-nulth woman weaving a red cedar bark hat on the Songhees reserve near Victoria. Smith wrote, "The Nootkas do not live here but had come from the west coast of Vancouver Island to this point to wait until sent for by the cannery people at the mouth of the Fraser River. Most of them were traveling in their Columbia River boats and they expected the cannery to send a tug boat to tow them across the Gulf of Georgia to the canneries."[35] Smith purchased the unfinished hat, which along with the photograph became source material for Taylor's painting *Industrial Arts* (fig. 7.2). Smith also photographed a Nuu-chah-nulth man who, while waiting to go to the canneries, was making a totem pole based on a picture of a Haida pole that had been provided by an art dealer in Victoria (fig. 7.3).[36] Although the pole suggested intercultural relationships, Smith was generally not interested in purchasing contemporary objects inscribed with evidence of recent economic interaction with tourism or other aboriginal cultural groups; he preferred objects animated by the conflation of age and authenticity.[37]

Taylor's mural *Potlatch Ceremony*, depicting a Kwakwaka'wakw ceremony, presented a romanticized but powerful view of this crucial economic and political institution. *Potlatch*, a Chinook word meaning "to give away" or "to gift," refers to a wide range of practices, including naming, marriage, and memorial feasts, and it generally consisted of property distribution and elaborate, spectacular displays of chiefly wealth, prestige, and ceremonial prerogative. Such ceremonies were at the center of Northwest Coast life, mediating social, economic, and political relationships among families and communities. Government officials and missionaries, who saw in the practice a wasteful throwing away of property accompanied by many "indiscretions" such as gambling and intemperance, generally considered the

Figure 7.2. William Taylor, mural *Industrial Arts, Tlingit*, 1911–1918. Photograph by Amir Gavriely, 2011.

potlatch a transgression of Christian and capitalist values. Some aboriginal Christian converts, such as Kwakwaka'wakw leader Ga'axsta'las (Jane Constance Cook), opposed the potlatch in their communities—Cook's opposition was a strategic response to colonialism's hardships informed by a concern for the position of women and children, increased poverty under colonialism, and the health and general well-being of Kwakwaka'wakw society as well as by the new economic opportunities made possible in the context of Protestantism.[38] In 1884, the federal government outlawed such ceremonial activity through its "potlatch ban." Section 3 of the Indian Act stated, "Every Indian or other person who engages in or assists in celebrating the Indian festival known as the 'Potlatch' or the Indian dance known as the 'Tamanawas' is guilty of a misdemeanour, and shall be liable to

Figure 7.3. A Nuu-chah-nulth man carves a pole for the tourist trade on the Songhees Indian Reserve, June 28, 1909. This photograph was one of the source images for the mural *Industrial Arts*. Harlan I. Smith photograph, Division of Anthropology Archives, American Museum of Natural History.

imprisonment for the term not more than six nor less than two months in any gaol or other place of confinement."[39] However, the law was not always able to curtail the activity as policy makers had hoped. As Smith observed, "I am informed now, however, that the cases are thrown out of court by the judges as being unconstitutional or else out of their jurisdiction."[40] The inability to monitor the activity led Deputy Superintendent of Indian Affairs Duncan Campbell Scott to declare the ban a summary offence, thereby facilitating enforcement by Indian agents in the field. Many anthropologists, such as Boas and Smith, supported First Nations in their assertions of cultural and political sovereignty but at the same time benefited from colonialism's dispossessions because they were able to materially build their collections from confiscated regalia.[41] The potlatch persisted, with creative adaptations, despite the law. In the mode of salvage ethnography, Taylor's murals celebrated the potlatch as a thing of the past, and by locating these traditions within the nebulous category "ceremony," the murals also understated their economical, political, and legal pertinence (fig. 7.4).

During the visit to Oweekeno territory at Rivers Inlet on the central coast (a major industrial salmon-canning center), Taylor surely found additional inspiration for his potlatch mural. The Rivers Inlet canneries were established in the late nineteenth century to supply canned sockeye

Figure 7.4. William Taylor, mural *Potlatch Ceremony, Kwakiult*, 1916. Photograph by Amir Gavriely, 2011.

salmon to international markets. The community comprised a multiethnic workforce of Oweekeno, Nuu-chah-nulth, and Kwakwaka'wakw First Nations; Japanese boatmen from the Fraser River; Norwegian colonists from the Bella Coola Valley; and Danish-speaking immigrants who had established a colony at Cape Scott on Vancouver Island.[42] Taylor and Smith were invited to a "cultus potlatch." At this feast, held on a Saturday night when provincial fishery regulations made fishing illegal, local Okweekeno leaders hosted visiting Kwakwaka'wakw from Alert Bay and Nuu-chah-nulth from Nootka Sound. Smith described the proceedings: "I realized that the Indians were having a labor agitation. Other canneries had been paying bounties to secure Indians to work for them, and the Indians wanted five dollars for each one who had come to work at the Rivers Inlet cannery. They also thought the women who put the salmon into the cans were not paid enough. They finally decided not to go out and tend the nets, unless the wages of the women were increased and the bounty was forthcoming."[43] The potlatch as a site of assembly and organization—in this case regarding a labor conflict—did not make it into Taylor's murals.

In July, following their visit to Rivers Inlet, Taylor and Smith traveled to Nuxalk territory, in the Bella Coola Valley. Steamship service connected the region to villages, salmon canneries, logging camps, and sawmills nestled along the central and north coasts of British Columbia. As in other northern communities, Nuxalk women and men took advantage of wage labor opportunities offered by the new fishing and forestry industries dominating the region's economy. When Taylor and Smith arrived, they found the village empty; most of the Nuxalk were away working at the fish canning plants, so Smith took numerous photographs of the Bella Coola village (divided, according to Smith, into "Christianized" and "pagan" sections), totem poles, and cemetery, and of an elderly man making a wooden spoon with an iron adze. He met with the Methodist missionary Reverend Gibson, who assisted with procuring a number of Nuxalk totem poles for the Northwest Coast hall's displays once community members had returned from the canneries.

However, it was the Nuxalk "bread-making industry" that drew Taylor's attention. The Nuxalk harvested the bark of the western hemlock, which was cooked to make a kind of "bread" consumed with eulachon grease and coho salmon skin:

> Down in the flats, near the mouth of the river, the families gather during the summer and make bread for themselves and their neighbors. Seated in a rope chair, high up in a hemlock tree, a native scrapes away the inside bark of the tree. Below in the sunlight children hold out a cedar blanket to catch the shreds as they fall. Near them is the large pit in the ground to which they carry the bark for cooking. Hot stones are put over the surface of the pit, and over these stones alternate layers of moist skunk cabbage leaves and scraped bark. Four days are required for the cooking, at the end of which time the bark is ground into a pulp by means of pestle and stone, and then is left in the sun to dry.[44]

Taylor and Smith learned of this practice from Fillip Jacobsen, a Norwegian-born resident of Bella Coola who with his brother Johan Adrian Jacobsen collected Northwest Coast objects for sale to museums and in 1882 had taken a group of Nuxalk dancers to Germany. Jacobsen had even built a full-scale model of an old hemlock-cooking place at a location where the Nuxalk prepared the bark.[45]

In selecting the subject matter that would represent Nuxalk "industry," Taylor chose not to depict one of the most remunerative industries carried out by Nuxalk people of the time: logging. By the late 1880s, most young

Nuxalk men were involved in logging—either working with the support of their families as independent hand loggers or employed in nonnative-owned logging operations within the traditional territory. The Nuxalk, like other aboriginal and nonaboriginal hand loggers, obtained provincial licenses to cut timber on specific tracts of land. Income from hand logging paid for and provided the timber for major building projects on the reserve, such as construction of the Methodist church and hospital, as well as providing the timber required for building the numerous homes that constituted the "modern" Bella Coola village.[46] The hand-logging tide was turning, however. By 1910 revisions to the British Columbia Forestry Act prioritized capital-intensive, large-scale production and increasingly alienated aboriginal loggers from the industry. In 1913, Nuxalk spokesperson Wilson told the Royal Commission on Indian Affairs, "When an Indian wants work at logging he cannot always get a license. In fact, we have great difficulty in getting these licenses."[47] The Nuxalk responded by forming their own commercial logging company; however, they again found that the provincial forestry branch did not want to provide logging licenses to aboriginal peoples, and so most tenures within their territory went to nonnative operations. Bella Coola Indian Loggers, as the Nuxalk company was called, applied through Department of Indian Affairs' processes for permits to log themselves or to sell the timber on their reserves, with the proceeds to be distributed among community members.

In 1909, Smith found that much had changed since his visit to the Northwest Coast with the Jesup expedition, twelve years earlier. Northern villages had become "modernized," and there were no longer many totem poles for sale, the remaining ones being too tall for the museum's hall or being rotted. "The only thing I feel sorry about are that the old days have gone for the Indian."[48] To stretch travel funds, in September Smith left Taylor to complete the trip on his own so that he could experience "the true spirit" of all regions of the coast and "paint with feeling."[49] The strategy paid off. Contemporary museum critics praised Taylor's work: "Landscapes, although idealized give the color and feeling of particular spots which a visitor to this northern country can locate, while each canvas shows good type portraits of the tribe represented." Lieutenant George Emmons, who, along with Smith, provided "scientific supervision" for the murals, pronounced them "rarely accurate presentations."[50] And more recently, the AMNH's murals have garnered international distinction. In 1987, museum artist Stephen C. Quinn highlighted the institution's long genealogy of painting excellence: "We stand on the shoulders of the great artists of the Museum's bright and illustrious past. Their works are ours to preserve and protect."[51]

On one level, Taylor's murals erase the historical and political context of the new industrial economy and indigenous peoples' assertions of aboriginal rights on the Northwest Coast. They ignore the complex histories of colonialism—that the Songhees Indian reserve in Victoria, British Columbia (a site of Taylor and Smith's research), was sold in 1911 to remove aboriginal people from the influence of urban centers, for example; that many of the villages Taylor and Smith visited were deserted because families had traveled to work in the salmon canneries; and that, by 1914, many aboriginal men were volunteering for the war effort. They obscure dispossession and colonialism's incursions—the unrelenting encroachment on indigenous territories and the restrictive legislation that made access to territories and resources increasingly difficult for aboriginal peoples. In their erasure of innovative indigenous adaptations to modern life and the emerging industrial economy, the paintings embraced salvage ethnography. Such representations that contained aboriginal peoples of the past and connected them to narratives of disappearance were also closely linked to the actual material dispossession of indigenous lands and territories. People who were "vanished" left behind their land and resources for the taking. As we would expect in this period of salvage anthropology, the murals captured aboriginal peoples, economies, and cultures in an "ethnographic past," the moment just before interaction with European cultures.

However, it is also important to note that Taylor's murals reference local economic activities, uses of the resources, and relationships to the natural and spiritual world. They point to complex economic and political systems of chiefly prestige and wealth; they describe an indigenous economy that persisted into the first half of the twentieth century, if in an altered form, despite colonialism's challenges. Taylor's recognition of the trade relationships between First Nations of the coast, even though they were depicted narrowly as "traditional" activities, pointed to commercial activity and trade as integral to the aboriginal right to fisheries and resources management. Furthermore, when we consider the much broader visual anthropology by examining the murals in conjunction with their source materials (photographs, correspondence, and cultural objects), they hint at how people actually lived and survived the unrelenting pressures of colonialism and how they influenced its shifts. The period during which Taylor painted was characterized by intense change and state expansion into the lives of aboriginal peoples. Despite these challenges, people moved through the land- and waterscapes of the Pacific Northwest on seasonal journeys to exploit resource sites, visit relatives, participate in ceremonial and political culture, adopt new technologies and ideas, and engage in the industrial economy.

Even though constrained by the discourses of salvage ethnography and by their idealism and romanticism, the murals of the Hall of Northwest Coast Indians represent the diversity and richness of local indigenous technologies, economies, and culture. They describe a high degree of movement, mobility, and formalized political and cultural interactions among Northwest Coast aboriginal families and communities. In other words, the paintings can be read with a kind of tension that in the context of the museum salvage paradigm suggests cultural loss but also highlights complex cultural innovation and dynamic sovereign societies. They also point to the interconnectedness of culture and nature of the kind the Tseshaht leader Mr. Bill referred to in his 1914 testimony to the Royal Commission on Indian Affairs, cited at the beginning of this chapter, when he demanded the right to sell fish despite the fisheries regulations: "The salmon were here even before we were—We claim the salmon ourselves and it should not have anything to do with the whites. . . . When this earth was made and this river with salmon in it and forests with deer in it and all that we use, they were made for us to use and everything that was in it."[52]

Acknowledgments

I wish to thank Amir Gavriely, Dianne Newell, and Dorothee Schreiber for their support of this project as well as Kristen Mable and Mai Qaraman of the American Museum of Natural History for their expert research assistance. I am also grateful for the support of the Hampton Research Grant at the University of British Columbia.

Notes

1. "A New Type of Mural Painting: Critical Note Relative to the Decorations in the North Pacific Hall of the American Museum," *Natural History* 18 (1918): 149.

2. Testimony of Tseshaht spokesperson Mr. Bill, May 11, 1914, RG10, vol. 11025, file AH13, Library and Archives of Canada (hereafter cited as LAC). Cited in Douglas C. Harris, *Landing Native Fisheries: Indian Reserves and Fishing Rights in British Columbia, 1849–1925* (Vancouver: University of British Columbia Press, 2008), 173.

3. Between 1913 and 1916, this commission visited indigenous communities throughout British Columbia to settle what was known as the "Indian land question." While community leaders stressed aboriginal rights, for the state this "question" was limited to determining Indian reserve acreage.

4. See, e.g., Julie Cruikshank, *Do Glaciers Listen? Local Knowledge, Colonial Encounters, and Social Imagination* (Vancouver: University of British Columbia Press, 2005); Keith Thor Carlson, *The Power of Place, the Problem of Time: Aboriginal Identity and Historical Consciousness in the Cauldron of Colonialism* (Toronto: University of Toronto Press, 2010); Susan Roy, *These Mysterious People: Shaping History and Archaeology in a Northwest Coast Community* (Montreal: McGill-Queen's University Press, 2010).

5. "A Guide to Works of Arts in New York," undated newspaper clipping, file 1605 (1916–1917–1918–1922), box 245, Central Archives, American Museum of Natural History (hereafter cited as AMNH).

6. Accompanied by George T. Emmons, in 1911 Taylor made a second trip to Alaska. Director to William Taylor, June 23, 1922, file 832 (1909–1911), box 203, Central Archives, AMNH.

7. Harlan I. Smith to Will S. Taylor, October 4, 1909, file 343, folder 8, Department of Anthropology, Correspondence, 1908–1926, Division of Anthropology Archives, AMNH.

8. William Taylor vertical file, Library and Special Collections, AMNH. In relation to Harlan Smith, see "Harlan Ingersoll Smith," http://www.civilization.ca/cmc/exhibitions/tresors/ethno/etp0400e.shtml.

9. F. W. Putman, "Anthropologic Miscellanea," *American Anthropologist* 11, no. 3 (1909): 537–38.

10. H. C. Bumpus to Mr. Taylor, June 11, 1909, file 832 (1909–1911), box 203, Central Archives, AMNH. Taylor was paid $600 per painting (an amount the museum director later considered insufficient) and was provided canvases, paints, brushes, models, and studio space at the museum.

11. Will S. Taylor, "Results of an Art Trip to the Northwest Coast: Mural Decorations Planned to Show Indian Industries," *Natural History* 10 (1910): 44. For an excellent history of the hall and the museum's collecting activities, see Aldona Jonaitis, *From the Land of the Totem Poles: The Northwest Coast Indian Art Collection at the American Museum of Natural History* (New York: American Museum of Natural History, 1988).

12. Cited in Jonaitis, *Land of the Totem Poles*, 218.

13. Jonaitis, *Land of the Totem Poles*. See also Douglas Cole, *Captured Heritage: The Scramble for the Northwest Coast Artifacts* (Seattle: University of Washington Press, 1985); Ira Jacknis, "Franz Boas and Exhibits: On the Limitations of the Museum Method of Anthropology," in *Objects and Others: Essays on Museums and Material Culture*, ed. George W. Stocking Jr. (Madison: University of Wisconsin Press, 1985), 75–111.

14. Jonaitis, *Land of the Totem Poles*, 219.

15. Stephen Christopher Quinn, *Windows on Nature: The Great Habitat Dioramas of the American Museum of Natural History* (New York: Abrams, 2006). Regarding notions of authenticity and its limits to understanding cultural change, see Paige Raibmon, *Authentic Indians: Episodes of Encounter from the Late Nineteenth Century Northwest Coast* (Durham, NC: Duke University Press, 2005).

16. Jonaitis, *Land of the Totem Poles*, 221.

17. M. C. D., "Foreword on the New Mural Paintings in the American Museum," *Natural History* 11 (1911): 130.

18. Ibid., 129.

19. William Taylor to Dr. Townsend, June 12, 1911, file 832 (1909–1911), box 203, Central Archives, AMNH.

20. Jacknis, "Franz Boas and Exhibits," 82.

21. George A. Dorsey, "The Anthropological Exhibits as the American Museum of Natural History," *Science* 25, no. 641 (1907): 585.

22. Carol Duncan, *Civilizing Rituals: Inside Public Art Museums* (London: Routledge, 1995), 5. On the distinctions between artifact, art, and commodity, see Ruth B. Phillips and Christopher B. Steiner, eds., *Unpacking Culture: Art and Commodity in Colonial and Postcolonial Worlds* (Berkeley: University of California Press, 1999).

23. E. C. B. Fassett, "The New Mural Paintings and the Industries They Portray," *Natural History* 11 (1911): 136.

24. Taylor, "Results of an Art Trip," 44.

25. M. C. D., "Foreword on the New Mural Paintings," 130.

26. Ibid., 129.

27. Jonaitis, *Land of the Totem Poles*, 222.

28. Taylor, "Results of an Art Trip," 49.

29. Dianne Newell, *Tangled Webs of History: Indians and the Law in Canada's Pacific Coast Fisheries* (Toronto: University of Toronto Press, 1993); Harris, *Landing Native Fisheries*.

30. George Thornton Emmons and Frederica de Laguna, eds., *The Tlingit Indians* (Seattle: University of Washington Press, 1991).

31. Harris, *Landing Native Fisheries*.

32. Interview with Siyémches te Yeqwyeqwi:ws (Chief Frank Malloway) by Heather Myles and Hychblo (Tracey Joe), June 1996, quoted in Keith Thor Carlson, ed., *You Are Asked to Witness: The Stó:lo in Canada's Pacific Coast History* (Chilliwack, BC: Stó:lo Heritage Trust, 1996), 3–4.

33. John Sutton Lutz, *Makúk: A New History of Aboriginal-White Relations* (Vancouver: University of British Columbia Press, 2008), 121–22.

34. Ibid., 189.

35. Harlan I. Smith, "Photographs from the North Pacific Coast, 1909" (scrapbook 1 of 6), Division of Anthropology Archives, AMNH, p. 72.

36. Ibid., 78.

37. Roy, *These Mysterious People*, 60–62.

38. Leslie A. Robertson, *Standing Up with Ga'axsta'las: Jane Constance Cook and the Politics of Memory, Church, and Custom* (Vancouver: University of British Columbia Press, 2013).

39. An Act Further to Amend "The Indian Act, 1880," SC 1884 (47 Vict.), c. 27, s. 3. See also Douglas Cole and Ira Chaikin, *An Iron Hand upon the People: The Law Against the Potlatch on the Northwest Coast* (Vancouver: Douglas and McIntyre, 1900); and Catherine Bell, "Recovering from Colonization: Perspectives of Community Members on Protection and Repatriation of Kwakwaka'wakw Cultural Heritage," in *First Nations Cultural Heritage and Law: Case Studies, Voices, and Perspectives*, ed. Catherine Bell and Val Napoleon (Vancouver: University of British Columbia Press, 2008).

40. Harlan I. Smith, "A Visit to the Indian Tribes of the Northwest Coast," *American Museum Journal* 10, no. 2 (1910): 39.

41. Julian Harrison and Regna Darnell, eds., *Historicizing Canadian Anthropology* (Vancouver: University of British Columbia Press, 2006).

42. Lester R. Peterson, "Fishing Rivers Inlet by Sail and Oar," in *Raincoast Chronicles First Five: Stories and History of the B.C. Coast*, ed. Howard White (Madeira Park, BC: Harbour, 1977).

43. Smith, "Visit to the Indian Tribes," 37.

44. Taylor, "Results of an Art Trip," 48. Margaret Siwallace, of Nuxalk, describes the preparation of western hemlock cambium in Nancy J. Turner, *Food Plants of Coastal First Peoples* (Victoria, BC: Royal British Columbia Museum, 1995), 34–53.

45. Smith, "Photographs of the Northwest Coast, 1909" (scrapbook 3 of 6), Division of Anthropology Archives, AMNH, p. 186. In relation to the Jacobsens, see Aaron Glass, "Northwest Coast Ceremonialism: The Works of J.A. Jacobsen (1853–1947)," in "The North-West Pacific in the 18th and 19th Centuries," special issue, *European Journal of American Studies* (2010), document 3, http://ejas.revues.org/8518.

46. "Correspondence Regarding Timber on Reserves in the Agency, 1903–1941," RG10, vol. 7858, file 30162-7, pt. 1, LAC.

47. Cited in Lutz, *Makúk*, 215.

48. Harlan I. Smith to Prof. H. C. Bumpus, Director, August 6, 1909, file 832 (1909–1911), box 203, Central Archives, AMNH.

49. Harlan I. Smith to Prof. H. C. Bumpus, Director, September 21, 1909, file 832 (1909–1911), box 203, Central Archives, AMNH.

50. M. C. D. "Foreword on the New Mural Paintings," 130.

51. Stephen C. Quinn, "A Guide to the Background Painters and Mural Artists of the Exhibit Halls of the American Museum of Natural History," February 1987, Library and Special Collections, AMNH.

52. Testimony of Tseshaht spokesperson Mr. Bill, May 11, 1914, RG10, vol. 11025, file AH13, LAC.

PART THREE

Narratives

CHAPTER EIGHT

Arrows and Sciences

Odd Displays for Another Brazil, 1840–1882

Maria Margaret Lopes, Mariza Corrêa, and Irina Podgorny

Caminhae um pouco pelo Brasil; estudae-lhe a terra, as plantas, os animaes, a gente . . . encontrareis, a cada passo, com as douradas pepitas que o velho Martius atirou à vossa estrada!

Walk around Brazil a bit; study the earth, the plants, the animals, the people . . . you will find with each step the golden nuggets that the wise Martius threw on your path.

—EDGAR ROQUETTE-PINTO[1]

Introduction

In 1838, several naturalists and men of letters gathered in Rio de Janeiro, capital of the Brazilian empire, to create the Instituto Histórico e Geográfico Brasileiro (IHGB).[2] Organized in committees or sections, the members of the institute, meeting on a regular basis, soon began to publish a journal. They organized competitions, promoted scientific expeditions, and gathered the colonial documents spread throughout Europe and all the provinces of Brazil. As the Brazilian historian Manoel L. L. S. Guimarães has shown, the IHGB soon became the privileged locus to discuss how to write the history of Brazil.[3] In Brazil, the discipline of history took shape in the framework of learned societies—modeled after the French academies of the eighteenth century—such as the IHGB.

The writing of Brazilian history accompanied the process of consolidation of a Brazilian constitutional monarchy, a centralized state, and an agrarian and slavery-based empire that began with the end of the wars of independence. The building of the country implied an emphasis on a national singularity relying on both an aggregate notion of the vast territory and the idea of a nation that would erase the existing social differences and turn the natural and cultural contrasts into marks of locality.[4] In this framework, contrary to the new republics of Spanish America, the Empire of Brazil was defined not by opposition to the Portuguese metropolis but as a continuation of the civilizing process that had begun with colonization.[5] Thus, the "philosophical voyages" from colonial times would be used as an inspiration and as a program to be continued by the naturalists of the empire.[6] In this context, the names of earlier Portuguese naturalists were honored everywhere; for instance, in the Sociedade Vellosiana—named after a botanist from the eighteenth century—a learned society was established to describe "the magnificent products of this land."[7] Tellingly, the society adopted as its emblem the branches of brazilwood (*Caesalpinia echinata*), recognizing that the history of Brazil could not be understood without reference to the early Portuguese commerce between India and the New World:[8] brazilwood, like other natural specimens, was also a monument to the early history of Brazil.

In 1840 the IHGB called for a prize to award to the author of the best guidelines on how to write the ancient and modern history of Brazil, a history that, as everybody agreed, was absolutely necessary. They decided to award the prize to Carl Friedrich von Martius, conservator of the botanical garden of Munich and professor of botany at the university there. Martius, who was sent by the king of Bavaria, had traveled in Brazil between 1817 and 1820. He produced an essay that, as many Brazilian scholars have already argued, became an important point of reference for contemporary and future historians. His suggestions would be followed not only by historians but, as the emblem of Sociedade Vellosiana shows, also by naturalists.

This chapter, in this vein, traces how the study of nature and the study of ancient history, as Martius suggested, were to be brought together by the initiatives of the IHGB in the decades to come. In particular, this chapter analyzes the materials collected to write the long history of the Native population as recommended by Martius and others, such as Peter Lund. As we will see, there was a shift in the practices of collecting and in the spaces where these materials were deposited: originally within the field of history—a field that was also to be organized by the pursuits of the

IHGB—their connection with expeditions, exhibitions, and the spaces of the museums transferred the materials almost exclusively to anthropology and to the discussions over the racial construction of Brazil. Thus, this chapter analyzes three important turning points in the writing of Brazilian history with regard to the past of the Natives: the publication of Martius's essay in the 1840s; the expedition to Ceará in the late 1850s; and finally, the anthropological exhibition at the Museu Nacional early in the 1880s—the latter an institution of growing importance for the institutionalization of Brazilian sciences.

How to Write the History of Brazil: The Materials for the History of the American Race

In his essay published in Brazil in 1844, Martius articulated several scientific models from the nineteenth century together with elements from eighteenth-century culture. He proposed that the history of Brazil should not lose sight of the diverse elements of nature that in Brazil had come together for the development of mankind. In particular, it had to include the history of the three ethnic groups that made up the present Brazilian population; namely, "the copper-colored or American race, the white or Caucasian race, and the black or Ethiopian race."[9] To write a Brazilian history meant to write the history of each group as an independent entity and of the interactions and mixtures among them over the last centuries. However, in order to do so, it was necessary to start collecting the materials indispensable to write such a history. Brazilians—as the IHGB's undertakings demonstrated[10]—had already begun to gather archival sources from colonial times, including Native vocabularies and missionaries' observations. But for Martius, Brazilian historians had still to investigate, minutely, the life and development of the aboriginal Americans—to extend their research to the period before the conquest and to scrutinize the history of the earliest inhabitants of Brazil, "a history that, at present, is neither divided in distinct epochs nor seems to offer visible monuments, a history that remains in obscurity, and for that very reason, highly excites our curiosity."[11]

By insisting on the investigation of precolonial periods, Martius questioned the prevailing idea that the Indians were a living representation of the primitive state of mankind—people who had no history because they had not changed abiding by the laws of time. On the contrary, argued Martius, the present-day population was the "relic of a very ancient history that was lost." Although he believed that the contemporary American race had degenerated from an opulent and vigorous state, this process implied the passage of a long—and as yet unknown—period of time.

However, where was one to find the documents to write such a long history if the Natives had left no written record and at a time when historians' privileged material basis was writing and inscriptions? For Martius, given the lack of written sources, it was important to study the outward manifestations of the "American race" as a physical entity and compare it with neighboring peoples. The next step would be to study their soul and intelligence, spiritual activity, and the manner in which "that manifested itself in historical documents" that is today the language of the Indians: their mythologies, theogonies, geogonies, superstitions, symbols and traditions of law, social and legal relationships, and their knowledge of nature.[12] Martius questioned the "scandalous work by Cornelius de Pauw" who had denigrated Native Americans as inferior. Instead, Martius invited Brazilian historians to take into account the recent discoveries of monumental buildings in Paupala, Uxmal, Copan, Quito, and Tiawanaco before starting to write the history of the American race. Although such monuments had not yet been discovered in Brazil, Martius remarked that the negative evidence did not preclude the possibility that in deep times there had not been a civilization similar to those discovered in other countries.[13] Local history, in such a way, implied also comparisons with other contexts, which furnished elements that predicted what kind of materials and data future investigations could provide.

The question about to how write the history of Brazil was also intrinsically connected with the study of Brazil's geography—with the study, collection, and description of Brazilian nature. Several questions brought natural history and history together: the search for origins, the study of Indian languages, and the vernacular names used to describe plants and animals. The study of native languages was not only a means for better understanding the indigenous names that designated natural products.[14] As Guimarães explained, it was "a manner of making sense of and approaching a nature (that was) so diverse."[15] On the other hand, archeology, paleontology, ethnography, and geology were seen as the disciplines that could give clues about origins based on what the investigations of fossils found in caves in Minas Gerais by the Danish naturalist Peter Wilhelm Lund (1801–1880) had proved: "the settlement in Brazil derives from rather remote eras undoubtedly prior to historical times . . . and the people that inhabited this part of the New World belonged to the same races as those that occupied the country during the period of the Discoveries."[16]

After having found in the caves of Lagoa Santa human remains associated with extinct fossil mammals, Lund placed himself in the arena of the new discipline that was going to be called "prehistory," a new science "in between geology and history."[17] For Lund, the antiquity of man in South America—namely, the contemporaneity of extinct fauna and humans that his discoveries seemed to prove—meant it was necessary to think about history in terms of geological times. Lund criticized the current opinions that held that the Natives of the Americas were the result of migrations and degeneration of the inhabitants of the Old World. After his findings in Lagoa Santa, anthropologists had to dismiss the idea that the American continent was geologically young.[18] Lund, like Martius, claimed that the American race of Brazil had a long history.

The question for both of them—as well as for the members of the IHGB—was how to collect reliable materials to write that history.[19] Lund was not only providing historical monuments for the history of Brazil: through him, the IHGB started corresponding with the Royal Antiquarian Society of Copenhagen, one of the most prestigious centers for the study of ancient monuments.[20] Thus, the discussions in the IHGB were fed from different sources, which they processed following their own interests and goals but that resulted in the collection of objects as diverse as fossils, antiquities, colonial documents, legends, and vocabularies.

Brazilians and Martius, on the other hand, were right when they compared their political and institutional stability with the situation of their republican neighbors from former Spanish America. While the writing of history and the compilation of documents and monuments was being organized and published by an institution such as the IHGB, in countries such as Argentina, the same initiatives were carried out by private entrepreneurs subject to the dynamics of the market.[21] Knowing the kind of support the IHGB could provide in terms of organizing funds and logistics, Martius suggested the IHGB should assist those traveling naturalists in pursuit of the historical monuments of the American race.[22]

The IHGB, in fact, backed several journeys of foreign naturalists and assessed the reliability of their results.[23] But the society went even further than that: as a national forum for the development of science in Brazil in 1856, it supported the proposal submitted by the Museu Nacional that the exploration of the country had to be done exclusively by local researchers and men of letters.[24] As a result, in 1859, a commission was dispatched to Ceará, in the northeastern part of Brazil, on the Atlantic coast.

Ethnology in the "Comissão das Borboletas"

On January 26, 1859, the Comissão Científica de Exploração, also known as Comissão do Ceará or "Commission of the Butterflies," left Rio de Janeiro aboard the steamboat *Tocantins* toward Ceará. Aiming at surveying the mineral resources and the topography for the construction of roads and the conversion of the Indians, the commission was one of the most important manifestations of the "inward expansion," as Ilmar Mattos has called the process of organizing the empire of Brazil.[25] Organized as a multidisciplinary undertaking, data were going to be collected divided in five sections: botany, geology and mineralogy, zoology, astronomy and geography, and ethnography. The commission was led by the directors of the National Museum and the faculty members from the schools for advanced studies based at court.[26] As they would say, Ceará was "among our provinces the one that has the fewest slaves and where the fewest individuals of pure Indian race can be found, is at the same time the province which presents the most beautiful and more characteristic types of the mixture of both races."[27]

Shaped by the ethnographic interest in indigenous names of plants, animals, and places and in the myths and costumes of the inhabitants of the *sertões*, or "backlands," the members of the ethnographical section followed special instructions, which repeated almost literally Martius's suggestions. The instructions indicated that they had to look for "the main elements that are useful to distinguish the human races: the physical organization, the intellectual and moral character, language and historical traditions."[28] However, they slightly shifted their interest considering that what they were collecting was not the basis for the writing of history but the "actual materials needed by the science of ethnology." The instructions to the zoological section explained that although "man occupies the top of the successive chain of animal creation," the zoologists were "dispensed from dealing with anthropology, for it was the exclusive responsibility of another member of the section of ethnography of the commission."[29]

On the other hand, the instruction for the ethnographic section, quoting Camper and Gall, said that they should take measurements of the bodies and heads of the Natives as "a necessary complement to the study of physical characters."[30] Alongside descriptions and drawings, heliographs, skulls, and molds of heads and faces, it was recommended to collect ornaments, tools, musical and war instruments; everything that could be used as evidence of their industry, habits, and customs, including mummies and sepultures, with special emphasis on the differences of behavior between men and women, the systems of beliefs, and myths.[31] This had to be accompanied by the study of language. Again, reminiscent of Martius's writings, the instructions insisted on the importance of grammars and dictionaries and on the words and names that structured Native languages. It was important also to gather all that referred to "strategic knowledge," namely, fortifications, medicine, surgery, meteorology, shape of their dwellings and towns, trade, time measurement, roads, means of orientations, use of plants, agriculture, and farming and animal husbandry. As Martius said, the instructions indicated that they gather the "acts of public law and those resembling international law" as well as those aspects connected with Native medicine, their tales, stories, and legends. The instructions also stated that "archeology by means of Vico's application and its ordinary tools could discover something about their origin or at least their particular history."[32] Even when the reference to Giambattista Vico (1668–1744) was a truism of those years, it reveals how the period's scholars perceived the role of the ethnographic section and the study of language: as Martius had expressed himself, it was the first step toward writing the history of those men and women they were going to meet. Language, myths, and laws were monuments that could reveal the past as well as the weapons and the mere human physical remains. Let us remember with Paolo Rossi and Arnoldo Momigliano that Giambattista Vico, in the *Scienza nuova*, spoke of "fossils" not referring to natural objects but to the "traces of a human presence": remains of skeletons and of ancient armor.[33] Myths, for Vico, were not just reconstructions of natural events but of events in social life: they are—as Rossi phrased it—"mythologized politics."[34] Asking for the languages and law of the American race in that sense was a first step to placing it within the history of nations. As Martius had suggested, collecting geogonies and theogonies had the same character as collecting historic monuments. Most importantly, they had to be recorded on paper, inscribing them into a medium that would definitively transform the vanishing sounds into a historic document. Therefore, the collections should be accompanied by a diary and, if possible, by copies of documents found in local archives related to the history and geography of the country. Praising the Indians, the inhabitants of the *sertão*, the fauna and flora in Brazilian romantic poetry, accompanied the search for the origins of humankind in the Americas supported by the idea that decadence and inevitable extinction were accelerated by contact with civilization. The Natives were seen as part of the history of the nation and, more importantly, there was an agreement on the fact that they had produced and were producing monuments and historical documents.[35]

The instructions brought together scientific interests, the preservation of Brazilian material culture, and the possibility of amassing materials for the national collections. It was also "very useful" to know the opinion of the Indians about "us, about their fundamental complaints, in order to study how to surpass these obstacles and to regain for industry such a lost workforce and to diminish the number of internal enemies."[36] This was the way by which "science put at the service of civilization" contributed to the debate about the free labor market and the promotion of industrialization as a road to progress in a period in which slave labor was at an end.[37]

The commission generated personal conflicts among its members and many controversies, which were published in the press and used as political accusations against the government.[38] Many of them originated in the fact that the commission did not fulfill the expectations it had raised. But whereas it did not find "half a dozen gold and silver mines," it succeeded in "gathering for the Museu Nacional a collection of products of the organic and inorganic kingdoms, everything that could be proof of the state of civilization, industry, uses and costumes of our Indians."[39] When the commission came back, the Museu Nacional organized the Exposição da Indústria Cearense (Ceará's Industry Exhibition), the first of a series of large public exhibitions that took place at the museum. Inspired by the world fairs, animals, samples of crops cultivated in the Northeast, and several kinds of wood were seen as close to the objects of Ceará's industry, such as the gourds, cups, plates, and bowls from the Inhamuns—"crafts that deserve to stand next to those from the Black Forest or Nuremberg"— the leather clothes of the *sertanejo*, or embroideries that could "compete with those from Flanders."[40]

The commission also revealed the anxieties of the period. To implant the natural sciences at home also meant to obtain recognition, fame, and prestige through the publicity of the work resulting from it. Brazilian naturalists were soon engaged in the consolidation of their scientific activities as autonomous fields of knowledge, which would bestow on them political prestige and professional recognition related to their supposed contribution to universal science. The Museu Nacional, which struggled since its origins in 1818 for more funds, more traveling naturalists, and more collections, profited enormously from the commission. Making its collections more representative of the natural resources of the country and consolidating itself as an official advisory body in matters of mining and agriculture, the Rio de Janeiro Museu Nacional lived its golden age in terms of scientific production from the middle of the 1870s onward. From then and up to the first decades of the twentieth century, the ethnographic and anthropological collections and researches, understood within the field of natural sciences, occupied the center of attention of the museum directors, in particular Ladislau Netto (1838–1894)—a botanist—who directed it from 1868 to 1893.[41] The making of the Brazilian Anthropological Exhibition at the Museu Nacional do Rio de Janeiro in 1882 was a sign of this lasting interest but also of the completion of the shift from history to anthropology. The institutionalization of anthropology at the Museu Nacional would fully absorb the study of the "copper-colored race."

The Exposição Antropológica Brasileira: An "Anthropological Boom"

As a landmark of the history of natural sciences and anthropology in Brazil, the Anthropological Exhibition from 1882 gathered more than just archaeological, ethnographical, and anthropological collections: it was mandatory for Brazil to be one of the first nations in the Americas to investigate its pre-Columbian past. In that sense, the exhibition displayed what had been done in that direction by the museum from the mid-nineteenth century on by bringing together the ethnographic materials from Ceará with the collections from several provincial museums and materials from different regions of the country.

Early in the 1870s, the national museum's fourth section, named "Numismatics, Liberal Arts, Archaeology and Uses and Costumes of Modern Nations" held the first collection of *sambaquis* (shell deposits similar to those found in Denmark). In 1872, the section of "Comparative Anatomy and Zoology" displayed eight human skeletons, and as the director was engaged in acquiring collections of skulls from different "races," in two years it had acquired twenty-four complete skeletons, sent by the presidents of the provinces, following Netto's request and instructions to take objects from indigenous burials.[42] In the institutional reform of 1876, the denomination "Anthropology" was added to the first section of zoology, and then animal paleontology was also incorporated.[43] The changes in the names and in the order of priority, besides showing the beginnings of a process of redrawing the limits of the disciplines, bear witness to the interests of the director himself and the relevance that the anthropological collections and research had already attained.[44] From 1888 onward, a fourth section was opened in the Museum, namely "Anthropology, Ethnology and Archaeology." As a consequence, anthropology was separate from zoology and became an independent section. In fact, from 1876, it became the domain of Netto, who aimed at transforming it into an independent archaeological and ethnographic museum. He was a follower of Ernest Théodore Hamy, who, distancing himself from anthropology as practiced by Paul Broca and his disciples, incorporated into his researches historical and ethnographical concerns.[45]

According to Netto, in Brazil, "shortly, the last vestiges of our indigenous tribes will no longer be visible. A large number of these noble and ancient nations—whose ethnic characters, the almost countless myths and chronicles could guide us in the study of their ancestors—would be gone forever." Fevers, smallpox and syphilis, as well as "the lack of food and the displacement from their ancient way of life, will reduce the populations still prosperous in the last century to a hundredth of a people. Many others had already been exterminated and their ruins engulfed by the forest."[46]

Praised by French anthropologists such as Broca and Quatrefages, Netto defined the museum's mission in the national and international panoramas: it was to outline the peculiarities of the Brazilian "race." Museum-based scientists were going to devote themselves to the study of the Natives on the verge of extinction, easily transformed into objects of science. Netto, who admired the ethnographic studies done by the North American geologist Charles Frederic Hartt in the Amazon, worried about the lack of funds and legislation that put at risk the work initiated by the naturalists of the museum. Netto would later not only hire Hartt for the museum[47] but also would arrange the purchase of 500,000 objects collected by the Imperial Geological Commission, organized by Hartt in the years 1877–1879. This collection, including numerous archeological and ethnographic objects, constituted the largest such collection ever incorporated into the museum.

In the museum journal, on the contrary, the articles devoted to zoological studies predominated over anthropology, ethnography, and archaeology, which represented 19% of a total of 131 papers published between 1876 and 1919. Interestingly, it published the first ethnological article written by a Brazilian woman, Maria do Carmo de Mello Rego, describing indigenous artifacts from Matto Grosso in the same year that Leolinda Daltro, another "sertanista," roamed the same region.[48] This paper reported on the quantity and quality of the materials taken to the Berlin Museum by Karl von Steinen, complaining again about the loss of materials to foreign collections. The Museu Nacional was also the institutional space where the first course in anthropology was taught in 1877. In the first year, the syllabus was devoted to human anatomy and physiology; in the second year, it was devoted to the study of races, especially in the Americas and in relation to heredity, miscegenation, and acclimatization. Monogenism, polygenism, and transformism were left for the end of the course. In the 1880s, the course was transformed into public lectures, and summaries were regularly published by Rio de Janeiro newspapers.

The allure of the Museu Nacional's anthropological collections and works was such that in 1882, Orville Adalbert Derby, the American director of the section of geology at the museum, reported that "there was a splendid opportunity for the Smithsonian to obtain the finest collection of Brazilian antiquities at a very low cost." Derby was rapidly forced to change his ideas and to inform his Washington friends that nothing could be done, for the museum lived a real "anthropological boom." In fact, its director dedicated a great deal of his time to gather "a very trustful exhibition in this field by means of which he managed to attract considerable attention of the public and assured the addition of a great amount of collections to the Museum." Derby promised to discuss this possibility further, considering "that the museum had a considerable debt towards the Smithsonian," and counseled the Smithsonian to send a model of a "Pueblo" to help him persuade Netto to send the archaeological collection to the American National Museum.[49]

To such an extent were the efforts of Netto that collections from almost all the provinces were sent to the Exposição Antropológica Brasileira, sponsored by the Ministry of Agriculture, including objects from the Indians in conflict in Manaus and casts of the bodies of Botocudos and Xerentes. From the Amazon, where Netto visited indigenous tribes to study their costumes and exhume bones from their cemeteries, came a collection gathered by the director of the Museu Paraense, inaugurated in Belem in 1871.[50]

The Exposição Antropológica Brasileira was indeed a success. Inaugurated in July 1882, it remained open for three months and received more than one thousand visitors, which was seen as a considerable public attendance. Some of the materials on display belonged to the emperor's cabinet, others to the National Museum's archaeological holdings or to private collections. It was accompanied by a collection of books and publications on ethnography and the Tupi and/or Guarani languages, all proceeding from the National Library. The collections were organized in eight rooms named after those who contributed to these studies in Brazil: Vaz de Caminha, Anchieta, and Rodrigues Ferreira (the three with ethnographic objects); Lery and Hartt (archaeological artifacts); Lund (materials related to anthropology); Martius (ethnography and archaeology); and Gabriel Soares (ethnography and archaeology). For this successful event, the emperor rewarded Netto with the Ordem da Rosa, the highest award of the empire.[51] In his opening speech, Netto summarized: "This is the largest national festival that the sciences and arts could proudly have imagined and transformed into reality with the aim of raising the Empire of Brazil to the level of universal erudition. . . . The National Museum is honored with the glory of undertaking it."[52] A German journalist resident in Brazil described the exhibition as it was in 1883, incorporated as part of the permanent exhibition:

> The famous Mundurucus room, after the most savage and warlike of the Brazilian tribes, was full of ethnological treasures, emphasis being given to the mummified heads—truly works of art, so well prepared that the art of the Egyptians looked pale in comparison to these realizations of the savages. There were also the plaster casts of the Indians, a teen in his seventeenth or eighteenth year and a 30-year-old warrior with his weapons. In contrast with these two figures, there were two mummies, rare and well preserved, proceeding from Bolivian and Peruvian tombs, a small man and a small woman, sitting in the position they were placed in the mortuary vases. There was also pottery, a large collection of stone weapons, and in the "Lund's Room" there were around 60 skeletons, besides the skulls of the savages, including the famous fossil skull of Lagoa Santa.[53]

The same journalist questioned the exhibition of objects from the Aleutian Islands and New Zealand, saying that while they were "very interesting things, they can be found in any European museum. The real treasures of our Museum are those that come from South America." Even today Brazilian historiography does not understand why the National Museum had Egyptian mummies or Etruscan collections: they were an essential part of the metropolitan character that Netto wanted for the museum. While the 1882 anthropological exhibition tended to address the local character of the collections, this did not involve abandoning the profile of a general and encyclopedic museum that characterized that institution from its origin. Netto combined the local with the universal, emphasizing the national contribution to the universality of science. Enthusiastic about the success of the exhibition, Netto started planning a Pan-American Anthropological Exhibition for 1884, dreaming of a monumental building to house it, and later, the museum.[54] He proposed that following the North American example, the government should open a national subscription to attract capitalists and rich landowners. The new exhibition, however, never took place, nor did the dreamed of construction of a new building.⁵⁵

Although the museums managed to keep a kind of hegemony over the national symbols, at the end of the nineteenth century some intellectuals began to lose interest in the past of the country as expressed in the museums and asked themselves how the present was preparing for the future. Soon after the abolition of slavery (1888) and the proclamation of the republic (1889), several Brazilian intellectuals came to realize "the impure and formidable mass of two million negroes, suddenly invested of constitutional prerogatives," which seemed at once to be too visible in the Brazilian population; thanks to the same "prerogatives," they all would be equal before the law from then on.

Martius's proposals, although ever present, were permanently reinterpreted in terms of a changing political situation but also in terms of the organization of scientific disciplines. In 1840, the history of Brazil was perceived as a dynamic totality that combined the history of three nations with the study of nature. The institutionalization of science in Brazil would divide history from ethnography and ethnology, but on the other hand, they were brought together with natural history in the space of expeditions and in the halls and deposits of the Museu Nacional. Martius's proposal would remain, as Edgar Roquette-Pinto, one of the future directors of the Museu Nacional, would say, a forgotten mark on a road that still had to be followed.

Acknowledgments

We would like to thank Philip L. Kohl and Stefanie Gänger for their comments. Maria Margaret Lopes and Mariza Corrêa would also like to thank Conselho Nacional de Desenvolvimento Científico e Tecnológico, Brazil for supporting their research.

Notes

1. Carl Friedrich Philipp von Martius, Pirajá da Silva,"Introdução" in *Natureza, doenças, medicina e remédios dos índios brasileiros (1844)* (Rio de Janeiro: Editora Nacional, 1939), xxii (all translations are ours). Accessed November 19, 2013, http://www.brasiliana.com.br/obras/natureza-doencas-medicina-e-remedios-dos-indios-brasileiros-1844/preambulo/6/texto.

2. Lúcia M. P. Guimarães, "Debaixo da imediata proteção de Sua Majestade Imperial," *Revista do Instituto Histórico e Geográfico Brasileiro* 388 (1995): 459–613;

F. de M. Figueirôa Silvia, "Associativismo científico no Brasil: O IHGB como espaço institucional para as ciências naturais durante o século XIX," *Interciencia* 7, no. 13 (1992): 141–46.

3. Manoel L. L. S. Guimarães, "Nação e civilização nos trópicos: O Instituto Histórico Geográfico Brasileiro e o projeto de uma história nacional," *Revista Estudos Históricos* 1 (1988): 5–27, accessed October 22, 2013, http://bibliotecadigital.fgv.br/ojs /index.php/reh/article/view/1935/1074; "História e natureza em von Martius: Esquadrinhando o Brasil para construir a nação," *História, Ciência, Saúde-Manguinhos* 7, no. 2 (2000): 391–41, accessed November 20, 2013, doi:10.1590/S0104-59702000 000300008.

4. Sandra J. Pesavento, "Acertar o passo com a história: O dilema da modernidade brasileira no século XIX," *Quipu* 9, no. 2 (1992): 217–36.

5. Guimarães, "Nação e civilização," 6. See Irina Podgorny and Maria M. Lopes, *El desierto en una vitrina: Museos e historia natural en la Argentina, 1810–1890* (Mexico City: Editorial Limusa, 2008), about the topic spread after independence all over Spanish America, about how Spain had ruled "dejando a sus pueblos en la más complete ignorancia."

6. Maria M. Lopes, "The Scientific Exploration Commission: An inward expansion," in *Comissão Científica do Império 1859–1861*, ed. Lorelay Kury (Rio de Janeiro: Andrea Jakobsson Editora, 2009), 233–38.

7. Friar Jose Mariano da Conceição Velloso (1741–1811) finished his *Flora fluminense* in 1790 with over 1,600 species described and drawn. His work remained unpublished until the mid-nineteenth century.

8. "Annual report read in the first session of 1852," in *Trabalhos da Sociedade Vellosiana* (Rio de Janeiro: Bibliotheca Guanabarense, 1853). As Carl von Martius had said, the history of Brazil was intrinsically related to the commercial history of the Asian sappanwood, a tree that as the so-called brazilwood from South America produced a valued type of reddish dye called "brazilian." Carl Friedrich Philipe von Martius, "Como se deve escrever a história do Brasil," *Revista do Instituto Histórico e Geográfico Brasileiro* 6, no. 24 (1845): 391.

9. Martius, "Como se deve escrever a história do Brasil," 381–82.

10. Kaori Kodama, *Os índios no Império do Brasil: A etnografia do IHGB entre as décadas de 1840 e 1860* (Rio de Janeiro: Editora Fiocruz/EDUSP, 2009).

11. Martius, "Como se deve escrever a história do Brasil," 384–85.

12. Ibid., 386–87.

13. Ibid., 388. See the recent discovery of two ancient pyramid complexes near the town of Jaen (in Peru, close to the border with Ecuador), on the western edge of the Amazon lowland by Quirino Olivera.

14. "Letters and Documents referent to Sociedade Vellosiana," Documents, folder 4, 1851, Museu Nacional Rio de Janeiro.

15. Guimarães, "História e natureza em von Martius," 393.

16. Peter W. Lund, "Letter Written to the Secretary of the IHGB by the Honorary Fellow Dr. W. Lund from Lagoa Santa (Minas Gerais)," *Revista do Instituto Histórico e Geográfico Brasileiro* 4 (1842): 84. See Maria M. Lopes, "Cenas de tempos profundos: Ossos, viagens, memórias nas culturas da natureza no Brasil," *História, Ciência, Saúde-Manguinhos* 15, no. 3 (2008): 615–34, accessed November 20, 2013, doi:10.1590/ S0104-59702008000300004.

17. Irina Podgorny, *El sendero del tiempo y de las causas accidentales: Los espacios de la prehistoria en la Argentina, 1850–1910* (Rosario: Prohistoria, 2009).
18. Maria M. Lopes, "Parentesco entre los muertos y los vivos nas cavernas de Lagoa Santa, no Brasil," *Anuario Instituto de Estudios Historico Sociales* 25 (2010): 353–76.
19. Paolo Rossi, *The Dark Abyss of Time: The History of the Earth and the History of Nations*, trans. Lydia G. Cochrane (Chicago: University of Chicago Press, 1984).
20. Lúcia. M. P. Guimarães, "Uma parceria inesperada: O Instituto Histórico e Geográfico Brasileiro e a Real Sociedade dos Antiquários do Norte," *Revista do Instituto Histórico e Geográfico Brasileiro* 155, no. 384 (1994): 499–511.
21. Irina Podgorny, "Fossil Dealers, the Practices of Comparative Anatomy and British Diplomacy in Latin America, 1820–1840," *British Journal for the History of Science* 46, no. 4 (2012): 647–74, accessed November, 23, 2013, doi:10.1017/S0007087412000702.
22. Martius, "Como se deve escrever a história do Brasil," 389.
23. Silvia F. de M. Figueirôa, *A formação das ciências geológicas no Brasil: Uma história social e institucional, 1875–1934* (Sao Paulo: Hucitec, 1997), 78–88.
24. Maria M. Lopes, "Mais vale um jegue que me carregue, que um camelo que me derrube . . . lá no Ceará." *História, Ciência, Saúde-Manguinhos* 7, no. 1 (1996): 50–64. For a detailed account of the commission, see Renato Braga, *História da Comissão Científica de Exploração* (Fortaleza: Imprensa Universitária do Ceará, 1962); Lorelai Kury, ed., *Comissão Científica do Império, 1859–1861* (Rio de Janeiro: Andrea Jakobsson Editora, 2009).
25. Ilmar R. de Mattos, "Construtores e herdeiros: A trama dos interesses na construção da unidade política," *Almanack Braziliense* 1 (2005): 8–26.
26. The heads of the sections of the commission were Francisco Freire Alemão (botany), professor of the School of Medicine and later director of the Museu Nacional—one of the main Brazilian botanists, he was president of the Sociedade Vellosiana and the commission; Guilherme Schüch de Capanema (geology); Manuel Ferreira Lagos (zoology)—adjunct to the first section of comparative anatomy and zoology of the Museu Nacional, secretary of the IHGB, and one of the main organizers of the commission; Giacomo Raja Gabaglia (astronomy and geography); and Antonio Gonçalves Dias (ethnography and journey narrative)—romantic poet and teacher of Latin in the main secondary school of Rio de Janeiro, the Colégio D. Pedro II.
27. "Letter from the Scientific Commission," *Jornal do Commercio*, May 30, 1859.
28. Luiz P. do Couto Ferraz, "Instrucções para a Commissão Scientífica encarregada de explorar o interior de algumas províncias do Brasil," in *Trabalhos da Comissão Científica às províncias Nordeste do Brasil* (Rio de Janeiro, 1862), xxxix.
29. Ibid., xxi.
30. Ibid., xl.
31. Ibid., xli.
32. Ibid., xliv.
33. Rossi, *Dark Abyss of Time*, 104. Arnaldo Momigliano, "Vico's *Scienza nuova*: Roman 'Bestioni' and Roman 'Eroi,'" *History and Theory* 5, no. 1 (1966): 3–23.
34. Lia Formigari, "Droit, mythe et langage dans la *Scienza nuova* de Giambattista Vico," in *Lingua et traditio: Geschichte der Sprachwissenschaft und der neueren

Philologien: Festschrift für Hans Helmut Christmann zum 65. Geburtstag, ed. R. Baum, K. Böckle, F. J. Hausmann, and F. Lebsanft (Tübingen: Gunter Narr, 1994), 89–96.

35. Kaori Kodama, "Em busca da gênese do Brasil nas províncias do norte: Gonçalves Dias e os trabalhos etnográficos da Comissão Científica de Exploração," in *Comissão Científica do Império (1859–1861)*, ed. Lorelai Kury (Rio de Janeiro: Andrea Jakobsson Editora, 2009), 115–53.

36. Couto Ferraz, "Instrucções," xliv.

37. Maria S. P. Alegre, "O Brasil descobre os Sertões, a Expedição Científica de 1859 ao Ceará," *Ciências Sociais Hoje* (1989): 209.

38. This seems to be the rule; see, e.g., Podgorny, chap. 6 in this volume, and also Irina Podgorny,"Los reyes del diluvio: La geología del cenozoico sudamericano en la década de 1880," in *Vida y Obra de Florentino Ameghino: Publicación Especial 12*, ed. Asociación Paleontológica Argentina (Buenos Aires: Asociación Paleontológica Argentina, 2011), 21–34, on the conflicts generated among the members of the scientific expeditions organized by the national governments.

39. Manoel F. Lagos, "Oficio apresentado em 30 de maio de 1856," *Revista do Instituto Histórico e Geográfico Brasileiro* 19 (1856): 12.

40. Ibid. The activities of the commission at the Museu Nacional continued until 1867. See Maria M. Lopes, *O Brasil descobre a pesquisa científica: As ciências naturais e os museus no século XIX*, 2nd ed. (São Paulo: HUCITEC, UnB, 2009), 128–43.

41. Lopes, *O Brasil descobre a pesquisa científica*, 158–204.

42. Maria M. Lopes, "O local musealizado em nacional: Aspectos da cultura das ciências naturais no século XIX, no Brasil," in *Ciência, Civilização e Império nos Trópicos*, ed. Alda Heizer and Antonio A. P. Videira (Rio de Janeiro: ACCESS, 2001), 77–96.

43. The sections of the museum were (1) Anthropology, General and Applied Zoology, Comparative Anatomy, and Animal Paleontology; (2) General and Applied Botany and Plant Paleontology; (3) Physical Sciences: Mineralogy, Geology, and General Paleontology.

44. Maria M. Lopes, "The Museums and the Construction of Natural Sciences in Brazil in the 19th Century," in *Cultures and Institutions of Natural History*, ed. Michael T. Ghiselin and Alan E. Leviton (San Francisco: California Academy of Sciences, 2000), 81–100.

45. Elizabeth A. Williams, "Art and Artifact at the Trocadero: Ars Americana and the Primitivist Revolution," in *Objects and Others: Essays on Museums and Material Culture*, ed. W. Stocking Jr. (Madison: University of Wisconsin Press, 1985), 146–66. This would lead to the establishment of the Musée d'ethnographie du Trocadéro (1878).

46. Ladislau de S. M. Netto, *Le Muséum national de Rio de Janeiro et son influence sur les sciences naturelles au Brésil* (Paris: Delagrave, 1889), 19.

47. Lopes, *O Brasil descobre a pesquisa científica*, 158–204.

48. Mariza Corrêa, "Os índios do Brasil elegante e a Professora Leonilda Daltro," *Revista Brasileira de História* 9, no. 18 (1989): 43–65.

49. Archives Record Unit 7078, Richard Rathbun Papers 1870–1918, Box 3, folder 6, Correspondence, Derby, Orville A. 1881–1904, Letters January 14, 1882, April 19, 1882, and August 4, 1882, Smithsonian Institution. Maria M. Lopes is grateful to Pamela Henson and the staff of the Smithsonian Institution Archives for access to that documentation.

50. When in 1894 the Swiss naturalist Emil August Goeldi left his position at the zoology section of the Museu National because of disagreements with Netto, he became director of the Museu Paraense, where he noted that several collections were lacking, and he accused the National Museum of growing at the expense of other institutions, taking objects as "loans" with the pretext of giving more volume to the anthropological exhibition. See Lopes, *O Brasil descobre a pesquisa científica*, 248–65.

51. Lopes, "O local musealizado em nacional," 77–96.

52. Ladislau de S. M. Netto, "Prefácio," in *Archivos do Museu Nacional do Rio de Janeiro* (Rio de Janeiro: Museo Nacional, 1885), 6:iii.

53. Carl von Koseritz, *Imagens do Brasil* (São Paulo: Belo Horizonte, 1980), 90.

54. Maria M. Lopes, "Nobles rivales: Estudios comparados entre el Museo Nacional de Río de Janeiro y el Museo Público de Buenos Aires," in *La ciencia en la Argentina entre siglos: Textos, contextos e instituciones*, ed. Marcelo Montserrat (Buenos Aires: Manantial, 2000), 277–96.

55. Luiz de Castro Faria, *As exposições de antropologia e arqueologia do Museu Nacional* (Rio de Janeiro: Imprensa Nacional, 1949).

CHAPTER NINE

Manifest Destiny as the Order of Nature

Alice Beck Kehoe

Guiana is a country that hath yet her maidenhead, never sacked, turned, nor wrought; the face of the earth hath not been torn, nor the virtue and salt of the soil spent by manurance. The graves have not been opened for gold, the mines not broken with sledges, nor the images pulled down out of their temples.

—WALTER RALEIGH[1]

America may with much Propriety be called the youngest Brother and meanest of Mankind; no Civil Government, no Religion, no Letters; the French call them Les Hommes des Bois, or Men-Brutes of the Forrest: They do not cultivate the Earth by planting or grazing: Excepting a very inconsiderable Quantity of Mays or Indian Corn, and of Kidney-Beans . . . which some of their Squaas or Women plant; they do not provide for To-Morrow, their Hunting is their necessary Subsistence not Diversion; when they have good luck in Hunting, they eat and sleep until all is consumed and then go a Hunting again.

—WILLIAM DOUGLASS[2]

Successful colonization raised questions of legitimacy. By what right did European invaders dispossess America's aborigines? The question was not purely philosophical, although John Locke framed it that way; it was contested by the European powers wanting to exploit America. Spain conquered with its armies while its clerics and philosophers debated Indians' rights. Britain and other latecomers appealed to international law, particularly the right of first discovery. To argue this doctrine, the occupiers had to obfuscate the obvious fact that North America was populated by millions of people when Europeans landed on its shores. Labeling those people "brutes of the forests," transliterating the French *sauvage* as "savage," transformed a question of sovereign rights into a matter of natural history.[3] Lacking native empires such as Tawantisuyu or that of the Mexica, North America was described as a wilderness. With the eighteenth-century Enlightenment's passion for ordering the things of this world, America's aborigines became objects for classification along with the continent's flora and other fauna. This Enlightenment attitude persisted in archaeology, tagging the precontact past as "prehistory" and detaching it from histories commencing with European imperial enterprises.

Michel Foucault invoked Don Quixote to characterize Enlightenment efforts to transcend the "classical" period in science, based on ordering phenomena by similarities, by finding actual objects already known by representations in the literature.[4] American archaeology reverses the image in that the discipline built windmills against which First Nations' descendants tilt with poor effect. Consolidating disjunction with ethnohistory, mainstream American archaeology constructed classifications for found data, rejecting "unscientific" terms such as "kingdom" in favor of academic models, for example, "chiefdoms."[5] The result has been barely concealed racism, acknowledged in the formation of the World Archaeological Congress in 1986 and tentatively addressed early in the present century by "indigenous archaeologies" and "historicizing" recapitulations such as Sassaman's 2010 study of the Eastern Archaic.[6] Both these twenty-first-century approaches reject the conventional position that North American Indians lived outside history on a continent unaffected, as Walter Raleigh alleged, by any forms of human labor.

The Sixteenth to the Nineteenth Century: Jefferson's Merciless Savages

In the fifteenth and sixteenth centuries, feudalism's decline and the rise of centralized states, abetted by Protestants' break with Rome, facilitated capitalist enterprise. Not only Columbus's patrons, the Spanish monarchs and their dynasty, but also governments and corporations of wealthy nobles and merchants in the rest of Europe sponsored and financed both industrial development in their own countries and colonization abroad. During the Elizabethan era, Englishmen likened wild nature to a seductive woman whose veil they will rip away, to thrust themselves in and penetrate her secret places, to possess her and take what she can produce with labor.[7]

This politico-economic view of nature pervaded seventeenth-century conflicts between Stuart royalists and English landed proprietors determined to keep their parliament and Magna Carta power. They rationalized estate agriculture through experiment and the Enclosure Acts permitting them to disrupt peasant subsistence by turning common grounds into agribusinesses. John Locke promoted this agrarian capitalism.[8] Employed by the Earl of Shaftesbury, leader of opposition to the royalists, and also one of the gentleman proprietors of the Carolina Colony, Locke brilliantly built the argument that "unimproved" nature was an affront to God:

> God and his [man's] reason commanded him to subdue the earth. . . .
> He gave it to the use of the industrious and rational (and labour was to be his title to it). . . . So that God, by commanding to subdue, gave authority so far to appropriate: and the condition of human life, which requires labour and materials to work on, necessarily introduces private possessions.[9]

An American Indian was "wild . . . knows no enclosure, and is still a tenant in common."[10] Indians did not use metallic money, the means of converting perishable products into durable wealth that can be used to enlarge landholding and production. Money is, logically according to Locke, the culmination of God's "great commission" to mankind to subdue the earth.[11] Christians transmogrify nature into money.

Leaders of the American Revolution used Locke's *Second Treatise of Government* as a "canonical text,"[12] justifying both appropriation of Indian lands and their own rejection of the British Crown's proclamation of sovereign title to those lands. The United States, no less than Canada, perpetuated the English ideology of divine mandate to create enclosures of plowed territory with carpentered structures, representing capital exchangeable for money. That which did not have written legal title documents was, as Locke said, "waste." Its inhabitants were wastrels, or worse. Thomas Jefferson claimed, in the Declaration of Independence, that they were "merciless Indian Savages, whose known rule of warfare, is an undistinguished destruction of all ages, sexes and conditions."[13] When he became president,

Jefferson professed a desire to "civilize" the Indians while telling Congress in 1803, in a secret message, that his real aim was to maneuver the Indian nations into moving west, giving up frontier territories.[14] He was constrained by that British proclamation of 1763 announcing Crown title to Indian lands, a principle adopted by the United States in 1792 as Article I of the U.S. Constitution.[15]

Duplicitous regarding American First Nations, Jefferson was straightforward about the value of taking over the continent and cataloging its riches. He encouraged gentlemen traveling along and beyond the frontier to take notes, make maps, and collect specimens of landscape, geology, flora, fauna, and Indian life,[16] culminating in his explicit instructions in 1803 to Captain Lewis for the Corps of Discovery. He also directed the creation of the U.S. Public Land Survey, accepted by the Continental Congress in 1785. By law, most of the United States was to be professionally surveyed and divided into regular, rectangular townships, mapping an immense grid on the continent. So systematic a project was fully in the Enlightenment spirit, epitomized perhaps by Linnaeus's powerful classification of all organisms into his *Systema naturae*.

The Nineteenth and Twentieth Centuries: Manifest Destiny

Anglo America in the early nineteenth century officially, under international law's doctrine of discovery, covered the entire continent north and east of Mexico and California, excluding Russian America in the far northwest. The United States actively pursued actual dominion, mapping and recording its domain. By the 1840s, its citizens were straining against the frontier of the Louisiana Purchase. Canada, too, was straining, its vast territory of Rupert's Land coming under governance by the Hudson's Bay Company chief officer, George Simpson. Like Jefferson, Simpson ordered his subordinates to collect artifacts and information about the Indian nations they dealt with. It would be another generation before Canadians obtained status as a British Commonwealth nation in 1867. The United States had by that time consolidated through wars its continental reach and national unity. It was fulfilling, said its citizens, its "manifest destiny."

That slogan was advanced in 1845 by a journalist, John O'Sullivan, in the magazine he edited, the *Democratic Review,* and then in the *New York*

Morning News. Urging U.S. title to Oregon Territory, O'Sullivan declared "that claim is by the right of our manifest destiny to overspread and to possess the whole of the continent which Providence has given us for the development of the great experiment of liberty and federated self-government."[17] Soon, "the whole of the continent" was seen to encompass Texas, Mexico, and California. Mexicans, and especially the majority, who were in fact Indians, were "degraded." Fortunately, "no race is so degenerate as to be beyond the influences of the agencies which a kind Providence has arranged in these latter days for the redemption of all his children."[18] Reflecting Locke, another newspaper editor called for "regenerating Mexico by the axe, the hoe and the plough."[19] Mexico, after three and a half centuries of Spanish development, could hardly be said to be wilderness, but its indigenous population was no better than savages and impossible to raise to the status of citizens.[20] Lewis Henry Morgan knew that none of them could possibly have built cities. In a magazine article in 1876 and then in his 1877 book *Ancient Society,* Morgan asserted that "The Aztec monarchy should be dismissed from American aboriginal history, not only as delusive, but as a misrepresentation of the Indians."[21] Typical of ideologues, Morgan made no effort to personally see the monuments recognized by Jefferson, von Humboldt, and others; nor to read several best-selling travel books; nor (most inexcusably, because they were acquainted) to consider the writings of the pioneer scientific archaeologist Daniel Wilson.[22]

Completing America's destiny to reach from sea to shining sea launched a set of exploring expeditions organized to secure a wide range of scientific data. Funding and arrangements were zealously pursued by the zoologist Spencer Baird, appointed assistant secretary of the Smithsonian Institution in 1850. Three years after his appointment, Baird boasted that "The string of scientific expeditions which I have succeeded in starting is perfectly preposterous."[23] Indian Affairs had been administered under the federal Department of War until 1849, when they were transferred to the newly created Department of the Interior. Twenty years later, Congress stated it was still permissible to "detail officers of the U.S. Army to act as Indian agents."[24] Until 1871 when Congress ended the practice of making treaties with Indian "tribes," the Indians held a peculiar status as "domestic dependent nations," a phrase created by Supreme Court Justice John Marshall in deciding *Cherokee Nation v. Georgia,* 1831. Throughout the nineteenth and twentieth centuries, U.S. courts continued to describe American Indians as "savages . . . wandering" lands to which they could not hold title.[25]

Consequences for Archaeology

Contrasting dramatically with nineteenth-century European nations, Anglo America recognized no patrimony within its territories for its citizens. Civilization was imported by emigrant settlers. Where in Denmark and Scotland prehistoric roots were sought and demonstrated,[26] in the United States and Canada the vestiges of earlier societies were often attributed to non-Indian precursors of contact-era indigenous nations or simply ignored.[27] Ohio's huge Hopewell geometric earthworks did draw interest, with a number of descriptions and diagrams published beginning in 1787, leading to the founding of the American Antiquarian Society in 1812 with its first publication the 1820 report of Caleb Atwater on the Newark (Ohio) works and to the Smithsonian's first monograph, the 1848 *Ancient Monuments of the Mississippi Valley* (including the Ohio River region).[28]

Perpetuating the picture of America as wilderness waste inhabited by "men-brutes," manifest destiny ideology focused post–Mexican War scientific fieldwork on finding and cataloging the country's resources, unveiling nature through expeditions led by military men. Primarily, these expeditions sought the best route for a transcontinental railroad. All the possibilities ran through territories defended by First Nations. An aftermath of the Civil War was President, formerly General, Grant's turning the otherwise unemployed U.S. Army to the final "pacification" of these nations. Among the veterans was John Wesley Powell, who made a heroic river traverse of the Grand Canyon—passing Havasupai villages that lived down there for centuries. Geology was Powell's principal interest, geological and geomorphological features being keys to minerals, agricultural potential, and transportation routes.[29] His and others' expeditions brought back artifacts as well as flora, fauna, and mineral specimens, eventually forcing Congress to approve in 1879 taking control of the Smithsonian and giving it a museum building. In 1879, Powell convinced Congress to create within this a Bureau of Ethnology (later, Bureau of American Ethnology) and appoint him its director. Despite being a disciple of Morgan's racist cultural evolution, Powell was remarkably broadminded in tolerating bureau employees whose convictions and research conclusions disagreed with Morgan's. Historian Dorothy Ross credits Powell with influencing social scientists as well as those engaged in natural history research.[30] Most relevant for archaeology was Cyrus Thomas's project to resolve the issue of who were the mound builders. Thomas's 1894 report, carrying the imprimatur of the U.S. government, said they were ancestors of the "domestic, dependent" Indian nations.

Aleš Hrdlička, curator of the division of physical anthropology at the Smithsonian National Museum of Natural History, 1903 until 1941, insisted in 1915 that

> the only possible conclusions on the two important questions . . . that the American aborigines represent a single race, and that the presence of this race on this continent is of no demonstrated geological antiquity . . . [the] beginning of migration into America . . . would be somewhere between ten thousand years ago and the dawn of the historic period in the Old World.[31]

Formidably energetic and strong in his opinions, Hrdlička did archaeological and museum collection research on all continents beginning in 1898. His 1915 conclusion was based on hard-nosed demand for well-supported data,[32] which in practice meant tangible collections of skeletal and geological specimens.[33] Hrdlička thus, as Ashley Montagu remarked, fit into nineteenth-century science's mode of natural history specimen comparisons. In Hrdlička's case his stringent empiricism freed him from racist pronouncements while precluding greater sensitivity to ideological issues.

Gordon Willey and Jeremy Sabloff label 1840–1960 the classificatory period of American archaeology.[34] This is certainly true so far as it goes. They state that between 1840 and 1914 (i.e., although they do not mention it, from the Mexican to the Great War), "archaeologists struggled to make archaeology into a systematic scientific discipline." Notwithstanding that Daniel Wilson was, they admit, "relatively advanced for the time," he merits in their view only one paragraph in a volume of 384 pages.[35] Focused on establishing chronology as the sine qua non of archaeology,[36] Willey and Sabloff did not see beyond Hrdlička's short-chronology argument to the pervasive racism Wilson sought to undermine by proclaiming that *all* humans are "a clothing, cooking, fire-making, tool-using animal . . . distinguished from all other animals by certain characteristics which seem to point to civilization as his normal condition."[37] Unequivocally challenging prevailing contrasts between civilized Europeans and the savages they dispossessed, Daniel Wilson has been disregarded by historians of archaeology while the copycat 1865 *Pre-Historic Times* by Wilson's rich, advantageously situated, plagiarizing contemporary Sir John Lubbock is routinely cited as the cornerstone of nonclassical archaeology.[38] Lubbock pictured for America such men-brutes as Tierra del Fuegians (whose subsistence had been destroyed by commercial seal hunting) nearly naked on a beach, witnesses for the continent's state of savagery.

If anyone doubts the force of colonialist ideology on archaeology in the Americas, let them visit a museum. Which museum for North American antiquities? Museums of natural history. That dichotomy between civilizations and the savages has multiple permanent monuments in stone in the form of museums of art and museums of natural history. Symbolically east and west in mid-Manhattan, the Metropolitan Museum of Art houses Classical archaeology and later formal art, while straight westward across Central Park, the American Museum of Natural History contains all the archaeology and historical ethnography of the Americas. The same division is seen in Washington, D.C., between the National Museum of American [U.S.] History and the National Gallery of Art, and the Museum of Natural History and the recent National Museum of the American Indian, where American First Nations artifacts are to be seen. Chicago has its Art Institute and a little south along the lakefront, the Field Museum of Natural History, with American Indian and other colonized continents' exhibits. (And to take colonization all the way, in Daniel Wilson's native Edinburgh, the National Museum of Scotland holds Sir George Simpson's collection from the Hudson's Bay Company's First Nations customers.)

Archaeology as a Colonial Enterprise

What did European imperial ideology mean to the archaeologist in the trench, he whose "jeans had been through the mud and the barbed-wire fences of countless field seasons, his hat had faded in the prairie sun, and his eyes had the kind of crow's feet known locally as the High Plains squint. [One] could tell he was an archeologist by his boots."[39] He (and it was preponderantly "he") was trained to meticulously lay out grids of squares; dig stratigraphically in arbitrary level segments; photograph, measure, and diagram every visible distinction; wash, measure, catalog, and classify every artifact. He understood how to knap cryptocrystalline stone and could identify the components of ceramics. All this was good science, replicable and observable by every sufficiently trained witness. It was also, Dorothy Ross remarked, "aggressively masculine."[40]

American archaeology's long-standing premise that North America had no history until Europeans invaded flattened interpretations. Martin, Quimby, and Collier's widely used 1947 textbook *Indians Before Columbus* taught that archaeology discerned three stages in the American Indian past: archaic—hunting and gathering from ca. 20,000 BCE to CE 900;

intermediate—CE 900–1300 (maize agriculture, ceramics); and late prehistoric—CE 1300–1600. Radiocarbon dating soon revolutionized chronologies, placing maize cultivation to second millennium BCE and ceramics to first millennium BCE without dislodging the flattened sociology of bands, tribes, and chiefdoms. The textbook assures readers that archaeological research into preconquest North America is more than an esoteric pastime: "If through anthropology we can understand all the facets of life in a relatively simple culture . . . then we are better able to understand and attack the greater and more complex problems" of our present atomic-bomb-threatened world.[41] America's past was not a patrimony; it was a case study for the anthropological laboratory, a passive land that "hath yet her maidenhead." Tearing off her mantle of soil, archaeologists could classify and systematize her ornaments, then shelve them with trilobite fossils and passenger-pigeon skins in the natural history museum. They came from Jefferson's "merciless savages beyond our frontiers."

Seventeenth-century philosopher and scientist Robert Hooke believed Nature to be female, "a power in itself wholly unactive" until awakened by men.[42] With this attitude, archaeologists could explain the American past as a record of ecological functionalism,[43] human groups adapting like other species in the wilderness to changes in the environment or demography. The American past lay beyond the frontier of civilization. Socialized in the dominant ideology, the majority of archaeologists accepted the meager remnants of the American past as sufficient to know it, just as the way paleontologists can know extinct organisms by their fossilized remains. Twentieth-century archaeologists prided themselves on not being antiquarians enthralled by texts and art. Scientific method and rigorous analysis yield hard truths to be expressed in professional terminology. Archaeological "cultures" are composed of imperishable artifacts classified binomially (e.g., Talking Crow Punctate) and diagrammed showing modification through time as established by stratigraphy. Changes in the environment provoked changes in shelter structures and diet. Given that North American aborigines had not achieved civilizations—Morgan's teaching—evidence that some sites seemed to indicate hierarchical relationships among the occupants drew the label "chiefdom," soon subdivided into "simple chiefdom" or "complex chiefdom." Never mind that ethnologists protested that the academic term is without actual exemplars.[44] Susan Alt illustrates the astounding reductionism coming out of mainstream American archaeology in her denouement of its standard interpretation of the great medieval city of Cahokia.[45]

Indigeneity

At the end of the twentieth century, increase in First Nations populations, especially an increase in formally educated members fluent in American political discourse, began to shift power over archaeological activities out of professional archaeologists' authority.[46] A 1992 amendment to the (1966) National Historic Preservation Act allowed "Indian tribes" to create Tribal Historic Preservation Offices (THPO) to supervise cultural resource management on tribal territories, removing that jurisdiction from State Historic Preservation Offices. Along with the Native American Grave Protection and Repatriation Act (NAGPRA, 1990), ordering American Indian physical remains and grave goods to be tallied and returned on request to affiliated tribes, the THPO amendment officially recognized that First Nations sites and relics originated with *fully human* communities. Against Locke's shadow hovering yet in public stereotypes, American aborigines now were held to have lived in civil societies where they exercised title to their lands (if not precisely in "fee simple") and improved on raw nature to make things of value. Taking a cue from the legal circumstances, some American archaeologists began emphasizing humanities-oriented "historical" data and models.[47] A few became active in groups debating indigenous issues of sovereignty and intellectual property rights.[48] Others planned archaeological projects training First Nations youth. Truly turning the tables, because the number of First Nations members who are qualified archaeologists has been too small to staff THPO needs, tribes brought in non-Indian archaeologists to be their employees. Their projects integrate landscapes and artifacts with First Nations histories stretching back centuries earlier than the European invasions. American First Nations, no longer part of the order of nature, can be seen within the millennia-old global ecumene.

Historicity raises its own issues. On one level, determining "descendant communities" with standing to request repatriation can become an adversarial court battle. On a deeper level, no histories are straightforward chronicles or lineages. Just look at Britain's royal family's German members— Georg of Hanover, Albert of Saxe-Coburg, Phillip Battenberg—expunged to counter antipathy to Germany in World War I.[49] The Kennewick Man controversy illustrates the opposite, a particular small community claiming a man who lived 9,400 years ago, with no known links in the intervening ten millennia.[50] If this man had children, if the children had children, on through the millennia, thousands of living American Indians could be his descendants, and they could be scattered throughout North America.

Complications do not stop at the issue of thousands or of no possible descendants of Kennewick. Claim to his skeleton has been led by Colville Reservation, a creation of the United States in 1872. The Confederated Tribes of the Colville Reservation comprise over 9,365 descendants of 12 aboriginal tribes of Indians enrolled in the confederation. The tribes, commonly known by English and French names, are the Colville, the Nespelem, the San Poil, the Lake, the Palus, the Wenatchi (Wenatchee), the Chelan, the Entiat, the Methow, the southern Okanogan, the Moses Columbia, and the Nez Perce of Chief Joseph's Bands.[51]

Before dispossession, these nations occupied territories stretching across Idaho and northern Washington states, most speaking Salish languages, Chief Joseph's Band speaking Sahaptin. On the National Park Service, U.S. Government website for "Kennewick Man Controversy," the leading claimants are listed as "Umatilla, Yakama, Nez Perce, Wanapum and Colville." Umatilla, with Walla Walla and Cayuse, form the Confederated Tribes of the Umatilla Indian Reservation near Pendleton, Oregon; the first two speak Sahaptin, while Cayuse is linguistically an isolate. Wanapum live as part of the Confederated Tribes and Bands of the Yakama Nation in Idaho, Yakama being the preferred name for the Nez Perce nation; these share a Sahaptin language.[52]

On its website, Colville declares that "The Confederated Tribes of the Colville Reservation is a Sovereign Nation. The Confederated Tribes of the Colville Reservation is a federally recognized American Indian Tribe."[53] Sovereignty rests on the treaties made with the nations beginning in 1855, resting on the statement in Felix Cohen's *Handbook of Federal Indian Law* that *"Those powers which are lawfully vested in an Indian tribe are not, in general, delegated power granted by express acts of Congress, but rather inherent powers of a limited sovereignty which has never been extinguished."* Each Indian tribe begins its relationship with the federal government as a sovereign power, recognized as such in treaty and legislation. What is not expressly limited remains within the domain of tribal sovereignty.[54]

Cohen quotes from Justice Marshall's 1832 decision in *Worcester v. Georgia*, "The Indian nations had always been considered as distinct independent, political communities."[55] Their independence did not end when in 1871 Congress ceased to make treaties with Indian nations, Cohen asserts.[56]

On the basis of the *Handbook of Federal Indian Law,* indigenous sovereignty is inherent in polities' existence. At its core, this position rests on the concept of natural law, that some truths are self-evident, as the

Declaration of Independence asserts. NAGPRA echoes the concept. Contested cases such as Kennewick Man seem to pit Euro-American culture against Indian, essentializing both as adversarial positions are constructed, cold rational disregard for emotional feelings versus "we are all kin" in a spiritually infused world.[57] Reluctance to rebury the bones of the man for whom no one has mourned for ten millennia carries the burden of children torn from their parents to be forced into Christian schools, wives put away at orders to break up polygynous marriages, villages massacred. In other words, colonialist denials of inherent sovereignty become outrages against natural law.

Indigeneity is bound to be as slippery as who on the Colville Reservation carries inherent sovereignty—Colville, Nespelem, San Poil, Lakes, Palus, Wenatchi, Chelan, Entiat, Methow, Okanogan, Moses Columbia, Chief Joseph's Nez Perce? The present elected tribal council? Its electorate? History is an ever-flowing stream with constantly shifting channels. Recent history's indigenous groups have rights in today's politics to territories taken from them by military power, and their communities should be allowed internal governance. Because they are existing polities in today's world, their histories as they know them should be listened to, that which they reverence should be respected—not because they manifest natural law as against Western states' imperialist greed or that their nations have eternally been in historic territories. Historicizing "the Other" recognizes complexities, shifts, factions, slave raids and destructive wars, trade empires, environmental effects, all the infinitude of billions of human decisions that mess up nice narratives. Perceiving the human realities of historically indigenous groups disbars both the picture of men-brutes in wildernesses and romantic paintings of noble children of nature.

Concluding Thought

Ethnohistorian Arthur Ray has grappled with indigeneity and its ramifications through several major court cases in Canada. In his analyses of these cases as he experienced them as expert witness, he came to understand the large difference between scholars' efforts to discover histories and judges' obligations to establish "findings of fact."[58] Courts of law attend to present circumstances, selecting proffered statements of historical circumstances and legal precedents as they seem relevant to particular claims. Socialization in Western culture may bias a judge, as notoriously it did Justice McEachern in *Delgamuukw v. Regina*.[59] It makes historians' work difficult, undermining their hope of achieving "that noble dream" of truth.[60] It mists perceptions of First Nations people, communities, and archaeological records. Manifest destiny and American savages abide yet in school texts, pageants, popular art, and folk knowledge. The ideology seeps into the concept of indigeneity. First Nations do not belong in museums of natural history or in separate National Museums of American Indians, a long walk from the United States National Museum of American History. Their national museums belong in their present communities, where many are indeed situated. Living communities descended from First Nations vitally confront invaders' projections of children of nature. Their legal and political challenges and demands against colonial domination are moving them from stereotyped exhibits of past cultures, into our contemporary pluralistic society.

Notes

1. Walter Raleigh, *The Discovery of Guiana* (1595; Memphis, TN: General Books), 63.
2. William Douglass, 1755, quoted in Ronald L. Meek, *Social Science and the Ignoble Savage* (Cambridge: Cambridge University Press, 1976), 137.
3. Joyce E. Chaplin, *Subject Matter: Technology, the Body, and Science on the Anglo-American Frontier, 1500–1676* (Cambridge, MA: Harvard University Press, 2001).
4. Michel Foucault, *The Order of Things* (New York: Vintage, 1973), 46–47, 238–45.
5. Alice Beck Kehoe, *The Land of Prehistory: A Critical History of American Archaeology* (New York: Routledge, 1998), 172–89; Timothy Pauketat, *Chiefdoms and Other Archaeological Delusions* (Lanham, MD: AltaMira, 2007).
6. Stephen W. Silliman, ed. *Collaborating at the Trowel's Edge: Teaching and Learning in Indigenous Archaeology* (Tucson: University of Arizona Press, 2008); Kenneth E. Sassaman Jr., *The Eastern Archaic, Historicized* (Lanham, MD: AltaMira, 2010).
7. Carolyn Merchant, *The Death of Nature* (San Francisco: Harper and Row, 1980), 131–32, 143–44.
8. Neal Wood, *John Locke and Agrarian Capitalism* (Berkeley: University of California Press, 1984).
9. John Locke, "Two Treatises of Government," in *Two Treatises of Government and a Letter Concerning Toleration*, ed. Ian Shapiro (New Haven, CT: Yale University Press, 2003), 113–14.
10. Locke, "Two Treatises of Government," 111. This sort of argumentation establishes what philosophers of science term fundamentalism, "a belief that some other realm is more fundamental—that is, it can provide deeper understanding, can correlate disparate insights, and so forth—than the one that has been studied. . . . The feature to be explained is a result only of the rules operative in that realm," Sahotra

Sarkar, *Genetics and Reductionism* (Cambridge: Cambridge University Press, 1998), 43, 46. Invoking a lower, fundamental realm to explain features is reduction. An example is George Milner's explanation for Cahokia mounds in which he invokes the fundamental realm that all Midwestern First Nations lived in simple villages. See Susan Alt, "Histories of Mound Building and Scales of Explanation in Archaeology," in *Ideologies in Archaeology*, ed. Reinhard Bernbeck and Randall H. McGuire (Tucson: University of Arizona Press, 2011), 194–211.

11. Genesis 1:24.

12. Robert A. Williams Jr., *The American Indian in Western Legal Thought* (New York: Oxford University Press, 1990), 242.

13. The Indians on Virginia's frontiers in 1776 were already known as the Five Civilized Tribes (Cherokee, Creeks, Chickasaw, Choctaw, and Seminole). Their agricultural plantations competed with those of the Virginia aristocracy.

14. Robert J. Miller, *Native America, Discovered and Conquered* (New York: Praeger, 2006; Lincoln: University of Nebraska Press, 2008), 96 (citations refer to the University of Nebraska edition); Anthony F. C. Wallace, *Jefferson and the Indians* (Ann Arbor: University of Michigan Press, 1999).

15. U.S. Const. art. 1, sec. 8: "The Congress shall have Power . . . To regulate Commerce with foreign Nations, and among the several States, and with the Indian Tribes."

16. Roger G. Kennedy, *Hidden Cities: The Discovery and Loss of Ancient North American Civilization* (New York: Free Press, 1994), 175.

17. Quoted in Albert K. Weinberg, *Manifest Destiny* (Baltimore, MD: Johns Hopkins University Press, 1935; Chicago: Quadrangle, 1961), 145. Citations refer to the Quadrangle edition.

18. Quoted in Weinberg, *Manifest Destiny*, 177.

19. Quoted in Weinberg, *Manifest Destiny*, 183.

20. Ibid., 179.

21. Lewis Henry Morgan, *Ancient Society* (1877; Tucson: University of Arizona Press, 1985), 196.

22. Alice Beck Kehoe, "Europe's Prehistoric Dawn Reproduced: Daniel Wilson's Magisterial Archaeology," in *New Perspectives on the Origins of Americanist Archaeology*, ed. David L. Browman and Stephen Williams (Tuscaloosa: University of Alabama Press, 2002), 136, 137.

23. Robert V. Bruce, *The Launching of Modern American Science, 1846–1876* (Ithaca, NY: Cornell University Press, 1987), 196–97, 204–5.

24. Felix S. Cohen and Rennard Strickland, *Felix S. Cohen's Handbook of Federal Indian Law* (Charlottesville, VA: Bobbs-Merrill, 1982), 119–20.

25. Robert A. Williams Jr., *Like a Loaded Weapon: The Rehnquist Court, Indian Rights, and the Legal History of Racism in America* (Minneapolis: University of Minnesota Press, 2005).

26. Kehoe, *Land of Prehistory*, 16–17.

27. Kennedy, *Hidden Cities*, 30.

28. Ibid., 137.

29. Bruce, *Launching of Modern American Science*, 321–22.

30. Dorothy Ross, *The Origins of American Social Science* (New York: Cambridge University Press, 1991), 62.

31. Aleš Hrdlička, *The Genesis of the American Indian* (Washington, DC, 1917), 563, 566.
32. Eugene Giles, "Principal Figures in Physical Anthropology Before and During World War II," in *Histories of American Physical Anthropology in the Twentieth Century*, ed. Michael A. Little and Kenneth A. Kennedy (Lanham, MD: Lexington, 2010), 144; Donald J. Ortner, "Aleš Hrdlička and the Founding of the *American Journal of Physical Anthropology*: 1918," in Little and Kennedy, *Histories of American Physical Anthropology*, 103.
33. M. F. Ashley Montagu, "Aleš Hrdlička, 1869–1943," *American Anthropologist*, no. 46 (1944): 115.
34. Gordon R. Willey and Jeremy A. Sabloff, *A History of American Archaeology*, 3rd ed. (New York: Freeman, 1993).
35. Ibid., 45.
36. Ibid., 188.
37. Daniel Wilson, *Prehistoric Man*, 2nd ed. (London: Macmillan, 1865), 574; Kehoe, *Land of Prehistory*, 70, 75, 80, 87.
38. Kehoe, *Land of Prehistory*, 20.
39. Kent V. Flannery, "The Golden Marshall Town: A Parable for the Archaeology of the 1980s, in *The Puzzle of the Newport Tower: Assembling the Pieces: The First Symposium* (Newport, RI: Newport Art Museum, 2007), 267.
40. Ross, *Origins of American Social Science*, 394.
41. Paul S. Martin, George I. Quimby, and Donald Collier, *Indians Before Columbus* (Chicago: University of Chicago Press, 1947), 4.
42. Quoted by Mary Midgely, *Science as Salvation: A Modern Myth and Its Meaning* (London: Routledge, 1992), chap. 8 (online as Gifford Lecture, 1989–1990: "Science as Salvation").
43. David A. Phillips Jr., "Introduction," in *Examining the Course of Southwest Archaeology: The Durango Conference, September 1995*, ed. David A. Phillips Jr. and Lynne Sebastian, Special Publication no. 3 (Albuquerque: New Mexico Archeological Council, 2001), 3.
44. William C. Sturtevant, "Tribe and State in the Sixteenth and Twentieth Centuries," in *The Development of Political Organization in Native North America*, ed. Elisabeth Tooker (Washington, DC: American Ethnological Society, 1983), 138–49; "Tupinambá Chiefdoms?" in *Chiefdoms and Chieftaincy in the Americas*, ed. Elsa M. Redmond (Gainesville: University Press of Florida, 1998), 3–16; Igor Kopytoff, "The Internal African Frontier: The Making of African Political Culture," in *The African Frontier: The Reproduction of Traditional African Societies*, ed. Igor Kopytoff (Bloomington: Indiana University Press, 1987), 78.
45. Alt, "Histories of Mound Building."
46. Joe E. Watkins, "Beyond the Margins: American Indians, First Nations, and Archaeology in North America," *American Antiquity* 68, no. 2 (2003): 273–85.
47. E.g., Sassaman, *Eastern Archaic*; Kenneth E. Sassaman Jr. and Donald H. Holly, *Hunter-Gatherer Archaeology as Historical Process* (Tucson: University of Arizona Press, 2011).
48. E.g., Intellectual Property Issues in Cultural Heritage (IPinCH) working to network indigenous archaeologists and projects and develop international open access and information systems (http://cgi.sfu.ca/~ipinch/cgi-bin/).

49. Proclamation by King George V: "Now, therefore, We, out of Our Royal Will and Authority, do hereby declare and announce that as from the date of this Our Royal Proclamation Our House and Family shall be styled and known as the House and Family of Windsor, and that all the descendants in the male line of Our said Grandmother Queen Victoria who are subjects of these Realms, other than female descendants who may marry or may have married, shall bear the said Name of Windsor," *London Gazette*, July 17, 1917.

50. David Hurst Thomas, *Skull Wars: Kennewick Man, Archaeology, and the Battle for Native American Identity* (New York: Basic Books, 2001); see also www.nps.gov/archeology/kennewick/.

51. Accessed September 21, 2013, http://www.colvilletribes.com/facts.php.

52. Alice Beck Kehoe, *North American Indians: A Comprehensive Account*, 3rd ed. (Upper Saddle River, NJ: Prentice-Hall, 2006), 355, 363.

53. Accessed September 21, 2013, http://www.colvilletribes.com/facts.php.

54. Felix S. Cohen, *Handbook of Federal Indian Law* (Washington, DC: Government Printing Office, 1942), 122 (italics in original).

55. Ibid., 123.

56. Ibid., 67.

57. Eric G. Schwimmer, "Symbolic Competition," *Anthropologica* 14, no. 2 (1972): 117–55.

58. Arthur J. Ray, *Telling It to the Judge: Taking Native History to Court* (Montreal: McGill-Queen's University Press, 2011), 154.

59. Ibid., 28–41.

60. Peter Novick, *That Noble Dream: The "Objectivity Question" and the American Historical Profession* (Cambridge: Cambridge University Press, 1988).

CHAPTER TEN

Saving the Natives

The Long Emergence and Transformation of Indigeneity

John S. Gilkeson

Since the 1980s, thanks in large part to the activism of indigenous peoples on all continents, the term *indigeneity* has gained wide currency. Now recognized by the United Nations and other NGOs, it has attained the status of a new global identity. By 2003, at least four thousand groups, comprising some three hundred million people, called themselves indigenous. Although indigeneity still has not entered the *Oxford English Dictionary*, indigenous peoples share common features. They claim descent from and historical continuity with the original inhabitants of nation-states before the arrival of settlers who have since become the dominant population; their cultures and languages remain distinct from those of the dominant population; and they share a history of dispossession, deculturalization, and demoralization. Today, indigenous peoples strive for a greater measure of self-determination, recognition of their collective rights, and, as "original peoples," control over land and resources. For these people, recovery of the past is not only essential to any demonstration of "unbroken ancestry," it is also a warrant for their future survival.[1]

Indigenous peoples have not always been seen in this light. In nineteenth-century North America, it was commonly assumed that Native Americans had not been in the New World very long, that their "primitive" languages shared a common grammatical structure, that they bore no historical relationship to the magnificent ruins that sprinkled the Americas, and that their cultures, static and unchanging before the arrival of European explorers, traders, and settlers, were rapidly disintegrating. The end result was that they had no future: they would either assimilate into Euro-American society or be doomed to extinction. It was also thought that Native Americans didn't have any past. In the absence of writing and written documents, they became "people without history" who could be neither actors in their own histories nor their own historians. Lacking "agency," they were "passive peoples," all too often "victims," but certainly not "agents of change in their own right."[2]

This essay traces the long emergence of indigeneity in the work of North American anthropologists, archaeologists, and historians since the early nineteenth century. It tells the story of how Native Americans, once viewed as people without history, have come to be seen as historical peoples. No longer viewed as frozen in time, without either past or future, Native Americans do indeed have histories, histories that stretch back at least fifteen thousand years.[3] Once regarded as static, their past has come to be seen as changing, even developmental, before contact with Europeans. Once regarded as always of external origin, change has come to be seen as endogenous, produced from within, as well as from without. Once conceived of in terms of major shifts in technology or subsistence, change has come to be seen as gradual and occurring on a small scale. And once seen as destroying Native American cultures, change has come to be seen as adding to them.

From their very first encounters with Native Americans in the late fifteenth century, Europeans questioned their "human status and capabilities." Were Native Americans, Europeans asked, "fully human"? Did they possess "reason"? Could they be converted to Christianity and civilized? By the mid-1700s, Native American humanity was no longer in question. Although deemed fully human, as the descendants of Adam, Native Americans were also seen as "benighted," owing to the "low" level of their technology and their paganism. In the developmental scheme that Euro-Americans derived from Scottish philosophic historians, Native Americans were also seen as "hunter-gatherers" who, in the march of civilization, must cede their land to European farmers. Also from the Scots, Americans derived the "comparative method," whereby observations of contemporary "primitive" societies could be used to reconstruct the undocumented past of civilized societies.[4]

Once Native Americans were seen as fully human, if benighted, a second question—not resolved until the late 1920s—arose: how and when did they arrive in the New World? It was generally assumed that their ancestors had crossed the Bering Strait from Asia and had then made their way south to the foot of the Western Hemisphere. Given the biblical temporal framework that prevailed until the 1860s, their past seemed of short duration, spanning no more than six thousand years.[5]

To answer the question of the origins of Native Americans, American scholars turned to comparative philology along the lines of European studies that had identified an Indo-European language family. As early as 1784, in his *Notes on the State of Virginia*, Thomas Jefferson urged the collection of Native American vocabulary lists. From 1799 on, at Jefferson's initiative, the American Philosophical Society distributed circulars calling for the systematic compilation of Native American word lists.[6]

For the next five decades, students of Native Americans systematically pursued the study of Native American languages. In 1819, Peter Duponceau characterized all Native American languages as "polysynthetic," incorporating the greatest number of ideas in the least number of words. From this putative linguistic affinity Duponceau inferred a common origin. In 1826, Lewis Cass emphasized the need for a "synonymy," given the wide variety of names by which most Native American tribes were known. Albert Gallatin expected his 1836 classification of all Native American languages east of the Rocky Mountains, which he revised shortly before his death in 1849, not only to throw light on Native American origins and migrations but also to demonstrate an affinity between Native American and Northeast Asian languages. Finally, in 1847, Henry Rowe Schoolcraft persuaded Congress to allocate money toward the expansion of Cass's synonymy into an encyclopedia. Nearly $130,000 was spent on the six-volume *Historical and Statistical Information Respecting the History, Condition, and Prospects of the Indian Tribes of the United States* published between 1851 and 1857.[7]

Collection of the relics of vanished Native American tribes supplemented the collection of vocabulary lists and other linguistic information. Applying the techniques of natural history, students of Native Americans sought to classify relics in the same manner that the flora and fauna of the New World were classified. Thomas Jefferson again led the way, excavating "a barrow," or Indian mound, in 1784. Subsequently, the enormous mounds that settlers discovered in the Ohio and Mississippi River valleys as they made their way west raised questions about the relationship of the mound builders to contemporary Native Americans. Early investigators, ranging from Caleb Atwater to Ephraim G. Squier and Edwin H. Davis, propagated the myth of a vanished race of mound builders to account for the discrepancy between the glories of the past and the degraded status of Native Americans.[8]

The "ruins" of the Southwest also stirred interest in the origins issue. Even before the opening of the Santa Fe Trail in 1821, American scholars had learned of the existence of "purportedly indigenous histories" claiming that the Aztec and Toltec peoples had migrated to the Valley of Mexico from the north.[9] The "ruined cities" of Middle America described by John Lloyd Stephens in *Incidents of Travel in Central America, Chiapas and Yucatan* (1841) only whetted popular interest in historical connections between Mexico and the Southwest.[10] Although Americans discovered even more ruins in the wake of the Mexican-American War (1846–1848), they had no way to "date" the ruins or to determine the course of their builders' migrations.[11]

Until roughly 1850, Native Americans loomed large in the American imagination. In the aftermath of the War of 1812, Native Americans figured prominently in Americans' "quest for cultural identity and nationalism."[12] In American history textbooks of the 1830s and 1840s, they were commonly depicted as "important" peoples whose customs, tools, and "probable origins" were of considerable interest.[13] Yet interest in Native Americans began to wane in the 1850s. By then, efforts to assimilate Native Americans, to civilize and Christianize them, had frequently proved unsuccessful. Indeed, the great majority of Native Americans who once lived east of the Mississippi had been removed, their lands now cultivated by Euro-American farmers. Although their resistance to the westward expansion of the "farming frontier" continued into the 1880s, Native Americans increasingly became objects of "objective," "scientific" study, much of it sponsored by the Smithsonian Institution, founded in 1846. "Pity" and "censure" gave way to the "scientific analysis" of Lewis Henry Morgan's *The League of the Ho-dé-no-sau-nee, or Iroquois* (1851).[14]

Also contributing to the declining importance of Native Americans was the "time revolution" of the 1850s and 1860s. The acceptance of man's antiquity, as documented by excavations of "cave men" in southwestern France and at Brixham Cave in southwestern England, spawned a new domain—"prehistory."[15] In Europe, there was a "close affinity" between prehistory, which lacked both "chronology" and "any specificity of time," and history. Indeed, nineteenth-century European nationalists seized on prehistoric archaeology, much as they did folklore, to bolster claims for autonomy, if not independence. In the twentieth century, the great prehistorian V. Gordon Childe regarded prehistoric Europeans as his "spiritual ancestors."[16]

American history, by contrast, dealt only with Euro-Americans; until the late 1960s, historians left the study of Native Americans to anthropologists and archaeologists.[17] Historians, moreover, emphasized the rupture that had occurred in American history with the coming of the Europeans to the New World. As John Lothrop Motley explained in 1869, "we of to-day have no filial interest in the man of Natchez. He was no ancestor of ours nor have he and his descendants left traces along the dreary track of their existence or induce a desire to claim relationship with them. We are Americans."[18]

The gap between history and prehistory in America widened as the discipline of history professionalized in the late nineteenth century. To stake out their academic turf, professional historians adopted the analysis of written documents as their "signature methodology." As the influential French historians Charles Langlois and Charles Seignobos declared in 1898, "no documents, no history."[19] Defining history as document based meant that Native Americans, who had no written languages and therefore were held to be unable to produce written documents, were people without history. It also meant that their own views of their past as recorded in oral traditions, which could not then be verified, were not taken into account. As anthropologist Robert H. Lowie explained in 1915, scholars could not "attach to oral traditions any value whatsoever under any circumstance whatsoever," because "we cannot know them to be true."[20]

If Native Americans constituted obstacles to white advance across the continent in Francis Parkman's romantic history *The Conspiracy of Pontiac* (1851), they did not figure at all in the 1880s in Herbert Baxter Adams's tracking of the transplantation of the "germs" of Teutonic institutions into the New World. And they figured only metaphorically in the seminal 1893 essay "The Significance of the Frontier in American History," in which Adams's student Frederick Jackson Turner famously described how the European settler became an "American" by briefly exchanging the "garments of civilization" for Native American "hunting shirt and moccasin."[21] From the late nineteenth century until the 1930s, Native Americans rarely appeared in historical monographs except those dealing with the fur trade and Spanish borderlands.[22] This marginalization of Native American agency in historical works had its counterpart in popular culture. In Wild West shows and in Westerns, Native Americans were depicted as noble but defeated savages.[23]

Where nineteenth-century American historians studied civilized peoples, anthropologists and archaeologists studied peoples whose cultures appeared to be static and unchanging.[24] As an evolutionary framework supplanted the biblical framework in the wake of the publication of Charles Darwin's *On the Origin of Species* in 1859, "the sequence of human prehistory," as "refined" by Sir John Lubbock in *Pre-historic Times* in 1865, gave way from "one of Adamite preceded by pre-Adamite" to a series of cultural stages—either the three stages (Stone, Bronze, and Iron Ages) of the Danish museum curator Jens J. A. Worsaae or the three stages (savagery, barbarism, civilization) of the pioneer American ethnographer Lewis Henry Morgan. Either way, Native Americans fell out of time. As Otis T. Mason, curator of the U.S. National Museum, explained, "when grade, or stage of culture, is the concept, the word 'prehistoric' does not refer to time at all."[25]

It is hardly surprising, then, that a "flat" view of Native American prehistory prevailed not only among American historians in the late nineteenth century but among anthropologists and archaeologists as well. Native American cultures were assumed to have a shallow time depth, to have "changed little, if at all," before the coming of the Europeans. Assuming that they would find little evidence of "internal cultural transformations" in the archaeological record and attributing any "major alterations" they did find to "external changes brought about by the tribal migration of cultures," American archaeologists felt little interest in developing "cultural chronologies" that would demonstrate "either cultural change or lack of it."[26]

Instead, anthropological and archaeological work in late-nineteenth- and early-twentieth-century America took the form of "salvage ethnology" recording the customs and languages of "the vanishing savage" before they became extinct. To recover precontact cultures and languages, anthropologists interviewed elderly informants to elicit "memory cultures" that could serve as baselines against which to measure the cultural demoralization and disintegration that had ensued from contact with Europeans. These memory cultures were treated as though they existed in an atemporal "ethnographic present," which D'Arcy McNickle likened to "a kind of cookie-cutter device that clipped away and discarded that which was antecedent and subsequent."[27]

Salvage ethnology found an institutional home in the Bureau of Ethnology (later the Bureau of American Ethnology [BAE]), established in 1879. Building on the activities of Jefferson, Gallatin, and other gentlemen-scholars, the BAE completed the linguistic classification and synonymy of North American tribes they had called for. Although BAE director John Wesley Powell was not as interested in archaeology as he was in linguistics and ethnology, BAE fieldworkers, from the early 1880s on, excavated prehistoric mounds and earthworks. One of them, Cyrus Thomas, finally resolved the identity of the mound builders, concluding in the BAE *Annual Report* for 1891 that the mound builders were the ancestors of the indigenous peoples found in eastern North America when the Europeans arrived.[28] Most of the BAE's researches were "firmly grounded in evolution," particularly Lewis Henry Morgan's three-stage sequence, which froze Native Americans in time. Yet at least two BAE fieldworkers documented Native American historicity. While Frank Hamilton Cushing's ethnographies of the Zuni addressed "questions of history and origins," James Mooney became one of the first American anthropologists to view Native Americans "as more than a dying cultural remnant."[29]

A flat view of the Native American past persisted even after the German émigré Franz Boas began in the late 1880s to reorient American anthropology around the intensive investigation of the history and culture of specific Native American tribes. As Boas explained in 1888, to find the Native American and study his culture, "we must visit him in his village, where he lives undisturbed by the contact with Europeans, according to his ancient customs." Although Boas recognized Native American historicity, he and his students felt the urgency of reconstructing precontact Native American cultures disintegrating before their eyes. For the Boasians, "history" meant context. Only by putting an ethnographic or archaeological specimen in its context could its "meaning" be discerned.[30] Not until the 1930s would the Boasians abandon salvage ethnology in favor of the study of cultural change.[31]

From the 1870s until the late 1920s, an "early man" debate raged among American prehistorians who, assuming that the prehistory of the New World paralleled that of the old, searched for evidence that would confirm man's great antiquity in the New World. In the 1870s, Charles C. Abbott thought that he had found such evidence in the "Trenton [New Jersey] Gravels," but his claims were not substantiated. As Cyrus Thomas admitted in 1898, claims for a "glacial or Paleolithic man of America" still "want[ed] the credibility which entitles him to a place in scientific circles." Evidence "hard" enough to confute skeptics was finally found in New Mexico in the late 1920s and early 1930s. Although the Folsom and Clovis finds pushed back man's antiquity in the New World by at least thirteen thousand years, New World prehistory still lacked "depth" comparable to that of the Old World.[32]

In fact, American archaeology long suffered from what Berthold Laufer in 1913 referred to as a "lack of a substantial chronology."[33] This lack was eventually remedied by the development of dating techniques—stratigraphy and seriation in the 1910s, dendrochronology between the world wars, and radiocarbon dating in the 1950s. In addition to gaining greater control over time, American archaeologists began to conceive of change as occurring gradually rather than invariably on a large scale. Beginning with the Pecos Classification of 1927, they worked out cultural chronologies for the Southwest, the Southeast, and other regions of the country.[34] If stratigraphy and seriation enabled archaeologists to assign relative dates to material objects and arrange them in sequences, dendrochronology and radiocarbon dating provided absolute dates.[35]

At the same time that archaeologists were becoming cultural historians, American anthropologists took up the study of acculturation or culture contact.[36] In so doing, they were heeding Franz Boas's 1920 call for anthropologists to turn their attention from "diffusion," or the "dissemination of elements," to the "problem of the 'inner development' of culture" conceived in terms of the study of "acculturation," the "interdependence of cultural activities," and "the relation of the individual to society." As anthropologists shifted their attention from the "elements" of culture to its "processes" and "patterns," their analytic perspective shifted from the diachronic to the synchronic, to "the dynamic changes in society that may be observed at the present time."[37]

Anthropologists had long chafed at the constraints of salvage ethnology and the reconstruction of memory cultures. Indeed, memory cultures were growing "very remote" by the late 1920s. Like her contemporaries Robert Redfield, Lloyd Warner, Alfonso Villa Rojas, and Fred Eggan, Elizabeth Colson wanted to study "living communities, using participant observation." Warner, Eggan, and others influenced by A. R. Radcliffe-Brown's "functionalism" redefined themselves as "social anthropologists" specializing in the study of "social organization."[38] Studies of acculturation, moreover, had an "obvious utility" during the Depression. In the wake of the Indian Reorganization Act of 1934, which encouraged Native Americans to organize tribal governments and then seek federal recognition, recent PhDs, whose numbers swelled as new doctoral programs opened at the University of Chicago and Yale, found positions as advisers to federal agencies at a time when academic positions were few and far between.[39]

Acculturation studies focused anthropologists' attention on the "sequence of changes" that indigenous cultures had undergone since their first European contact.[40] Whereas studies of diffusion traced the movement of a cultural trait or complex of traits, acculturation studies focused on "reception." Although they were two-way in theory, in practice they tended to be one-way, focusing more on the indigenous "receptor" culture than on the mainstream American "donor" culture.[41]

Acculturation studies also reflected the growing recognition, on the part of anthropologists and the federal officials whom they advised, that far from vanishing, Native American populations were increasing. By 1930, Native Americans' demographic gains were becoming noticeable as the rate of Native American population growth began to exceed that of the general population of both the United States and Canada. If only because of these demographic gains, it became ever more difficult for anthropologists to ignore Native American persistence.[42]

Yet until after the Second World War, the "master story" of American anthropology remained, in the words of Edward Bruner, a story of "past glory, present disorganization, future assimilation."[43] In a pioneering study of acculturation, *The Changing Culture of an Indian Tribe* (1932), Margaret Mead traced the breakdown of "Antler" (Omaha) culture owing to "white invasion." Mead saw only one alternative to the total "disorganization" of the Omaha: their "gradual amalgamation . . . into the white population."[44] In *Patterns of Culture* (1934), Ruth Benedict famously told the story of the "broken cup" of the Digger Indians, who had grown demoralized because of the disintegration of their culture.[45] In *Acculturation in Seven American Indian Tribes* (1940), Ralph Linton saw no alternative other than eventual Native American assimilation. "Everything indicates that the ultimate end of situations of close and continuous contacts is the amalgamation of the societies and cultures involved," although Linton did admit that "this conclusion may be postponed almost indefinitely."[46] As late as 1945, Julian Steward could declare that "anthropologists are in general agreement that it is purely a question of time before all Indians lose their identity."[47]

The situation, however, changed quickly after 1945. By the mid-1950s, the assimilation of Native Americans into "the normal stream of American life" no longer appeared inevitable, and the long-held belief that "Indian tribes and communities [would] disappear" no longer appeared to have any factual basis. In 1954, a conference of experts on acculturation predicted the persistence, into the foreseeable future, of Native American communities as "cultural islands, more or less well adjusted to or integrated into the American system."[48] Discussions of acculturation now emphasized "cultural creativity" rather than assimilation. Acculturation, declared a committee of the Social Science Research Council in 1954 that had studied the matter, was "neither a passive nor a colorless absorption," but rather "a culture-producing, as well as a culture-receiving process." Indeed, "when not forced," acculturation was "essentially creative."[49] In 1957, Evon Vogt, citing dramatic demographic growth, declared that Native Americans were no longer "vanishing." Vogt did not deny that Native American material culture was changing. Yet even as Native Americans were rapidly adopting "goods, techniques, and technological equipment of the white American way of life," their "systems of social structure and culture" were "persist[ing] with variable vigor." In what Vogt termed "Pan-Indianism," "reasonably well educated" Native Americans, many of them greatly removed "from their aboriginal ways of life," were forging a new pan-tribal "Indian" identity by means of participating in powwows, attending intertribal ceremonial gatherings, and engaging in intertribal visiting and even intermarriage.[50]

Even as Vogt called attention to Native American perseverance, cultural persistence, and ability to adapt to changing conditions, practitioners of the new interdisciplinary field of ethnohistory were rediscovering Native American historicity.[51] The first generation of ethnohistorians cut their teeth on the some 550 native land claims and termination cases heard by the Indian Claims Commission between 1946 and 1978 that awarded over $500 million in damages to Native American plaintiffs. To make the strongest argument they could that Native American plaintiffs constituted "identifiable groups" that had maintained "historical continuity" with the signatories of earlier treaties with federal and state governments, ethnohistorians turned to documentary sources. Because oral testimony was considered much less reliable in the claims cases than were written documents produced by literate nonnatives, ethnohistorians not only mined archives and museums for such documents but learned how to compensate for the documents' ethnocentric bias—for example, systematic underreporting of Native Americans' active management of the lands they occupied.[52]

Until the 1950s, historians had been slow to acknowledge Native American persistence, cultural creativity, and, perhaps most surprisingly, agency. Before the Second World War, they had begun to pay more attention to Native American history, but usually out of preoccupation with the seemingly larger issues of the fur trade, the Spanish borderlands, and imperial and federal Indian policy. Among the relatively few historians whose primary interest lay in Native Americans themselves, white–Native American relations served as "the overarching focus of study." Yet even Angie Debo, who attempted to see Native American life from the inside, portrayed Native Americans more as victims than as agents.[53]

In 1952, Bernard De Voto, editor of *Harper's* and an accomplished Western historian, complained that "most American history" continued to be "written as if history were a function solely of white culture."[54] As a graduate student, Robert Berkhofer was told that "Indian history was not part of American history." When Berkhofer persisted in writing a dissertation on Protestant missionaries to the American Indians from the 1770s to the 1860s, it was listed in *Dissertation Abstracts* under the heading of anthropology, not history. As late as the 1950s, Native American history remained largely the province of anthropologists.[55]

Native American "militancy," however, soon transformed the "master story" from one of victimhood to a "narrative of resistance." In 1961, representatives from ninety tribes issued "A Declaration of Indian Purpose"; in 1964, the three-year-old National Indian Youth Council organized the first "fish-in," and the *Indian Historian* published its first number; in 1968, the American Indian Movement was established; and in 1969, some of its adherents occupied Alcatraz.[56] By then, it was clear that for Native Americans the "golden age" no longer lay in the past as captured by the ethnographic present, but in the future. The challenge for students of Native Americans was to tell the story of how Native Americans had maintained their "tradition and ethnicity" despite all the pressures on them to assimilate.[57] In 1970, Margaret Mead, an accomplished practitioner of salvage ethnology, acknowledged that Native Americans had become far more "concerned with the well being of their people" than "with the preservation of vestigial and ancient parts of ancient cultures."[58]

An "academic Indian history" quickly developed in the late 1960s and early 1970s. Native American studies programs were founded at San Francisco State University in 1968, the University of Minnesota and UCLA in 1969, and at the University of California, Berkeley, in 1972. Also in 1972, the Newberry Library appointed the distinguished Native American scholar D'Arcy McNickle as the director of its new Center for the History of the American Indian. Native American history subsequently became a "growth field" at a time when history enrollments were declining in many other areas.[59]

In 1971, Robert Berkhofer called for a "New Indian History." The "Indian-centered history" that Berkhofer envisioned would put "more of the Indians into [it]," move beyond historians' traditional focus on white–Native American relations, take up such topics as Indian-Indian relations and internal divisions within Indian tribes, and emphasize Native American "cultural persistence and change."[60] Yet historians who studied Native Americans remained more interested in Native American societies and cultures "only as they once were" and viewed "changes from pre–white contact days" as losses of "Indian ways" rather than as products of "dynamic, innovative Indian leadership and adaptive societies." Indeed, in the view of many of these historians, change "destroyed Indian cultures, never added to them."[61]

If ethnohistorians wanted to understand how Native Americans reacted to the coming of the Europeans, they had to made use of artifacts to supplement the documents on which they customarily relied.[62] In a decisive break with the ethnographic present, they turned to prehistoric archaeology, to works such as Bruce Trigger's *The Children of Aataentsic: A History of the Huron People to 1660* (1976), to understand precontact Native American cultures. It was clear by then that most ethnographic descriptions of precontact cultures did not actually describe "pristine" cultures but rather cultures that had already been affected by contact with Europeans. A growing body of evidence showed that far from being static or unchanging before European contact, Native American cultures were "evolving internally" as manifested in expanded trade, shifting patterns of warfare, more elaborate ritual, and more complex political alliances.[63]

If ethnohistory truly came of age in the 1980s, the publication of Eric Wolf's *Europe and the People Without History* in 1982 helped to make this so.[64] In tracing the history of European expansion since 1400, Wolf incorporated the people without history, treating them as agents of world history rather than as its victims. He showed that indigenous peoples had their own histories, which were not only separate and distinct from those of European states but also began long before the arrival of the Europeans. In a chapter on "The Fur Trade," Wolf drew on ethnohistory and prehistoric archaeology to emphasize Native American conventions such as kinship and gift giving, their active management of natural resources, and "ethnogenesis"—the birth of new ethnic groups, such as the métis, composed of people of mixed biological and cultural descent.[65]

However, if the world was as truly "interconnected" as Wolf contended, it became hard "to imagine even the possibility of autonomous societies in recent history." In his interpretation of world history since 1400, indigenous peoples shared the same fate: incorporation into a European-dominated "capitalist world-system."[66] It is perhaps not surprising that Marshall Sahlins criticized Wolf's rendering of indigenous peoples as "passive objects of their own history, and not its authors" and regretted that Wolf had not paid more attention to how these peoples "attempt to organize what is afflicting them in their own cultural terms."[67]

In his 1985 *Islands of History*, Sahlins declared "different cultures, different historicities." "Different cultural orders," he contended, have "their own historical practice" that is, "their own modes of historical action, consciousness, and determination." Historicity, in short, is "culturally variable."[68] Since then, ethnohistorians, invoking historicity, have rejected the notion that the prehistories of indigenous peoples are "unknowable," static, and of short duration rather than of "deep antiquity." They now recognize that the history of Native Americans and the history of European settlers are interdependent, that one cannot be written without taking the other into account.[69]

Finally, and this is Sahlins's point, Native American histories did not end with the coming of the Europeans to the New World in 1492. Now that Native Americans are becoming their own historians, the question becomes, who gets to write their history? And must this history always depend on written documents and artifacts? Ultimately, how much validity should historians attribute to Native American "historiography," specifically, to the origin stories and oral traditions that lie at its heart?[70] In a valedictory published a year before his death in 1999, Native American anthropologist Alfonso Ortiz insisted that scholars "must develop respect for" oral traditions, for "tribes' own accounts of their origins, early migrations, and statements of how they came to be where they are." While conceding that oral traditions "may not explain the distant past with the factual accuracy of careful historical research," Ortiz maintained that they nonetheless "present meaningful, comforting, and useful windows on the past for Indian people."[71]

Native Americans' growth in both numbers and political power, the redefinition of acculturation to emphasize giving as well as receiving, the development of an Indian-centered history, the blurring of the distinction between pre- and postcontact archaeology, and the acknowledgment of the historicity of nonwritten sources—all have transformed the study of the Native American past. Views emphasizing the rupture caused by European conquest are giving way to emphasis on continuity. In the continuity of the Native American past (and that of indigenous groups elsewhere) lies a strong warrant not only for their future survival but also for their sovereignty.

Acknowledgments

I wish to thank Susan Gray, Peter Iverson, Sharon Kirsch, Christine Szuter, and the editors for their helpful comments on earlier drafts.

Notes

1. Ronald Niezen, *The Origins of Indigenism: Human Rights and the Politics of Identity* (Berkeley: University of California Press, 2003), esp. 1–28; Rebecca Tsosie,

"The New Challenge to Native Identity: An Essay on 'Indigeneity' and 'Whiteness,'" *Washington University Journal of Law and Policy* 55 (2005): 55–98.

2. D'Arcy McNickle, "American Indians Who Never Were," *American Indian* 3 (Summer 1971): 6; Donald L. Fixico, "The Literature of American Indian History," in *A Century of American Historiography*, ed. James M. Banner Jr. (Boston: Bedford/St. Martin's, 2010), 180.

3. Peter Iverson, "Native Peoples and Native Histories," in *The Oxford History of the American West*, ed. Clyde A. Milner II, Carol A. O'Connor, and Martha A. Sandweiss (New York: Oxford University Press, 1994), 13.

4. Don D. Fowler and David R. Wilcox, "From Thomas Jefferson to the Pecos Conference: Changing Anthropological Agendas in the North American Southwest," in *Surveying the Record: North American Scientific Exploration to 1930*, ed. E. C. Carter II (Philadelphia: American Philosophical Society, 1999), 199–200; J. W. Burrow, *Evolution and Society: A Study in Victorian Social Theory* (Cambridge: Cambridge University Press, 1966), 10, 18.

5. A. Irving Hallowell, "The Beginnings of Anthropology in America," in *Contributions to Anthropology: Selected Papers of A. Irving Hallowell* (Chicago: University of Chicago Press, 1976), 41; Andrew Shryock and Daniel Lord Smail, *Deep History: The Architecture of Past and Present* (Berkeley: University of California Press, 2011), 271.

6. Fowler and Wilcox, "From Thomas Jefferson to the Pecos Conference," 199–200; Julie Tetel Andresen, *Linguistics in America, 1769–1924: A Critical History* (London: Routledge, 1990), 60–63.

7. Fowler and Wilcox, "From Thomas Jefferson to the Pecos Conference," 201–2; Mary R. Haas, "The Problem of Classifying American Indian Languages: From Duponceau to Powell," in *Language, Culture, and History: Essays by Mary R. Haas*, ed. Anwar S. Dil (Stanford, CA: Stanford University Press, 1978), 131–33, 136–39; Andresen, *Linguistics in America*, 97–104, 110–13.

8. Hallowell, "Beginnings of Anthropology in America," 108–12, 114–16; Gordon R. Willey and Jeremy A. Sabloff, *A History of American Archaeology*, 3rd ed. (New York: Freeman, 1993), 33–34.

9. Fowler and Wilcox, "From Thomas Jefferson to the Pecos Conference," 203.

10. Curtis M. Hinsley, "Hemispheric Hegemony in Early American Anthropology, 1841–1851: Reflections on John Lloyd Stephens and Lewis Henry Morgan," in *Social Contexts of American Ethnology, 1840–1984*, ed. June Helm (Washington, DC: American Ethnological Society, 1985), 30; Willey and Sabloff, *History of American Archaeology*, 65.

11. Fowler and Wilcox, "From Thomas Jefferson to the Pecos Conference," 205–6.

12. Robert F. Berkhofer Jr., *The White Man's Indian: Images of the American Indian from Columbus to the Present* (1978; repr., New York: Vintage, 1979), 95; A. I. Hallowell, "The Impact of the American Indian on American Culture," *Contributions to Anthropology: Selected Papers of A. Irving Hallowell* (Chicago: University of Chicago Press, 1976), 487–89.

13. Frances FitzGerald, *America Revised: History Schoolbooks in the Twentieth Century* (New York: Vintage, 1980), 90.

14. Roy Harvey Pearce, *Savagism and Civilization: A Study of the Indian and the American Mind* (Berkeley: University of California Press, 1988), 66, 129.

15. Jacob W. Gruber, "Brixham Cave and the Antiquity of Man," in *Context and Meaning in Cultural Anthropology*, ed. Melford E. Spiro (New York: Free Press, 1965), 373–402; Shryock and Smail, *Deep History*, 23–29.

16. Bruce G. Trigger, "Ethnohistory and Archaeology," *Ontario Archaeology* 30 (1978): 17; Steven Conn, *History's Shadow: Native Americans and Historical Consciousness in the Nineteenth Century* (Chicago: University of Chicago Press, 2004), 214.

17. Bruce G. Trigger, "Archaeology and the Ethnographic Present," *Anthropologica* 23 (1981): 4.

18. Jurgen Herbst, *The German Historical School in American Scholarship: A Study in the Transfer of Culture* (Ithaca: Cornell University Press, 1965), 115–20; Berkhofer, *White Man's Indian*, 95–96; Motley quoted in Conn, *History's Shadow*, 215.

19. Shryock and Smail, *Deep History*, 6–7.

20. Robert H. Lowie, "Oral Tradition and History," *American Anthropologist* 17 (July–September 1915): 598; Conn, *History's Shadow*, 21–22.

21. John Joseph Buss, *Winning the West with Words: Language and Conquest in the Lower Great Lakes* (Norman: University of Oklahoma Press, 2011); Conn, *History's Shadow*, 222–25; Turner quoted in Hallowell, "Impact of the American Indian," 483.

22. Kerwin Lee Klein, *Frontiers of Historical Imagination: Narrating the European Conquest of Native America, 1890–1990* (Berkeley: University of California Press, 1997), 144.

23. L. G. Moses, *Wild West Shows and the Images of American Indians, 1883–1933* (Albuquerque: University of New Mexico Press, 1996); Philip Deloria, *Playing Indian* (New Haven, CT: Yale University Press, 1998).

24. Bruce G. Trigger, "Prehistoric Archaeology and American Society," in *American Archaeology Past and Present: A Celebration of the Society for American Archaeology, 1935–1985*, ed. David J. Meltzer, Don D. Fowler, and Jeremy A. Sabloff (1986; repr., Washington, DC: Smithsonian Institution Press, 1994), 189.

25. David J. Meltzer, "The Antiquity of Man and the Development of American Archaeology," *Advances in Archaeological Method and Theory* 5 (1983): 5; Conn, *History's Shadow*, 214–15.

26. Trigger, "Prehistoric Archaeology," 193–95.

27. Jacob W. Gruber, "Ethnographic Salvage and the Shaping of American Anthropology," *American Anthropologist* 72 (December 1970): 1294, 1297; John W. Burton, "Shadows at Twilight: A Note on History and the Ethnographic Present," *Proceedings of the American Historical Society* 132 (December 1988): 423; D'Arcy McNickle, "Americans Called Indians," in *North American Indians in Historical Perspective*, ed. Eleanor Burke Leacock and Nancy Oestreich Lurie (New York: Random House, 1971), 30.

28. Regna Darnell, *And Along Came Boas: Continuity and Revolution in Americanist Anthropology* (Amsterdam: John Benjamins, 1998), 11; Fowler and Wilcox, "From Thomas Jefferson to the Pecos Conference," 209–11; Meltzer, "Antiquity of Man," 11–13.

29. Curtis M. Hinsley Jr, *Savages and Scientists: The Smithsonian Institution and the Development of American Anthropology, 1846–1910* (Washington, DC: Smithsonian Institution Press, 1981), 196, 213.

30. Franz Boas, "The Indians of British Columbia," *Popular Science Monthly* 32 (1888): 628; Jacob W. Gruber, "Archaeology, History, and Culture," in *American*

Archaeology Past and Present: A Celebration of the Society for American Archaeology, 1935–1985, ed. David J. Meltzer, Don D. Fowler, and Jeremy A. Sabloff (1986; repr., Washington, DC: Smithsonian Institution Press, 1994), 178.

31. Michael E. Harkin, "(Dis)pleasures of the Text: Boasian Anthropology on the Northwest Coast," in *Gateways: Exploring the Legacy of the Jesup North Pacific Expedition, 1897–1902*, ed. Igor Krupnick and William Fitzhugh (Washington, DC: Arctic Studies Center, Smithsonian Institution, 2002), 94–96; Michael E. Harkin, "Ethnohistory's Ethnohistory: Creating a Discipline from the Bottom Up," *Social Science History* 34 (Summer 2010): 120.

32. Hallowell, "Beginnings of Anthropology in America," 124; Meltzer, "Antiquity of Man," 1–2, 9–10, 23–25, 33–34, 37–38, 40.

33. Berthold Laufer, "'Remarks' on 'Some Aspects of North American Archaeology,' by Roland E. Dixon," *American Anthropologist* 15 (October–December 1913): 576–77; Fowler and Wilcox, "From Thomas Jefferson to the Pecos Conference," 219.

34. Fowler and Wilcox, "From Thomas Jefferson to the Pecos Conference," 220–22; Willey and Sabloff, *History of American Archaeology*, 56–57, 98–105, 109–12.

35. Bruce G. Trigger, *A History of Archaeological Thought*, 2nd ed. (Cambridge: Cambridge University Press, 2006), 382.

36. Harkin, "(Dis)pleasures of the Text," 95; Hallowell, "Impact of the American Indian," 484; May Ebihara, "American Ethnology in the 1930s: Contexts and Currents," in *Social Contexts of American Ethnology, 1840–1984*, ed. June Helm (Washington, DC: American Ethnological Society, 1985), 103–4.

37. George W. Stocking Jr., "Ideas and Institutions in American Anthropology: Thoughts Toward a History of the Interwar Years," in *The Ethnographer's Magic and Other Essays in the History of Anthropology* (Madison: University of Wisconsin Press, 1992), 137.

38. Ralph Beals, "Acculturation," in *Anthropology Today: An Encyclopedic Inventory*, ed. A. L. Kroeber (Chicago: University of Chicago Press, 1953), 621–22; Elizabeth Colson, "Defining American Ethnology," in *Social Contexts of American Ethnology, 1840–1984*, ed. June Helm (Washington, DC: American Ethnological Society, 1985), 179–80.

39. Beals, "Acculturation," 622; Colson, "Defining American Ethnology," 179; Lawrence C. Kelly, "Why Applied Anthropology Developed When It Did: A Commentary on People, Money, and Changing Times," in *Social Contexts of American Ethnology, 1840–1984*, ed. June Helm (Washington, DC: American Ethnological Society, 1985), 126.

40. Bruce G. Trigger, "Ethnohistory: Problems and Prospects," *Ethnohistory* 29 (Winter 1982): 4; Trigger, "Ethnohistory and Archaeology," 18.

41. Betty J. Meggers, "Recent Trends in American Ethnology," *American Anthropologist* 48 (April–June 1946): 188–89; "Acculturation: An Exploratory Formulation," *American Anthropologist* 56 (December 1954), 973; McNickle, "American Indians Who Never Were," 6.

42. D'Arcy McNickle, *Native American Tribalism: Indian Survivals and Renewals* (New York: Oxford University Press, 1973), 5, 8.

43. Edward M. Bruner, "Ethnography as Narrative," in *The Anthropology of Experience*, ed. Victor W. Turner and Edward M. Bruner (Urbana: University of Illinois Press, 1986), 142.

44. Margaret Mead to Clark Wissler, August 6, 1930, quoted in Maureen A. Molloy, *On Creating a Usable Culture: Margaret Mead and the Emergence of American Cosmopolitanism* (Honolulu: University of Hawaii Press, 2008), 95; Margaret Mead, *The Changing Culture of an Indian Tribe* (1932; repr., New York: Capricorn, 1965), 192, 220.

45. Ruth Benedict, *Patterns of Culture* (1934; repr., Boston: Houghton Mifflin, 1959), 21–22.

46. Ralph Linton, ed., *Acculturation in Seven Indian Tribes* (1940; repr., Gloucester, MA: Peter Smith, 1963), 519; Bruner, "Ethnography as Narrative," 142.

47. Julian H. Steward, "The Changing American Indian," in *The Science of Man in the World Crisis*, ed. Ralph Linton (New York: Columbia University Press, 1945), 290.

48. John Provinse et al., "The American Indian in Transition," *American Anthropologist* 56 (June 1954): 388–89.

49. "Acculturation: An Exploratory Formulation," *American Anthropologist* 56 (December 1954): 985.

50. Evon Z. Vogt, "The Acculturation of American Indians," *Annals of the American Academy of Political and Social Science* 311 (May 1957): 137–39, 145–46.

51. Klein, *Frontiers of Historical Imagination*, 211.

52. Shephard Krech III, "The State of Ethnohistory," *Annual Review of Anthropology* 20 (1991): 347–48; Harkin, "Ethnohistory's Ethnohistory," 117–18.

53. Ellen Fitzpatrick, *History's Memory: Writing America's Past, 1880–1980* (Cambridge, MA: Harvard University Press, 2002), 101–2, 124–25, 129–30; Fixico, "Literature of American Indian History," 171.

54. De Voto quoted in Hallowell, "Impact of the American Indian," 484.

55. Robert F. Berkhofer Jr., "Cultural Pluralism Versus Ethnocentrism in the New Indian History," in *The American Indian and the Problem of History*, ed. Calvin Martin (New York: Oxford University Press, 1987), 35.

56. Bruner, "Ethnography as Narrative," 144; Harkin, "Ethnohistory's Ethnohistory," 123; Edward H. Spicer, *A Short History of the Indians of the United States* (New York: Van Nostrand, 1969), 142–46.

57. Bruner, "Ethnography as Narrative," 139–40.

58. Margaret Mead, "The American Indian as a Significant Determinant of Anthropological Style," in *Anthropology and the American Indian: A Symposium* (San Francisco: Indian Historian Press, 1973), 71–73.

59. Philip J. Deloria, "Historiography," in *A Companion to American Indian History*, ed. Philip J. Deloria and Neal Salisbury (Malden, MA: Blackwell, 2002), 17–18; Melissa L. Meyer and Kerwin Lee Klein, "Native American Studies and the End of Ethnohistory," in *Studying Native America: Problems and Prospects*, ed. Russell Thornton (Madison: University of Wisconsin Press, 1998), 185, 190; Harkin, "Ethnohistory's Ethnohistory," 124.

60. Robert F. Berkhofer Jr., "The Political Context of a New Indian History," *Pacific Historical Review* 40 (August 1971): 357–62.

61. Robert F. Berkhofer Jr., "Native Americans and United States History," in *The Reinterpretation of American History and Culture*, ed. William H. Cartwright and Richard L. Watson (Washington, DC: National Council for Social Studies, 1973), 37–39.

62. Nancy Oestreich Lurie, "Indian Cultural Adjustment to European Civilization," in *Seventeenth-Century America: Essays in Colonial History*, ed. James Morton Smith (Chapel Hill: University of North Carolina Press, 1959), 33–60.

63. Trigger, "Archaeology and the Ethnographic Present," 12–13; J. Frederick Fausz, "Anglo-Indian Relations in Colonial North America," in *Scholars and the Indian Experience*, ed. W. R. Swagerty (Bloomington: Indiana University Press, 1984), 84; Neal Salisbury, "The Indians' Old World: Native Americans and the Coming of Europeans," in *Indians in American History*, ed. Frederick E. Hoxie and Peter Iverson (Wheeling, IL: Harlan Davidson, 1998), 59.

64. Harkin, "Ethnohistory's Ethnohistory," 115.

65. Eric R. Wolf, *Europe and the People Without History* (1982; repr., Berkeley: University of California Press, 1997); Meyer and Klein, "Native American Studies and the End of Ethnohistory," 192–93.

66. Richard Borshay Lee, "Twenty-First Century Indigenism," *Anthropological Theory* 6 (December 2006): 464–65.

67. Marshall Sahlins, "Cosmologies of Capitalism: The Trans-Pacific Sector of 'The World System,'" in *Culture in Practice: Selected Essays* (New York: Zone Books, 2000), 416–17; Wolf, *Europe and the People Without History*, x, 23.

68. Marshall Sahlins, *Islands of History* (Chicago: University of Chicago Press, 1985), x, 34.

69. Neil L. Whitehead, introduction to *Histories and Historicities in Amazonia*, ed. Neil L. Whitehead (Lincoln: University of Nebraska Press, 2003), viii, xi, xvi, xix–xx.

70. Deloria, "Historiography," 15–17.

71. Thomas E. Sheridan, "Strategic Essentialism and the Future of Ethnohistory in North America," *Reviews in Anthropology* 34 (2005): 63–78; Alfonso Ortiz, "Indian/White Relations: A View from the Other Side of the 'Frontier,'" in *Indians in American History*, ed. Frederick E. Hoxie and Peter Iverson (Wheeling, IL: Harlan Davidson, 1998), 13–14.

Selected Bibliography

This bibliography is by no means a complete record of all the works and sources used by the authors of this book. It indicates a wide range of readings on which the several contributors to this volume have formed their ideas. It serves as a convenience for those who wish to pursue the study of these topics in languages such as Portuguese, Spanish, and German.

Achim, Miruna. "Signos y piedras: La literatura anticuaria en búsqueda de la historia mexicana." In *Entre textos e imágenes,* edited by Fermín del Pino-Díaz, Pascal Riviale, and Juan J. R. Villarías-Robles, 17–26. Madrid: Consejo Superior de Investigaciones Científicas, 2009.

Achim, Miruna, and Irina Podgorny, eds. *Museos al Detalle: Colecciones, antigüedades e historia Natural, 1790–1870.* Rosario: Prohistoria Ediciones, 2013.

Aguirre, Robert D. *Informal Empire: Mexico and Central America in Victorian Culture.* Minneapolis: University of Minnesota Press, 2005.

Alberti, Samuel J. M. M. *Nature and Culture: Objects, Disciplines and the Manchester Museum.* Manchester: Manchester University Press, 2009.

Alcina Franch, José. *Arqueólogos o anticuarios: Historia antigua de la arqueología en la América española.* Barcelona: Serbal, 1995.

Allen, David Elliston. *The Naturalist in Britain: A Social History.* London: Allen Lane, 1976.

Alt, Susan M. "Histories of Mound Building and Scales of Explanation in Archaeology." In *Ideologies in Archaeology,* edited by Reinhard Bernbeck and Randall H. McGuire, 194–211. Tucson: University of Arizona Press, 2011.

Altekamp, Stefan. *Rückkehr nach Afrika: Italienische Kolonialarchäologie in Libyen 1911–1943.* Cologne: Böhlau, 2000.

Andresen, Julie Tetel. *Linguistics in America, 1769–1924: A Critical History.* London: Routledge, 1990.

Auroux, Sylvain, and Francisco Queixalós. *Pour une histoire de la linguistique amérindenne en France*. Paris: AEA-CNRS, 1984.
Barnes, Monica. "The Role of Eighteenth-Century French Explorers in the Development of Andean Archaeology." In *Ancient Travellers: Proceedings of the Twenty-Seventh Annual Conference of the Archaeological Association of the University of Calgary*, edited by Claire Allum, 268–76. Calgary: University of Calgary, 2002.
Barnhart, Terry A. *Ephraim George Squier and the Development of American Anthropology*. Lincoln: University of Nebraska Press, 2005.
Bellin, Joshua David. "Taking the Indian Cure: Thoreau, Indian Medicine, and the Performance of American Culture." *New England Quarterly* 79, no. 1 (2006): 3–36.
Benedict, Barbara. *Curiosity: A Cultural History of Early Modern Inquiry*. Chicago: University of Chicago Press, 2001.
Bergh, Susan. *Wari: Lords of the Ancient Andes*. New York: Thames and Hudson, 2012.
Berkhofer, Robert F., Jr. "Cultural Pluralism Versus Ethnocentrism in the New Indian History." In *The American Indian and the Problem of History*, edited by Calvin Martin, 35–45. New York: Oxford University Press, 1987.
———. *The White Man's Indian: Images of the American Indian from Columbus to the Present*. 1978. Reprint, New York: Vintage, 1979.
Bernal, Ignacio. *Historia de la Arqueología en México*. Mexico City: Editorial Porrúa, 1992.
Bieder, Robert E. *Science Encounters the Indian, 1820–1880: The Early Years of American Ethnology*. Norman: the University of Oklahoma Press, 1986.
Blair, Anne. *Too Much to Know: Managing Scholarly Information Before the Modern Age*. New Haven, CT: Yale University Press, 2010.
Blanckaert, Claude. "Les conditions d'émergence de la science des races au début du XIXe siècle." In *L'idée de "race" dans les sciences humaines et la littérature (XVIIIe et XIXe siècles)*, edited by Sarga Moussa, 33–49. Paris: L'Harmattan, 2003.
Blanckaert, Claude, Claudine Cohen, Pietro Corsi, and J.-L. Fischer. *Le muséum dans le premier siècle de son histoire*. Paris: Muséum National d'Histoire Naturelle, 1997.
Bleichmar, Daniela. *Visible Empire: Botanical Expeditions and Visual Culture in the Hispanic Enlightenment*. Chicago: University of Chicago Press, 2012.
Bleichmar, Daniela, and Peter C. Mancall, eds. *Collecting Across Cultures: Material Exchanges in the Early Modern Atlantic*. Philadelphia: University of Pennsylvania Press, 2011.
Braga, Renato. *História da Comissão Científica de Exploração*. Fortaleza: Imprensa Universitária do Ceará, 1962.
Brockmann, Andreas, and Michaela Stüttgen. *Spurensuche: Zwei Erdwissenschaftler im Südamerika des 19. Jahrhunderts*. Unna: Kreis Unna Kulturamt, 1994.
Browman, David L., and Douglas R. Givens, "Stratigraphic Excavation: The First 'New Archaeology.'" *American Anthropologist* 86, no. 1 (1996): 80–95.
Bruce, Robert V. *The Launching of Modern American Science, 1846–1876*. Ithaca, NY: Cornell University Press, 1987.
Bruner, Edward M. "Ethnography as Narrative." In *The Anthropology of Experience*, edited by Victor W. Turner and Edward M. Bruner, 139–55. Urbana: University of Illinois Press, 1986.
Burke, Peter. "From Antiquarianism to Anthropology." In *Momigliano and Antiquarianism: Foundations of the Modern Cultural Sciences*, edited by Peter N. Miller, 229–47. Toronto: University of Toronto Press, 2007.

Buss, John Joseph. *Winning the West with Words: Language and Conquest in the Lower Great Lakes*. Norman: University of Oklahoma Press, 2011.

Cañizares-Esguerra, Jorge. *How to Write the History of the New World: Histories, Epistemologies, and Identities in the Eighteenth-Century Atlantic World*. Stanford, CA: Stanford University Press, 2001.

———. "Iberian Colonial Science." *Isis* 96 (2005): 64–70.

———. "Travel Accounts." In *Guide to Documentary Sources for Andean Studies, 1530–1900*, edited by Joanne Pillsbury, 291–314. Norman: University of Oklahoma Press, 2008.

Carlson, Keith Thor. *The Power of Place, the Problem of Time: Aboriginal Identity and Historical Consciousness in the Cauldron of Colonialism*. Toronto: University of Toronto Press, 2010.

Chaiklin, Martha. "Ivory in World History: Early Modern Trade in Context." *History Compass* 8, no. 6 (2010): 530–42.

Chaplin, Joyce E. *Subject Matter: Technology, the Body, and Science on the Anglo-American Frontier, 1500–1676*. Cambridge MA: Harvard University Press, 2001.

Clark, William. *Academic Charisma and the Origins of the Research University*. Chicago: University of Chicago Press, 2006.

Cole, Douglas. *Captured Heritage: The Scramble for Northwest Coast Artifacts*. Seattle: University of Washington Press, 1985.

Conder, Claude R., Horatio Kitchener, and Edward Palmer. *The Survey of Western Palestine: Arabic and English Name Lists*. London: Committee of the Palestine Exploration Fund, 1881.

Conn, Steven. *History's Shadow: Native Americans and Historical Consciousness in the Nineteenth Century*. Chicago: University of Chicago Press, 2004.

Cook, Harold. *Matters of Exchange: Commerce, Medicine, and Science in the Dutch Golden Age*. New Haven, CT: Yale University Press, 2007.

Cook, James W. *The Arts of Deception: Playing with Fraud in the Age of Barnum*. Cambridge: Harvard University Press, 2001.

Corrêa, Mariza. "Os Indios do Brasil Elegante e a Professora Leonilda Daltro," *Revista Brasileira de História* 9, no. 18 (1989): 43–65.

Cruikshank, Julie. *Do Glaciers Listen? Local Knowledge, Colonial Encounters, and Social Imagination*. Vancouver: University of British Columbia Press, 2005.

DaCosta Kaufmann, Thomas. *The Mastery of Nature: Aspects of Art, Science, and Humanism in the Renaissance*. Princeton, NJ: Princeton University Press, 1993.

Darnell, Regna. *And Along Came Boas: Continuity and Revolution in Americanist Anthropology*. Amsterdam: John Benjamins, 1998.

Daston, Lorraine, and Peter Galison. *Objectivity*. New York: Zone Books, 2007.

Daston, Lorraine, and Katherine Park. *Wonders and the Order of Nature, 1150–1750*. New York: Zone Books, 1998.

Delbourgo, James. "Slavery in the Cabinet of Curiosities: Hans Sloane's Atlantic World." 2007. http://www.britishmuseum.org/research/research_news/hans_sloanes _atlantic_world.aspx.

Deloria, Philip L. "Historiography." In *A Companion to American Indian History*, edited by Philip J. Deloria and Neal Salisbury, 6–24. Malden, MA: Blackwell, 2002.

———. *Playing Indian*. New Haven, CT: Yale University Press, 1998.

Desmet, Piet. *La linguistique naturaliste en France (1867–1922)*. Leuven: Peeters, 1996.

Desmond, Adrian, and James Moore. *Darwin's Sacred Cause: How a Hatred of Slavery Shaped Darwin's Views on Human Evolution*. New York: Houghton Mifflin Harcourt, 2009.

Díaz-Andreu, Margarita. *A World History of Nineteenth-Century Archaeology: Nationalism, Colonialism, and the Past*. Oxford: Oxford University Press, 2007.

Díaz-Andreu, Margarita, and Timothy Champion. "Nationalism and Archaeology in Europe: An Introduction." In *Nationalism and Archaeology in Europe*, edited by Margarita Díaz-Andreu and Timothy Champion, 1–23. London: UCL Press, 1996.

Elsner, John, and Roger Cardinal. "Introduction." In *The Cultures of Collecting*, edited by John Elsner and Roger Cardinal, 1–7. London: Reaktion Books, 1994.

Evans, R. Tripp. *Romancing the Maya: Mexican Antiquity in the American Imagination, 1820–1915*. Austin: University of Texas Press, 2004.

Fabian, Ann. *The Skull Collectors: Race, Science, and America's Unburied Dead*. Chicago: University of Chicago Press, 2010.

Farro, Máximo. "Colecciones de cráneos, fotografías y manuscritos en el desarrollo de la antropología física y de la etnografía lingüística en la Argentina de fines del siglo XIX." In *Colecionismos, práticas de campo e representações*, edited by Maria Margaret Lopes and Alda Heizer, 93–104. Campina Grande: EDUEPB, 2011.

———. *La formación del Museo de La Plata: Coleccionistas, comerciantes, estudiosos y naturalistas viajeros a fines del siglo XIX*. Rosario: Prohistoria ediciones, 2009.

———. "Imágenes de cráneos, retratos antropológicos y tipologías raciales: Los usos de las primeras colecciones de fotografías del Museo de La Plata a fines del siglo XIX." In *Los secretos de Barba Azul: Fantasías y realidades de los archivos del Museo de La Plata*, edited by Tatiana Kelly and Irina Podgorny, 69–104. Rosario: Prohistoria ediciones, 2012.

———. "Las lenguas indígenas argentinas como objeto de colección: Notas acerca de los estudios lingüísticos de Samuel A. Lafone Quevedo a fines del siglo XIX." *Revista de Indias* 73, no. 258 (2013): 525–52.

Fausz, J. Frederick. "Anglo-Indian Relations in Colonial North America." In *Scholars and the Indian Experience*, edited by W. R. Swagerty, 79–105. Bloomington: Indiana University Press, 1984.

Fielding, Penny. *Scotland and the Fictions of Geography: North Britain, 1760–1830*. Cambridge: Cambridge University Press, 2008.

Figueirôa, Silvia F. de M. *A Formação das ciências geológicas no Brasil: Uma História Social e Institucional, 1875–1934*. São Paulo: Hucitec, 1997.

Finlay, Robert. *The Pilgrim Art: Cultures of Porcelain in World History*. Berkeley: University of California Press, 2010.

Fischer, Manuela. "Adolf Bastian's Travels in the Americas (1875–1876)." In *Adolf Bastian and His Universal Archive of Humanity: The Origins of German Anthropology*, edited by Manuela Fischer, Peter Bolz, and Susan Kamel, 191–206. Hildesheim: G. Olms, 2007.

FitzGerald, Frances. *America Revised: History Schoolbooks in the Twentieth Century*. New York: Vintage, 1980.

Fitzpatrick, Ellen. *History's Memory: Writing America's Past, 1880–1980*. Cambridge, MA: Harvard University Press, 2002.

Fixico, Donald L. "The Literature of American Indian History." In *A Century of American Historiography*, edited by James M. Banner Jr., 170–82. Boston: Bedford/St. Martin's, 2010.

Foucault, Michel. *The Order of Things: An Archaeology of Knowledge*. New York: Pantheon Books, 1971.

Fowler, Don D., and David R. Wilcox. "From Thomas Jefferson to the Pecos Conference: Changing Anthropological Agendas in the North American Southwest." In *Surveying the Record: North American Scientific Exploration to 1930*, edited by E. C. Carter II, 197–223. Philadelphia: American Philosophical Society, 1999.

Gänger, Stefanie. "Disjunctive Circles: Modern Intellectual Culture and the Journeys of Incan Antiquities, c. 1877–1921." *Modern Intellectual History* 10, no. 2 (2013): 399–414.

———. "La mirada imperialista? Los alemanes y la arqueología peruana." *Histórica* 30, no. 2 (2006): 69–90.

———. *Relics of the Past: The Collecting and Study of Pre-Columbian Antiquities in Peru and Chile, 1837–1911*. Oxford Studies in the History of Archaeology. Oxford: Oxford University Press, 2014.

Giles, Eugene. "Principal Figures in Physical Anthropology Before and During World War II." In *Histories of American Physical Anthropology in the Twentieth Century*, edited by Michael A. Little and Kenneth A. Kennedy, 141–54. Lanham MD: Lexington, 2010.

Grafton, Anthony, April Shelford, and Nancy Siraisi. *New Worlds, Ancient Texts: The Power of Tradition and the Shock of Discovery*. Cambridge, MA: Harvard University Press, 1992.

Gruber, Jacob W. "Archaeology, History, and Culture." In *American Archaeology, Past and Present: A Celebration of the Society for American Archaeology, 1935–1985*, edited by David J. Meltzer, Don D. Fowler, and Jeremy A. Sabloff, 163–86. 1986. Reprint, Washington, DC: Smithsonian Institution Press, 1994.

Guimarães, Lúcia M. P. "Debaixo da imediata proteção de Sua Majestade Imperial." *Revista do Instituto Histórico e Geográfico Brasileiro* 388 (1995): 459–613.

———. "Uma parceria inesperada: O Instituto Histórico e Geográfico Brasileiro e a Real Sociedade dos Antiquários do Norte." *Revista do Instituto Histórico e Geográfico Brasileiro* 155, no. 384 (1994): 499–511.

Guimarães, Manoel L. L. S. "História e natureza em von Martius: Esquadrinhando o Brasil para construir a nação." *História Ciência Saúde-Manguinhos* 7, no. 2 (2000): 391–413. Accessed November 20, 2013. doi:10.1590/S0104-59702000000300008.

———. "Nação e civilização nos trópicos: O Instituto Histórico Geográfico Brasileiro e o projeto de uma história nacional." *Revista Estudos Históricos* 1 (1988): 5–27.

Haas, Richard. *Keramikfunde aus Ancón, Peru: Die Tonobjekte der Sammlung Reiss und Stübel im Museum für Völkerkunde Berlin*. Berlin: Mann, 1986.

Halttunen, Karen. *Confidence Men and Painted Women: A Study of Middle-Class Culture in America, 1830–1870*. New Haven, CT: Yale University Press, 1982.

Hamann, Byron. "Drawing Glyphs Together." In *Past Presented: Archaeological Illustration and the Ancient Americas*, edited by Joanne Pillsbury, 231–82. Washington, DC: Dumbarton Oaks Research Library and Collection, 2012.

Harkin, Michael E. "(Dis)pleasures of the Text: Boasian Anthropology on the Northwest Coast." In *Gateways: Exploring the Legacy of the Jesup North Pacific Expedition*,

1897–1902, edited by Igor Krupnick and William Fitzhugh, 93–106. Washington, DC: Arctic Studies Center, Smithsonian Institution, 2002.
———. "Ethnohistory's Ethnohistory: Creating a Discipline from the Bottom Up." *Social Science History* 34, no. 2 (Summer 2010): 113–28.
Harris, Douglas C. *Landing Native Fisheries: Indian Reserves and Fishing Rights in British Columbia 1849–1925*. Vancouver: University of British Columbia Press, 2008.
Harrison, Julian, and Regna Darnell, eds. *Historicizing Canadian Anthropology*. Vancouver: University of British Columbia Press, 2006.
Henare, Amiria J. M. *Museums, Anthropology and Imperial Exchange*. Cambridge: Cambridge University Press, 2005.
Hill Boone, Elizabeth. "The Defining Sample: How We Pursue the Pre-Columbian Past." In *A Pre-Columbian World*, edited by Jeffrey Quilter and Mary Miller, 21–53. Washington, DC: Dumbarton Oaks Research Library and Collection, 2006.
Hinsley, Curtis M., Jr. *Savages and Scientists: The Smithsonian Institution and the Development of American Anthropology, 1846–1910*. Washington, DC: Smithsonian Institution Press, 1981.
Jacknis, Ira. "Franz Boas and Exhibits: On the Limitations of the Museum Method of Anthropology." In *Objects and Others: Essays on Museums and Material Culture*, edited by George W. Stocking Jr., 75–111. Madison: University of Wisconsin Press, 1985.
Jardine, Nicholas, and Emma Spary. "The Natures of Cultural History." In *Cultures of Natural History*, edited by Nicholas Jardine, Emma Spary, and James A. Secord, 3–13. Cambridge: Cambridge University Press, 1996.
Jonaitis, Aldona. *From the Land of the Totem Poles: The Northwest Coast Indian Art Collection at the American Museum of Natural History*. New York: American Museum of Natural History/Seattle: University of Washington Press, 1988.
Kaeser, Marc-Antoine. "On the International Roots of Prehistory." In *Histories of Archaeology*, edited by Tim Murray and Christopher Evans, 378–91. Oxford: Oxford University Press, 2008.
Kaulicke, Peter. *Gräber von Ancón, Peru: Nach den Arbeiten von W. Reiss/A. Stübel, M. Uhle, R. Ravines, G.R. Willey und C. Huapaya*. Munich: C. H. Beck, 1983.
Keen, Benjamin, *The Aztec Image in Western Thought*. New Brunswick, NJ: Rutgers University Press, 1971.
Kehoe, Alice Beck. "Europe's Prehistoric Dawn Reproduced: Daniel Wilson's Magisterial Archaeology." In *New Perspectives on the Origins of Americanist Archaeology*, edited by David L. Browman and Stephen Williams, 133–47. Tuscaloosa: University of Alabama Press, 2002.
———. *The Land of Prehistory: A Critical History of American Archaeology*. New York: Routledge, 1998.
———. *North American Indians: A Comprehensive Account*. 3rd ed. Upper Saddle River, NJ: Prentice-Hall, 2006.
Kennedy, Roger G. *Hidden Cities: The Discovery and Loss of Ancient North American Civilization*. New York: Free Press, 1994.
Klein, Kerwin Lee. *Frontiers of Historical Imagination: Narrating the European Conquest of Native America, 1890–1990*. Berkeley: University of California Press, 1997.
Kodama, Kaori. "Em busca da gênese do Brasil nas províncias do Norte: Gonçalves Dias e os trabalhos etnográficos da Comissão Científica de Exploração." In

Comissão Científica do Império (1859–1861), edited by Lorelai Kury, 115–53. Rio de Janeiro: Andrea Jacobsson Editora, 2009.

———. Os índios no Império do Brasil: A etnografia do IHGB entre as décadas de 1840 e 1860. Rio de Janeiro: Editora Fiocruz/EDUSP, 2009.

Kohl, Philip. "Nationalism and Archaeology: On the Constructions of Nations and the Reconstructions of the Remote Past." *Annual Review of Anthropology* 27 (1998): 223–46.

Kohl, Philip, and Claire Fawcett, eds. *Nationalism, Politics, and the Practice of Archaeology*. Cambridge: Cambridge University Press, 1995.

Kopytof, Igor. "The Internal African Frontier: The Making of African Political Culture." In *The African Frontier: The Reproduction of Traditional African Societies*, edited by Igor Kopytoff, 3–84. Bloomington: Indiana University Press, 1987.

Kury, Lorelai, ed. *Comissão Científica do Império, 1859–1861*. Rio de Janeiro: Andrea Jakobsson Editorial, 2009.

Langebaek Rueda, Carl Henrik. *Arqueología colombiana: ciencia, pasado y exclusión*. Bogotá: Inst. Colombiano para el Desarrollo de la Ciencia y la Tecnología F. J. de Caldas, 2003.

Lee, Richard Borshay. "Twenty-First Century Indigenism." *Anthropological Theory* 6, no. 4 (2006): 455–79.

Le Goff, Armelle, and Nadia Prévost-Urkidi. "Comission de l'exploration scientifique du Mexique (1862–1893)" (2009). Accessed March 29, 2013, http://www.nadiaprevosturkidi.net/publications/?lang=es.

Levenson, Jay A., ed. *Circa 1492: Art in the Age of Exploration*. Washington, DC: National Gallery of Art, 1991.

Levine, Philippa. *The Amateur and the Professional: Antiquarians, Historians and Archaeologists in Victorian Britain, 1838–1886*. Cambridge: Cambridge University Press, 1986.

Lewis, Daniel. *The Feathery Tribe: Robert Ridgway and the Modern Study of Birds*. New Haven, CT: Yale University Press, 2012.

Lopes, Maria M. "Cenas de tempos profundos: ossos, viagens, memórias nas culturas da natureza no Brasil." *História, Ciência, Saúde-Manguinhos* 15, no. 3 (2008): 615–34. Accessed November 20, 2013, doi:10.1590/S0104-59702008000300004.

———. "The Museums and the Construction of Natural Sciences in Brazil in the 19th Century." In *Cultures and Institutions of Natural History*, edited by Michael T. Ghiselin and Alan E. Leviton, 81–100. San Francisco: California Academy of Sciences, 2000.

———. *O Brasil descobre a pesquisa científica: As ciências naturais e os museus no século XIX*. 2nd ed. São Paulo: Hucitec, 2009.

———. "The Scientific Exploration Commission: An Inward Expansion." In *Comissão Científica do Império 1859–1861*, edited by Lorelai Kury, 233–38. Rio de Janeiro: Andrea Jakobsson Editorial, 2009.

Lopes, Maria Margaret, and Irina Podgorny. "The Shaping of Latin American Museums of Natural History, 1850–1890." *Osiris: Nature and Empire: Science and the Colonial Enterprise* 2nd ser., 15 (2000): 108–18.

López Luján, Leonardo. "El capitán Guillermo Dupaix y su álbum arqueológico de 1794." *Arqueología mexicana* 19, no. 109 (2011): 71–81.

MacGregor, Arthur. *Curiosity and Enlightenment: Collectors and Collections from the Sixteenth to the Nineteenth Century.* New Haven, CT: Yale University Press, 2007.
Majluf, Natalia. "De la Rebelión al Museo: Genealogías y Retratos de los Incas, 1781–1900." In *Los Incas, Reyes del Perú*, edited by Natalia Majluf, Thomas Cummins, Luis Eduardo Wuffarden, Gabriela Ramos Cárdenas, and Elena Phipps, 253–317. Lima: Banco de Crédito, 2005.
———. "Photographers in Andean Visual Culture: Traces of an Absent Landscape." *History of Photography* 24, no. 2 (2000): 91–100.
———. *Reproducing Nations: Types and Costumes in Asia and Latin America, ca. 1800–1860.* New York: Americas Society, 2006.
Majluf, Natalia, and Luis Eduardo Wuffarden, eds. *La recuperación de la memoria, Perú, 1842–1942.* 2 vols. Lima: Fundación Telefónica/Museo de Arte de Lima, 2001.
Martin, Paul S., George I. Quimby, and Donald Collier. *Indians Before Columbus.* Chicago: University of Chicago Press, 1947.
Mattos, Ilmar R. de. "Construtores e herdeiros: A trama dos interesses na construção da unidade política." *Almanack Braziliense* 1 (2005): 8–26.
McElroy, Keith. "Ephraim George Squier: Photography and the Illustration of Peruvian Antiquities." *History of Photography* 10 (April–June 1986): 99–129.
Meek, Ronald L. *Social Science and the Ignoble Savage.* Cambridge: Cambridge University Press, 1976.
Meltzer, David J. "The Antiquity of Man and the Development of American Archaeology." *Advances in Archaeological Method and Theory* 6 (1983): 1–51.
Merchant, Carolyn. *The Death of Nature.* San Francisco: Harper and Row, 1980.
Merrill, Lynn L. *The Romance of Victorian Natural History.* New York: Oxford University Press, 1989.
Midgely, Mary. *Science as Salvation: A Modern Myth and Its Meaning.* London: Routledge, 1992.
Miller, Peter N. Introduction to *Momigliano and Antiquarianism: Foundations of the Modern Cultural Sciences*, edited by Peter N. Miller, 3–65. Toronto: University of Toronto Press, 2007.
Miller, Robert J. *Native America, Discovered and Conquered.* Lincoln: University of Nebraska Press, 2008.
Molloy, Maureen A. *On Creating a Usable Culture: Margaret Mead and the Emergence of American Cosmopolitanism.* Honolulu: University of Hawaii Press, 2008.
Momigliano, Arnaldo. "Ancient History and the Antiquarian." *Journal of the Warburg and Courtauld Institutes* 13 (1950): 285–315.
———. "Vico's Scienza nuova: Roman 'Bestioni' and Roman 'Eroi.'" *History and Theory* 5, no. 1 (1966): 3–23.
Morgan, Lewis Henry. *Ancient Society.* 1877. Tucson: University of Arizona Press, 1985.
Morpurgo Davis, Anna. *Nineteenth-Century Linguistics.* London: Longman Pearson, 1998.
Moses, L. G. *Wild West Shows and the Images of American Indians, 1883–1933.* Albuquerque: University of New Mexico Press, 1996.
Murray, Tim, and Christopher Evans, eds. *Histories of Archaeology: A Reader in the History of Archaeology.* Oxford: Oxford University Press, 2008.
Myrone, Martin, and Lucy Peltz, eds. *Producing the Past: Aspects of Antiquarian Culture and Practice, 1700–1850.* London: Ashgate, 1999.

Naylor, Simon. "Collecting Quoits: Field Cultures in the History of Cornish Antiquarianism." *Cultural Geographies* 10 (2003): 309–33.
———. *Regionalizing Science: Placing Knowledges in Victorian England.* London: Pickering and Chatto, 2010.
Niezen, Ronald. *The Origins of Indigenism: Human Rights and the Politics of Identity.* Berkeley: University of California Press, 2003.
Novick, Peter. *That Noble Dream: The "Objectivity Question" and the American Historical Profession.* Cambridge: Cambridge University Press, 1988.
Olsen Bruhns, Karen. *Ancient South America.* Cambridge World Archaeology. Cambridge: Cambridge University Press, 1994.
Pauketat, Timothy. *Chiefdoms and Other Archaeological Delusions.* Lanham, MD: AltaMira, 2007.
Pearce, Roy Harvey. *Savagism and Civilization: A Study of the Indian and the American Mind.* Berkeley: University of California Press, 1998.
Pearce, Susan M. *On Collecting: An Investigation into Collecting in the European Tradition.* London: Routledge, 1995.
———, ed. *Visions of Antiquity: The Society of Antiquaries of London 1707–2007.* Oxford: Oxbow, 2007.
Penny, Glenn H. *Objects of Culture: Ethnology and Ethnographic Museums in Imperial Germany.* Chapel Hill: University of North Carolina Press, 2002.
Penny, Glenn, and Matt Bunzl, eds. *Worldly Provincialism: German Anthropology in the Age of Empire.* Ann Arbor: University of Michigan Press, 2003.
Phillips, David A., Jr. Introduction to *Examining the Course of Southwest Archaeology: The Durango Conference, September 1995,* edited by David A. Phillips Jr. and Lynne Sebastian, 1–10. Special Publication, no. 3. Albuquerque: New Mexico Archeological Council, 2001.
Pickstone, John V. *Ways of Knowing: A New History of Science, Technology and Medicine.* Manchester: Manchester University Press, 2000.
Pillsbury, Joanne, ed. *Guide to Documentary Sources for Andean Studies, 1530–1900.* Norman: University of Oklahoma Press, 2008.
———, ed. *Past Presented: Archaeological Illustration and the Ancient Americas.* Washington, DC: Dumbarton Oaks Research Library and Collection, 2012.
Pillsbury, Joanne, and Lisa Trever. "The King, the Bishop, and the Creation of an American Antiquity." *Ñawpa Pacha* 29 (2008): 192–219.
Pinto, John. *Speaking Ruins: Piranesi, Architects and Antiquity in Eighteenth-Century Rome.* Ann Arbor: University of Michigan Press, 2012.
Pi-Suñer Llorens, Antonia, ed. *México en el Diccionario Universal de Historia y de Geografía.* Vol. 3, *La contribución de Manuel Orozco y Berra.* Selected and introduced by Aurora Flores Olea, Miguel Ángel Castro, and Othón Nava Martínez. Mexico City: UNAM, 2004.
Pocock, John G. A. *Barbarism and Religion.* Vol. 4, *Barbarians, Savages and Empires.* Cambridge: Cambridge University Press, 2008.
Podgorny, Irina. *Charlatanes: Crónicas de remedios incurables.* Buenos Aires: Eterna Cadencia, 2012.
———. "Fossil Dealers, the Practices of Comparative Anatomy, and British Diplomacy in Latin America." *British Journal for the History of Science* 46, no. 4 (2013): 647–74.
———."The Reliability of the Ruins." *Journal for Spanish Cultural Studies* 8, no. 2 (2007): 213–33.

———. *El sendero del tiempo y de las causas accidentales: Los espacios de la prehistoria en la Argentina, 1850–1910.* Rosario: Prohistoria, 2009.

———. "'Silent and Alone': How the Ruins of Palenque Were Taught to Speak the Language of Archaeology." In *Comparative Archaeologies: A Sociological View of the Science of the Past*, edited by Ludomir R. Lozny, 527–53. New York: Springer, 2011.

———. "Travelling Museums and Itinerant Collections in Nineteenth-Century Latin America." *Museum History Journal* 6, no. 2 (2013): 127–46.

———. *Los viajes en Bolivia de la Comisión Médico-Científico Quirúrgica Italiana.* Santa Cruz de la Sierra: Fundación Nova, 2011.

Podgorny, Irina, and Maria Margaret Lopes. *El Desierto en una Vitrina: Museos e historia Natural en la Argentina, 1810–1890.* México: LIMUSA, 2008.

Pomian, Krzysztof. *Collectors and Curiosities: Paris and Vienna, 1500–1800.* Cambridge: Polity Press, 1990.

Poovey, Mary. *A History of the Modern Fact: Problems of Knowledge in the Sciences of Wealth and Society.* Chicago: University of Chicago Press, 1998.

Porter, David L. "Monstrous Beauty: Eighteenth-Century Fashion and the Aesthetics of the Chinese Taste." *Eighteenth-Century Studies* 35, no. 3 (2002): 395–411.

Quinn, Stephen Christopher. *Windows on Nature: The Great Habitat Dioramas of the American Museum of Natural History.* New York: Abrams, 2006.

Quiñoz Flores, Georgina, Indira Salavarría Pedrero, and Elia Guadalupe, *Estado de Campeche: Informes de Gobierno 1862–1910.* Campeche: CONACULTA/PAC-MIC, 2003.

Qureshi, S. *Peoples on Parade: Exhibitions, Empire, and Anthropology in Nineteenth-Century Britain.* Chicago: University of Chicago Press, 2011.

Raibmon, Paige. *Authentic Indians: Episodes of Encounter from the Late Nineteenth Century Northwest Coast.* Durham, NC: Duke University Press, 2005.

Ranney, Edward. "Images of a Sacred Geography." In *The New World's Old World: Photographic Views of Ancient America*, edited by May Castleberry, 89–122. Albuquerque: University of New Mexico Press, 2003.

Ravines, Rogger. *Los Museos del Perú: Breve historia y Guía.* Lima: Dirección General de Museos, Instituto Nacional de Cultura, 1989.

Ray, Arthur J. *Telling It to the Judge: Taking Native History to Court.* Montreal: McGill-Queen's University Press, 2011.

Redford, Bruce. *Dilettanti: The Antic and the Antique in Eighteenth-Century England.* Los Angeles: J. Paul Getty Museum, 2008.

Riviale, Pascal. "Europe Rediscovers Latin America: Collecting Artifacts and Views in the First Decades of the Nineteenth Century." In *Collecting Across Cultures: Material Exchanges in the Early Modern Atlantic*, edited by Daniela Bleichmar and Peter C. Mancall, 254–68. Philadelphia: University of Pennsylvania Press, 2011.

Robertson, Leslie A., and the Kwagu'l Gixsam Clan. *Standing Up with Ga'axsta'las: Jane Constance Cook and the Politics of Memory, Church, and Custom.* Vancouver: University of British Columbia Press, 2013.

Robertson, Lindsay G. *Conquest by Law.* New York: Oxford University Press, 2005.

Rossi, Paolo. *The Dark Abyss of Time: The History of the Earth and the History of Nations.* Translated by Lydia G. Cochrane. Chicago: University of Chicago Press, 1984.

Roy, Susan. *These Mysterious People: Shaping History and Archaeology in a Northwest Coast Community.* Montreal: McGill-Queen's University Press, 2010.
Rudwick, Martin J. S. *Bursting the Limits of Time: The Reconstruction of Geohistory in the Age of Revolution.* Chicago: University of Chicago Press, 2005.
———. *The Meaning of Fossils: Episodes in the History of Palaeontology.* 2nd ed. Chicago: University of Chicago Press, 1976.
Rugeley, Terry. *Maya Wars: Ethnographic Accounts from Nineteenth-Century Yucatan.* Norman: University of Oklahoma Press, 2001.
———. *Rebellion Now and Forever: Mayas, Hispanics, and Caste War Violence in Yucatán, 1800–1880.* Stanford, CA: Stanford University Press, 2009.
Safier, Neil. *Measuring the New World: Enlightenment Science and South America.* Chicago: University of Chicago Press, 2008.
Sahlins, Marshall. "Cosmologies of Capitalism: The Trans-Pacific Sector of 'The World System.'" In *Culture in Practice: Selected Essays,* 415–69. New York: Zone Books, 2000.
———. *Islands of History.* Chicago: University of Chicago Press, 1985.
———. "'Sentimental Pessimism' and Ethnographic Experience; or, Why Culture Is Not a Disappearing 'Object.'" In *Biographies of Scientific Objects,* edited by Lorraine Daston. 158–202. Chicago: University of Chicago Press, 2000.
Said, Edward. *Culture and Imperialism.* New York: Knopf, 1993.
Sassaman, Kenneth E., Jr. *The Eastern Archaic, Historicized.* Lanham MD: AltaMira, 2010.
Sassaman, Kenneth E., Jr., and Donald H. Holly. *Hunter-Gatherer Archaeology as Historical Process.* Tucson: University of Arizona Press, 2011.
Schlanger, Nathan. "Series in Progress: Antiquities of Nature, Numismatics and Stone Implements in the Emergence of Prehistoric Archaeology." *History of Science* 48 (2010): 343–69.
Schnapp, Alain. "Between Antiquarians and Archaeologists: Continuities and Ruptures." In *Histories of Archaeology: A Reader in the History of Archaeology,* edited by Tim Murray and Christopher Evans, 392–405. Oxford: Oxford University Press, 2008.
———. *La conquête du passé: Aux origines de l'archéologie.* Paris: Carré, 1993.
———. *The Discovery of the Past: The Origins of Archaeology.* Paris: British Museum Press, 1993.
———. "Eduard Gerhard: Founder of Classical Archaeology?" *Modernism/Modernity* 11, no.1 (2004): 169–71.
Schwimmer, Eric G. "Symbolic Competition." *Anthropologica* 14, no. 2 (1972): 117–55.
Sellen, Adam. "Los padres Camacho y su museo," *Península* 5, no. 1 (2010): 67–70.
Shapin, Steven. *A Social History of Truth: Civility and Science in Seventeenth-Century England.* Chicago: University of Chicago Press, 1994.
Sheets-Pyenson, Susan. *Cathedrals of Science: The Development of Colonial Natural History Museums During the Late Nineteenth Century.* Montreal: McGill-Queens University Press, 1988.
Sheridan, Thomas E. "Strategic Essentialism and the Future of Ethnohistory in North America." *Reviews in Anthropology* 34 (2005): 63–78.
Shryock, Andrew, and Daniel Lord Smail. *Deep History: The Architecture of Past and Present.* Berkeley: University of California Press, 2011.

Silliman, Stephen W., ed. *Collaborating at the Trowel's Edge: Teaching and Learning in Indigenous Archaeology*. Tucson: University of Arizona Press, 2008.

Stocking, George W., Jr. "Essays on Museums and Material Culture." In *Objects and Others: Essays on Museums and Material Culture*, edited by George W. Stocking Jr., 3–14. Madison: University of Wisconsin Press, 1985.

———. "Ideas and Institutions in American Anthropology: Thoughts Toward a History of the Interwar Years." In *The Ethnographer's Magic and Other Essays in the History of Anthropology*, 114–77. Madison: University of Wisconsin Press, 1992.

Sturtevant, William C. "Tribe and State in the Sixteenth and Twentieth Centuries." In *The Development of Political Organization in Native North America*, edited by Elisabeth Tooker, 3–16. Washington, DC: American Ethnological Society, 1983.

Sweet, Rosemary. *Antiquaries: The Discovery of the Past in Eighteenth-Century Britain*. London: Hambledon, 2004.

Szegedy-Maszak, Andrew. Introduction to *Antiquity and Photography: Early Views of Ancient Mediterranean Sites*, edited by Claire L. Lyons. Los Angeles: J. Paul Getty Museum, 2005.

Taracena Arriola, Arturo. *De la nostalgia por la memoria a la memoria nostálgica: La prensa literaria y la construcción del regionalismo yucateco en el siglo XIX*. Mérida: UNAM, 2010.

Taracena Arriola, Arturo, and Adam Sellen. "Emmanuel von Friedrichsthal: Su encuentro con las ruinas yucatecas y el debate sobre el origen de la civilización maya." *Península*, 1, no. 2 (2006): 49–79.

Te Heesen, Anke. "Accounting for the Natural World." In *Colonial Botany: Science, Commerce and Politics in the Early Modern World*, edited by Londa Schiebinger and Claudia Swan, 237–51. Philadelphia: University of Pennsylvania Press, 2005.

Thomas, David Hurst. *Skull Wars: Kennewick Man, Archaeology and the Battle for Native American Identity*. New York: Basic Books, 2000.

Thurner, Mark. "Peruvian Genealogies of History and Nation." In *After Spanish Rule: Postcolonial Predicaments of the Americas*, edited by Mark Thurner and Andrés Guerrero, 141–75. Durham, NC: Duke University Press, 2003.

Trever, Lisa, and Joanne Pillsbury, "Martínez Compañón and His Illustrated 'Museum.'" In *Collecting Across Cultures*, edited by Peter Mancall and Daniela Bleichmar, 236–53. Philadelphia: University of Pennsylvania Press, 2011.

Trigger, Bruce G. *A History of Archaeological Thought*. 2nd ed. Cambridge: Cambridge University Press, 2006.

Vos, Paula de. "The Rare, the Singular, and the Extraordinary: Natural History and the Collection of Curiosities in the Spanish Empire." In *Science in the Spanish and Portuguese Empires, 1500–1800*, edited by Daniela Bleichmar, Paula de Vos, Kristin Huffine, and Kevin Sheehan, 271–89. Stanford, CA: Stanford University Press, 2009.

Wallace, Anthony F. C. *Jefferson and the Indians*. Ann Arbor: University of Michigan Press, 1999.

Webster, David. "The Mystique of the Ancient Maya." In *Archaeological Fantasies: How Pseudoarchaeology Misrepresents the Past and Misleads the Public*, edited by Garrett G. Fagan, 129–53. London: Routledge, 2006.

Welch, Margaret. *The Book of Nature: Natural History in the United States, 1825–1875*. Boston: Northeastern University Press, 1998.
Whitehead, Christopher. *Museums and the Construction of Disciplines: Art and Archaeology in Nineteenth-Century Britain*. London: Duckworth, 2009.
Whitehead, Neil L., ed. *Histories and Historicities in Amazonia*. Lincoln: University of Nebraska Press, 2003.
Willey, Gordon R., and Jeremy A. Sabloff. *A History of American Archaeology*. 1974. 3rd ed., New York: Freeman, 1993.
Williams, Elizabeth A. "Art and Artifact at the Trocadero: Ars Americana and the Primitivist Revolution." In *Objects and Others: Essays on Museums and Material Culture*, edited by George W. Stocking Jr., 146–66. Madison: University of Wisconsin Press, 1985.
Williams, Robert A., Jr. *The American Indian in Western Legal Thought*. New York: Oxford University Press, 1990.
———. *Like a Loaded Weapon: The Rehnquist Court, Indian Rights, and the Legal History of Racism in America*. Minneapolis: University of Minnesota Press, 2005.
Wolf, Eric R. *Europe and the People Without History*. 1982. Reprint, Berkeley: University of California Press. 1997.
Young-Sánchez, Margaret. "Reiss, Wilhelm (1838–1908) and Alphons Stübel (1835–1904)." In *Guide to Documentary Sources for Andean Studies, 1530–1900*, vol. 3, edited by Joanne Pillsbury, 568–72. Norman: University of Oklahoma Press, 2008.

Editors and Contributors

Editors

Philip L. Kohl is professor of anthropology and the Kathryn W. Davis Professor of Slavic Studies at Wellesley College. He received his BA from Columbia University (1969, Greek and Latin) and his MA (1972) and PhD (1974) in anthropology from Harvard University. He has taught at Wellesley College since 1974. He is coeditor of *Nationalism, Politics, and the Practice of Archaeology* (1995) with Clare Fawcett and of *Selective Remembrances: Archaeology in the Construction, Commemoration, and Consecration of National Pasts* (2007). He is the author of more than 150 articles and reviews and has delivered the distinguished lecture at the archaeological division of the American Anthropological Association Meeting in 2007.

Irina Podgorny, head researcher at Consejo Nacional de Investigaciones Científicas y Técnicas, has been a research scholar at Museo de La Plata in Argentina since 1995 and at the Max Planck Institute for the History of Science in 2009 and 2010. She received her BA in anthropology and archaeology and her PhD from Universidad Nacional de La Plata. A Humboldt Fellow, Senior Fellow of Internationale Kolleg für Kulturtechnikforschung und Medienphilosophie-Bauhaus-Universität Weimar, corresponding member of Shanghai Archaeological Forum (Institute of Archaeology, Chinese Academy of Social Sciences), visiting professor at the University of Paris 7, École des Hautes Études en Sciences Sociales, and Wofford College, she was awarded the Georg Forster Research Award in

2013. She is the author of *El desierto en una vitrina: Museos e historia natural en la Argentina* (with M. M. Lopes, 2008); *El sendero del tiempo y de las causas accidentales: Los espacios de la prehistoria en la Argentina, 1850–1910* (2009); *Guido Bennati: Los viajes en Bolivia de la Comisión Médico Científico Quirúrgica italiana* (2010); and *Charlatanes: Crónica de remedios incurables* (2012). She has extensively published on the history of comparative anatomy, paleontology, and archaeology in journals such as *British Journal for the History of Science*, *Nuncius*, and *Science in Context*. In Argentina, she is the director of the book collection *Historia de la ciencia*, published by Prohistoria Ediciones. Podgorny specializes in the trade in ruins and fossils. In the last years, she has started working on charlatans, confidence men, and quack doctors as agents of the circulation of knowledge and as dealers in antiquities, remedies, and natural history collections.

Stefanie Gänger is an assistant professor at the Institute for Iberian and Latin American History at Cologne University. She studied European and Latin American history at the universities of Augsburg, Seville, and Cambridge and received her PhD in history from the University of Cambridge in 2011. During work on her PhD, she was a visiting fellow at the Max Planck Institute for the History of Science in Berlin and at the University of Pennsylvania. Before coming to Cologne, she held postdoctoral fellowships at the Institute for Latin American Studies in Berlin and at the University of Konstanz. She is the author of *Relics of the Past: The Collecting and Study of Pre-Columbian Antiquities in Peru and Chile, 1837–1911* (2014). Her recent articles have addressed the history of antiquarianism and archaeology in Peru, of botany and trade in medicinal plants, and of discourses about indigeneity.

Contributors

Miruna Achim is an associate professor in the humanities department at the Universidad Autónoma Metropolitana-Cuajimalpa, Mexico City, where she has taught since 2004. She received her BA from Harvard University in the field of art history and her MA and PhD from Yale University in the fields of Spanish and Portuguese literature. Professor Achim specializes in the history of science and medicine in Latin America and collections, museums, and the public sphere in eighteenth-century Mexico. She is the author of *Lagartijas medicinales: Remedios americanos y debates* *ilustrados* (2008) and is currently working on two other books, *El Museo Nacional de México y los guiones de la historia, 1825–1867*, and *The Astrological Tradition in Colonial Mexico.*

Mariza Corrêa is an anthropologist. She was a full professor at the Department of Anthropology at the Institute of Philosophy and Human Sciences at Campinas State University (UNICAMP) for thirty years and a former president of the Brazilian Association of Anthropology. Presently she is a researcher at UNICAMP's Pagu/Center for Gender Studies, and she is a faculty member in the area of gender in the Ph.D. Program in Social Sciences at UNICAMP.

Máximo Farro graduated in anthropology and archaeology. He is currently working as a researcher at Consejo Nacional de Investigaciones Científicas y Técnicas in Argentina and as curator of the archival collections in the Archivo Histórico del Museo de La Plata, Argentina. He works mainly in the area of history of science, studying the historical nexus between anthropology, archaeology, and collections in nineteenth-century Argentina with particular emphasis on material culture, associated sets of practices, and epistemic infrastructures. He currently works on the history of linguistic ethnography from collections of manuscripts and vocabularies understood as "paper tools" used for classificatory purposes. He is the author of *La formación del Museo de La Plata: Coleccionistas, comerciantes, estudiosos y naturalistas viajeros a fines del siglo XIX* (2009).

John S. Gilkeson is professor of history in the School of Humanities, Arts, and Cultural Studies of Arizona State University. He holds a PhD from Brown University, an MA from the University of Oklahoma, and a BA from Amherst College. His work focuses on the borderland between the humanities and the social sciences, with special attention to cultural historians in American studies, anthropology, folklore, geography, and linguistics. He is the author of *Middle-Class Providence, 1820–1940* (1986) and *Anthropologists and the Rediscovery of America, 1886–1965* (2010).

Alice Beck Kehoe studied at Barnard College and Harvard University, from which she received her PhD in anthropology. She taught at the University of Nebraska–Lincoln and later at Marquette University, from which she retired in 2000 as professor emerita. She is the author of numerous books on Native American history. Among her publications are *North American Indians: A Comprehensive Account* (1981; 3rd ed., 2006); *The Ghost Dance:*

Ethnohistory and Revitalization (2nd ed., 2006); *Land of Prehistory: A Critical History of American Archaeology* (1998); *Shamans and Religion* (2000); *America Before the European Invasions* (2002); *Controversies in Archaeology* (2008); and *Expanding Anthropology, 1945–1980* (edited with P. L. Doughty, 2011). Her research also includes archaeological and ethnographic fieldwork on the Northwestern Plains, ethnographic fieldwork in an Aymara Indian village in Bolivia, and continued collaboration with Amskapi Pikuni, Blackfeet Reservation, Montana, for whom she prepared a history, *Amskapi Pikuni: The Blackfeet People* (2012).

Maria Margaret Lopes holds a degree in geology, a MS in education, and a PhD in social history and history of science. She carried out postdoctoral research at the University of Louisiana (1997) and at the Ethnographic Museum of Buenos Aires University (1998). As a professor at Campinas University (1986–2009), she was the head of the Pagu Centre for Gender Studies (2000–2004), coordinator of the Post-Graduate Program in Teaching and History of Earth Sciences (2006–2007), and a technical assistant of the Special Secretariat for Women's Policies of the Brazilian Presidency of Republic (2007–2009). Researcher in CEHFCi-Evora Portugal (2009–2011) and director of the Museum of Astronomy (2011–2012), she is invited professor at Universidade de Brasília (since 2013). A researcher within the National Council for Scientific and Technological Development, she has published widely on the history of geology and paleontology, gender, and the history of museums in Latin America.

Joanne Pillsbury is the Andrall E. Pearson Curator of Ancient American Art at the Metropolitan Museum of Art, New York. A specialist in the art and archaeology of the ancient Americas, she holds a BA in anthropology from the University of California, Berkeley, and a PhD in art history and archaeology from Columbia University. Previously associate director of the Getty Research Institute, and before that director of pre-Columbian studies at Dumbarton Oaks, she has also taught at the University of Maryland and the University of East Anglia. She is the editor of *Guide to Documentary Sources for Andean Studies, 1530–1900* (2008), *Moche Art and Archaeology in Ancient Peru* (2001), and *Past Presented: Archaeological Illustration and the Ancient Americas* (2012). She is coeditor of several volumes, including *Merchants, Markets, and Exchange in the Pre-Columbian World* (with Kenneth Hirth, 2013). Her recent articles have addressed special topics in the history of archaeology and collecting and architectural sculpture at Chan Chan, Peru.

Susan Roy is an assistant professor at the University of Waterloo in Canada. Before coming to the University of Waterloo, she was a postdoctoral fellow in the Department of History at York University, Canada, and in the First Nations Studies Program at the University of British Columbia. Her work examines the politics of expressions of history and culture as they relate to aboriginal rights assertions of Canadian First Nations. She has also worked as a historical research consultant for indigenous communities in Canada. She is the author of *These Mysterious People: Shaping History and Archaeology in a Northwest Coast Community* (2010).

Adam Sellen, born in Ontario, Canada, studied Latin American studies at the University of Toronto. He holds a PhD in Mesoamerican studies from the Universidad Nacional Autónoma de México (UNAM). Since 2004, he is a researcher at the Centro Peninsular en Humanidades y Ciencias Sociales of UNAM in Mérida, Yucatán. He is the author of *El Cielo compartido: Deidades y ancestros en las vasijas efigie zapotecas* and of various other publications on Zapotec iconography. His recent interest is in the history of archaeology and archaeological collecting in Yucatán and Oaxaca in the nineteenth century.

Index

Acculturation of Seven American Indian Tribes, 210
acculturation studies, 209–10, 214
Adam, Lucien, 70, 81
agency, 99, 203, 206, 211, 213
Alt, Susan, 194
Alzate y Ramírez, José Antonio, 27
American Academy of Natural Sciences, 25, 31
American Indian Movement, 212
American Museum of Natural History, 146, 147–48, 150, 161–62, 179, 193
Ancient Monuments of the Mississippi Valley, 191
Ancient Society, 190
Ancón, 48, 50, 54, 58, 59, 60
anthropology, 171, 174–79, 205–6, 212
Antigüedades peruanas, 53–54, 61
antiquarianism: Americanists and, 72, 103, archaeology and, 4, 5–6, 47, 72, 194; Camacho Museum and, 91, 93; Chinese porcelain and, 116; comparative anatomy and, 26–27, 29, 36, 39–40, 42; development of 5–6, 29, 42, 47, 51, 72, 93; history and, 71, 82; importance of, 28–29, 41; indigenous peoples and, 119; Lafone Quevedo, Samuel Alexander and, 82–83;
language studies and, 13, 80, 82–83; literary canon of, 37; natural history and, 13, 71, 78, 81–83; natural science and, 27, 73; origins of humans and, 28; scholarly societies and 72; Stephens, John Lloyd and, 23–24, 26, 39; Toltecs and, 37; vocabulary of, 57; written documents and, 103
antiquarian method, 27, 29, 37–38, 70–71, 73, 78, 80
archaeology: antiquarianism and, 4, 5–6, 39; biases in, 10; chronology and, 192, 208–9; classification and, 50, 187, 192, 194; collecting and, 50; colonialism and, 193; cultural sciences and, 71; dating techniques and, 7, 55–57, 61, 194, 208; development of, 6–14, 42, 47–50, 57, 71–72, 93, 118; early excavations and, 6; historiography of, 9–10, 12; illustrations and, 6, 50, 56–58; indigenous peoples and, 191, 193–94, 213–14; interdisciplinarity and, 4, 5–6, 42, 47, 83, 137; as male centric, 193; mining and, 57; nationalism and, 205; natural history and, 7; natural sciences and, 6, 8, 48–50, 57, 61, 78, 80; Pan-American perspective of, 8, 10; politics and, 9,

archaeology: antiquarianism (*continued*) 11, 12; private collectors and, 9, 71, 95, 97, 138, 139; racism in, 187; reductionism and, 194; written records and, 11
Argentina, 128, 130, 173
assimilation, 153, 205, 210
Atwater, Caleb, 191, 204
Aztecs, 3, 28, 32, 103, 190, 205

Baird, Spencer, 190
Bancroft, Hubert Howe, 97
Bardsley, Charles Wareing, 74, 76
Bella Coola, 149, 150, 152, 160. See also Nuxalk
Bella Coola Indian Loggers, 161
Benedict, Ruth, 210
Bennati, Guido, 128, 129–31, 132, 134–36, 139
Bering Strait, 203
Berkhofer, Robert, 211–12
Blumenbach, Johann Friedrich, 30, 31, 33
Boas, Franz, 146–50, 158, 208, 209
Bogotá, 136, 137
Bolivia, 58, 81, 126, 128–29, 130, 131–36
botany, 15, 49, 54, 78, 132, 137, 174
Boucher de Crèvecoeur de Perthes, Jacques, 7
Brackebusch, Ludwig, 77
Brazilian Anthropological Exhibition, 177–78
Brazilian history, 15, 170–72, 175–76, 178–81
Brinton, Daniel Garrison, 70, 81
British Columbia Forestry Act, 161
Broca, Paul, 133, 178
Buenos Aires Public Museum, 115
Buffon, Georges Louis Leclerc (Comte de Buffon), 29–30, 105
Bureau of Ethnology, 191, 207
Bureau of Indian Affairs, 153, 190
Burke, Peter, 51, 70

Cahokia, 194
Camacho, José María, 14, 91–94, 97, 99, 105, 107

Camacho, Leandro, 14, 91–94, 97, 99, 105, 107
Camacho Museum: antiquarianism and, 93; Charnay, Désiré and, 100–101; Clavijero, Francisco Javier and, 103; Cubas, Antonio García and, 95; cult of the phallus and, 102–4; daguerreotypes and, 98–99; disbursement of, 91, 95; Doutrelaine, Louis Toussaint and, 95, 103; establishment of, 93; Echevarría, Florentino Gimeno and, 106; Friedrichstal, Emmanuel von and, 98–99; importance of, 91–92, 94, 97, 102; Ministerio de Fomento and, 95; Museo Nacional and, 95, 101; Norman, Benjamin Moore and, 98; objects in, 94–98, 99–101, 102, 106, 107; opinions about, 92–94, 97, 99; Orozco y Berra, Manuel and, 101; preservation of, 94, 95, 99–100, 105, 106; Sierra O'Reilly, Justo and, 94, 95, 99; Stephens, John Lloyd and, 99; taxonomy and, 105
Campeche, 98, 105
Camper, Petrus, 30
Carrillo y Ancona, Crescenio, 99
Cass, Lewis, 204
Catamarca, 71, 73, 75, 76, 82
Catherwood, Frederick, 23, 52
Centeno, Ana María, 14, 110, 112–14, 116–18
Centeno collection, 110–19
Chaco (province), 70, 71, 77, 79, 82
Chaco (province), languages of, 70, 77, 79, 80, 82, 179
Chan Chan, 54, 58
Changing Culture of an Indian Tribe, The, 210
Cherokee Nation v. Georgia, 190
Chichén Itzá, 40
Childe, V. Gordon, 205
Children of Aataentsic, The, 213
Cholula, 28
chromolithographs, 48, 56, 59
Cieza de León, Pedro, 51, 58
Clovis, 208
Coast Salish, 150, 155–56

Cohen, Felix, 196
Collier, Donald, 193. See also *Indians Before Columbus*
Colombia, 136–39
Colombian Scientific Commission, 136–37
colonialism, 9
Colson, Elizabeth, 209
Columbus, Christopher, 187
Combe, George, 33, 35–36
Comissão Científica de Exploração, 15, 56, 174–75, 176
Comission Scientifique du Mexique, 95
comparative anatomy, 30–31, 33–40, 42, 98, 133, 174, 177
comparative philology, 73, 82
con men, 127–28
Conder, Claude Reignier, 74–75
Consejo de Instrucción Pública, 128
Conspiracy of Pontiac, The, 206
Copán, 23, 41–42
Corps of Discovery, 189
crania, 24–25, 31, 33–39, 54, 177
Crania Aegyptiaca, 31, 35
Crania Americana, 33, 35, 37, 38, 39, 98
cult of the phallus, 102–4
cultural change, 207, 208
cultural relativism, 149
cultural-diffusion, 152
culture-area approach, 149
curiosities, 114–16, 119
Cushing, Frank Hamilton, 208
Cuvier, Georges, 30, 61, 105
Cuzco, 14, 77, 111, 113, 116, 117

daguerreotypes, 40, 56, 98–99
Darwin, Charles, 7, 33, 48, 78, 206
dating techniques, 55–56, 57, 61, 194, 208
Dávalos y Lissón, Ricardo, 112–13, 115
Davis, Edwin H., 204
De generis humani varietate naturae, 30
De Voto, Bernard, 211
Debo, Angie, 211
Declaration of Independence, 188, 197
Declaration of Indian Purpose, A, 212
Delafield, John, 38
Delgamuukw v. Regina, 197–98

Derby, Orville Adalbert, 179
Description of Egypt, 51
Description of the Ruins of an Ancient City, Discovered near Palenque, 37
Diderot, Denis, 51
diffusion, 209
doctrine of discovery, 186–87, 189
Dombey, Joseph, 49
Dorsey, George, 150
double-entry tables, 81–82
Douglas Treaties of 1850–1854, 154
Doutrelaine, Louis Toussaint Simon, 95, 101, 102–3, 106
Dupaix, Guillermo, 51, 136
Duponceau, Peter, 204

earthworks, 191, 207
ecological functionalism, 194
Edmonds, Frederick, 32, 36
Eggan, Fred, 209
Emmons, George T., 146, 150, 161
empiricism, 192
Enclosure Acts, 188
Encyclopédie, 51
Enlightenment, The, 93, 113, 187, 189
ethnography, 71, 147, 149, 174, 176–77, 179
ethnohistory, 15–16, 211
ethnology, 73, 177
etymology, 71, 77
Europe and the People Without History, 213
Exposição da Indústria Cearense, 176, 179–81

facial angle, 30, 33
Ferrocarril, El, 134, 136
Field Museum (Chicago), 150
first salmon ceremony, 153, 154–55
"fish-in," 212
folklore, 82
Folsom, 208
fossils, 116, 129, 130, 173
Foucault, Michel, 71, 115, 187
Friedrichsthal, Emmanuel von, 40, 42, 98–99
functionalism, 194, 209

Galicia Chimalpopoca, Fausto, 103
Galindo, Juan, 29
Gallatin, Albert, 204, 207
Geoffrin, Marie Thérèse Rodet, 113
geography, 137, 174
geology, 48, 55, 57–58, 132, 137, 174, 191
Gimeno Echevarría, Florentino, 105–6
Guimarães, Manoel L. L. S., 169

Haida, 148, 150, 152, 156
Hall of Northwest Coast Indians, 146, 147–49, 152, 154, 161–62, 163
Hamy, Ernest Théodore, 178
Handbook of Federal Indian Law, 196–97
Hartt, Charles Frederic, 178
Heller, Karl Bartolomeus, 92, 99
Historical and Statistical Information Respecting the History, Condition, and Prospects of the Indian Tribes of the United States, 204
historicity, 187, 197, 213–14
Hrdlička, Aleš, 192
human remains, 23–25, 30–32, 39, 173, 192
Humboldt, Alexander von, 16, 28–29, 35, 38, 53, 61, 79, 190

illustrations, 6, 50–51, 54–61. *See also* chromolithographs; daguerreotypes; lithographs; photography
imperialism, 9
Inca: antiquities of, 49, 113, 116, 119, 135; monuments of, 6, 131; opinions about, 3; origins of, 28, 47–48, 52–54, 58, 60–61
Inca, El, 133
Incidents of Travel and Exploration in the Land of the Incas, 52
Incidents of Travel in Central America, Chiapas and Yucatan, 23, 205
Incidents of Travel in Egypt, Arabia Petrae and the Holy Land, 23
Incidents of Travel in Greece, Turkey, Russia and Poland, 23
Incidents of Travel in Yucatan, 23, 26, 99
Indian Act (Canada), 153, 157–58
Indian Claims Commission, 211

Indian Reorganization Act of 1934, 209
Indian reserves, 153, 154
Indian schools, 153, 197
Indians Before Columbus, 193
indigenous peoples: agency of, 99, 203, 206, 211, 213; anthropology and, 205–7, 209, 212; archaeology and, 205–9; artifact classification and, 204; assimilation of, 153, 205, 210; attitudes about nature of, 146; Brazilian history and, 171, 175; caricatures of, 206; ceremonial life of, 153, 156, 163; classification of, 187; collection of culture of, 189; common history of, 193–94, 202; common mission of, 202; descendent communities and, 195–96; disappearance of, 178, 192, 210; diseases and, 178; dispossession of, 15, 153, 178, 186, 188–89, 196; economy of, 154, 155–56, 157, 158–61, 162–63; historicity of, 208, 211; Indian Acts and, 153, 157–58; Indian reserves and, 153; Indian schools and, 153; Kennewick Man and, 196; logging by, 160–61; Manifest Destiny and, 189; massacres of, 197; memory cultures of, 207; missionaries and, 154, 156–57, 171, 186, 197, 212; mobility of, 153, 162–63; money and, 188; mythology of, 172; as natural history, 117, 147, 149–51, 187, 195, 198, 204; opinions about, 40–41, 150–51, 187, 188, 190, 203; opinions held by, 176; oral traditions of, 203, 206; origins of, 35, 39, 40–42, 191, 202–4, 208, 214; "pacification" of, 191; as people without history, 203, 206, 213; philology and, 171, 172, 175, 202, 204; resistance of, 212; rights of, 146–47, 154–58, 162–63, 186–87, 195–97; as "savages," 187–89, 190–92, 198, 203, 206–7; trade and, 152–53, 155; treaties with, 190, 196
Ingapirca, 6, 49
Inquiry on the Antiquities of America, An, 38
Instituto Histórico e Geográfico Brasileiro (IHGB), 169–70, 171, 173

interdisciplinarity, 8, 12, 42, 47, 49, 78, 82–83
Islands of History, 213
Italian Scientific and Medico-Chirurgical Commission, 128–36

Jefferson, Thomas, 188–89, 190, 204, 207
Jesup, Morris Ketchum, 148
Jesup North Pacific Expedition, 146–48
Jiménez de la Espada, Marcos, 76. See also *Relaciones geográficas de Indias: Perú*

Kennewick Man, 195, 196–97
Kluckwan, 153
Kuhn, Thomas, 7
Kwakwaka'wakw, 150, 156, 157, 159

La Condamine, Charles-Marie de, 6, 49
Lafone Quevedo, Samuel Alexander: agglutination and, 70, 79, 82; antiquarian method and, 75, 82; archaeology and, 73, 80; as businessman, 81; Catamarca and, 71, 73, 75, 76; data collection by, 70, 76, 81; double-entry tables and, 81–82; education of, 72; etymology and, 80; geographical etymology and, 75; history of, 72; intellectual pursuits of, 71, 72–73; interviews by, 77; linguistic ethnography and, 71, 75; linguistic studies of, 13, 78–79; methodology of, 70, 74–75; mining and, 72, 81; note taking and, 81–82; paleontology and, 80; philology and, 70, 79, 80; pronominal structure and, 79, 82; sources of, 70, 75, 76–77, 81, 82, 83; surnames and, 76; tabulation art and, 81–82; Taylor, Isaac and, 75–76; toponymy and, 75–76, 82
Laufer, Berthold, 208
League of the Ho-dé-n-sau-nee, or Iroquis, The, 205
León y Gama, Antonio de, 27
linguistic classification, 70, 77, 78, 82–83, 204, 207

linguistic ethnography, 13, 69–70, 71, 74–75, 76
linguistic ethnology, 82
Linnaeus, Carl, 29–30, 189
Linton, Ralph, 210
lithographs, 33, 52, 54, 55–57. See also chromolithographs
Locke, John, 186, 188, 190, 195
Louisiana Purchase, 189
Lowie, Robert H., 206
Lozano, Pedro, 76
Lubbock, John, 192, 206
Lund, Peter, 170, 172–73
Lutz, John, 155
Lyell, Charles, 48, 55

Manifest Destiny, 189, 191, 198
Manó, Joseph Charles: Bennati, Guido and, 129–31, 133; in Bolivia, 131–36; collection of, 125, 132; Colombian Scientific Commission and, 137; in Colombia, 136–39; as con man, 127, 138, 139; death of, 125; description of, 126–27, 139; expeditions of, 129–31; Gill, Emilio and, 129; goals of, 134–35, 136; Guatemala and, 136, 138; impact of, 139–40; Isaacs, Jorge and, 137–38; Montalvo, Juan and, 136; occupations of, 125–27, 128, 136–37, 138–39; pamphlets and, 131–32; in Paraguay, 128–31; Paraguay national museum and, 129; Perillán y Buxó, Eloy and, 133–35; personal history of, 126; Peru and, 136; politics and, 135–36; propaganda and, 127, 128, 131–32; Société de Géographie and, 125, 126, 138–39; Society of Medicine and Natural Sciences of Bogotá and, 138; travels of, 136; travels with wife of, 125–26; Veintimilla, Ignacio and, 136;
Marshall, John, 190, 196
Martin, Paul S., 193. See also *Indians Before Columbus*
Martínez Compañón, Baltasar Jaime (Bishop), 57
Martius, Carl Friedrich von, 15, 170, 171–72, 173, 181

Marx, Karl, 127–28
Mason, O. T., 149–50, 207
Matto de Turner, Clorinda, 113
Matto Grosso, 178
Maudslay, Alfred, 54, 56–57
Maya, 54, 56, 91, 97, 99, 102
McNickle, D'Arcy, 207, 212
Mead, Margaret, 210, 212
Metropolitan Museum of Art, 150, 193
Mexican-American War, 192, 205
Miller, Daniel, 70–71
mineralogy, 54–55, 60, 132, 137, 174
missionaries, 154, 156–57, 171
Momigliano, Arnaldo, 70, 175
Montalvo, Juan, 136
Montesinos, Fernando de, 54, 77
Mooney, James, 208
Moore, Arthur William, 74, 76
Morelet, Arturo, 92, 97, 98
Morgan, Lewis Henry, 190, 194, 205, 207, 208
Morton, Samuel George, 24–26, 31–40, 98
Motley, John Lothrop, 205–6
mounds, 28, 35, 38, 191, 204, 207
Moussy, Martin de, 77
Müller, Friedrich Max, 73, 78, 80
mummies: of Ancón, 48, 55, 59, 60; in collections, 5, 110, 180; Comissão Científica de Exploração and, 174; comparative anatomy and, 38; procurement of, 31, 32, 134–35
Museo Nacional (Mexico), 32, 95, 101, 102, 115
Museo Yucateco, 99
Museo Yucateco, El, 40, 41, 94
Museu Nacional (Brazil), 169, 171, 173, 176–81
myths, 82, 172, 175

National Historic Preservation Act, 195
National Indian Youth Council, 212
National Museum of History, 193
National Museum of the American Indian, 193

Native American Graves Protection and Repatriation Act (NAGPRA), 15, 24, 195–97
Native American studies programs, 212
nature: antiquities and, 5, 16, 71, 78, 117, 128, 130, 132, 138–39; archaeology and, 4, 13; art and, 105, 115; culture and, 146–47, 151, 163 curiosities and, 114; exploration of, 191; feminization of, 188, 194; history and, 3, 170, 181; importance of studying, 128; indigenous peoples and, 4–5, 14–15, 117, 146–147, 151, 163, 172, 195, 197–98; industry and, 131, 132; Isaacs, Jorge and, 137; language studies and, 78, 172; money and, 188; museum displays of, 129, 131–33, 147, 151, 163; perceptions of, 146, 151, 188, 194; politics and, 131; study of, 8
Necropolis of Ancon in Peru, The, 48, 50, 56, 59–60, 61
Netto, Ladislau, 177–78, 179–80
New York Morning News, 189–90
Nootka, 149, 150, 156. See also Nuuchah-nulth
Norman, Benjamin Moore, 25, 92, 93, 98
note-taking, 81–82
Nuuchah-nulth, 148, 149, 156, 159. *See also* Nootka
Nuxalk, 149, 150, 160, 161. *See also* Bella Coola

On the Origin of Species, 7, 206
oral traditions, 153, 203, 206, 211, 214
Orozco y Berra, Manuel, 95, 101, 102, 103
Ortiz, Alfonso, 214
Osborn, Henry Fairfield, 147, 148–49
O'Sullivan, John, 189–90
Oweekeno, 158–59

Pachacamac, 32
Palenque, 13, 23, 27, 28, 37, 39, 100–101
Pan-American Anthropological Exhibition, 180–81
Paraguay, 125–26, 128–31

Paraguayan War, 128, 130
Parkman, Francis, 206
Parte primera de la chronica del Peru, 51
Patria, La, 129
Patterns of Culture, 210
Pauw, Cornelius de, 172
Peabody Museum of Archaeology and Ethnology, 5
Pecos Classification, 208
Perillán y Buxó, Eloy, 133–35, 139
Pérou et Bolivie, 52
Peru, 28, 29
philology, 51, 60, 71, 72, 78, 79, 80
photography, 52, 53, 54
phrenology, 31, 33, 174
Pictet, Adolphe, 80
Piranesi, Giovanni Battista, 51
Poinsett, Joel Robert, 32, 34, 98
potlatch, 149, 153, 156–59
"potlatch ban," 153, 157–58
Powell, John Wesley, 191, 207
pre-Columbian: antiquities, 4–5, 14, 16, 112, 116; scholarly focus on, 11–12, 49, 52–53, 58, 118–19, 177. *See also* Camacho Museum; Centeno collection.
Pre-Historic Times, 192, 206
pre-Incan, 48, 53, 77

Quimby, George I., 193. See also *Indians Before Columbus*

race, 30, 33–39, 98, 174
Radcliffe-Brown, A. R., 209
Raimondi, Antonio, 58, 60
Ray, Arthur, 197
Redfield, Robert, 209
Registro Yucateco, El, 41, 93, 94
Reiss, Wilhelm, 48, 50, 52–56, 59–61
Relaciones geográficas de Indias: Perú, 76. *See also* Jiménez de la Espada, Marcos
Revista Médica, 138
Rio, Antonio del, 37, 38
Rivero, Mariano, 53, 54, 61
Robertson, William Parish, 92, 93, 97, 104
Rojas, Alfonso Villa, 209

Romainville, Pierre de, 110, 117
Rond d'Alembert, Jean, 51
Ross, Dorothy, 191, 193
Royal Commission on Indian Affairs, 146, 158, 161, 163
Rupert's Land, 189

Sabloff, Jeremy, 192
Sahlins, Marshall, 213–14
Saint-Hilarie, Étienne Geoffroy, 105
salvage anthropology, 158
salvage ethnography, 154, 158, 162–63, 207–09, 212
salvage ethnology. *See* salvage ethnography
Sassaman, Kenneth, 187
Schnapp, Alain, 27
Scienza nuova, 175
Scott, Duncan Campbell, 158
shell middens, 147, 177
shells, 104, 111, 114, 116, 155
Sierra O'Reilly, Justo, 40, 41, 94–95, 99, 104, 105
Simpson, George, 189, 193
Siyémches to Yeqwyeqwi:ws, 155
Smith, Harlan I., 147–48, 150, 153–54, 156–58, 160
Smithsonian Institution, 179, 190, 191, 205
Smithsonian National Museum of Natural History, 149–50, 192, 193, 207
Social Science Research Council, 210
Sociedade Vellosiana, 170
Société de Géographie, 125, 126, 138
Society of Medicine and Natural Sciences of Bogotá, 138
Squier, E. George, 52, 204
Stephens, John Lloyd: Camacho Museum and, 99; Copan and, 41–42; Friedrichsthal, Emmanuel von and, 40; monuments and, 205; origins of indigenous peoples and, 25–26, 39; Sierra O'Reilly, Justo and, 99; Toltecs and, 99; trading and, 132; travel writings of, 13, 23, 42, 52, 99
Steward, Julian, 210

Stübel, Alphons: in Ancón, 59; geology and, 60; history of, 48; Humboldt, Alexander von and, 52–53; illustrations and, 50, 54, 54–56, 59, 61; influence of, 61; mummies and, 60; objectivity and, 53, 59, 61; Squier, E. George and, 52; stratigraphy and, 60; travels of, 58–59; Wiener, Charles and, 52; writings of, 48
Syme, Patrick, 56
Systema naturae, 189

Tarayre, Guillemin, 39
taxidermy, 114, 116
taxonomy, 56, 98, 105, 106, 115–16
Taylor, Isaac, 74–76
Taylor, William: as absentee artist, 152; American Museum of Natural History and, 146; first salmon ceremony and, 154–55; Hall of Northwest Coast Indians and, 146; importance of, 161–62; as instructor, 147; murals of, 14, 150, 154–56; National Society of Mural Painters and, 147; personal history of, 147; trade and, 152–53; travels of, 147, 148, 150, 153–54, 160
Temple of the Moon, 32, 36
Temple of the Sun, 32, 36
Teotihuacan, 28, 32, 36
Tesoro de Catamarqueñismos, 76
Thomas, Cyrus, 191, 207, 208
Ticul, 24–25, 39
Tiwanaku, 54, 58, 135
Tlaxcaltecas, 28
Tlingit, 146, 148, 149, 150, 152, 153
Toltecs, 26, 28, 32, 34–37, 42, 99, 205
Tonatiuh-Nanahuatzin, 103
topography, 73
toponymy, 70–77, 82, 172
totem poles, 148, 149, 156, 160, 161
Tribal Historic Preservation Offices (THPO), 195

Trigger, Bruce, 213
Troya, Rafael, 50
Tschudi, Johann Jakob von, 53, 54, 61
Tseshaht, 145, 146, 153, 163
Tsimshian, 150, 152, 155
Tucumán, 73
Tula, 28
Tupi, 179

Uhle, Max, 60
U.S. Public Land Survey, 189
Ussher, James (Bishop), 57–58
Uxmal, 23, 40, 99, 172

Vico, Giambattista, 15, 175
Vogt, Evon, 210, 211
Von den äußerlichen Kennzeichen der Foßilien, 56
Vues des Cordillères, et monumens des peuples indigènes de l'Amérique, 28, 53

Wari culture, 60
Warner, Lloyd, 209
Werner, Abraham Gottlob, 55–56
Whitney, Dwight, 78
Wiener, Charles, 52
Willey, Gordon, 192
Wilson, Daniel, 190, 192, 193
Wolf, Eric, 213
Worcester v. Georgia, 196
Words and Places, 74–75
World Archaeological Congress, 187
Worsaae, Jens J. A., 207

Yucatán: human remains of, 25–26, 39; indigenous peoples of, 24–25, 39, 41; John Lloyd Stephens and, 23–26, 39; Mexico and, 41; ruins of, 24, 40–41, 98–99

Zahn, Wilhelm, 56